THE BARTENDER'S BEST FRIEND

UPDATED AND REVISED

THE

BARTENDER'S

BEST FRIEND

UPDATED AND REVISED

A Complete Guide to

Cocktails, Martinis,

and Mixed Drinks

MARDEE HAIDIN REGAN

WILEY

JOHN WILEY & SONS, INC.

This book is printed on acid-free paper.

Copyright © 2010 by Mardee Haidin Regan. All rights reserved

Published by John Wiley & Sons, Inc., Hoboken, New Jersey

Published simultaneously in Canada

For general information on our other products and services or for technical support, please contact our Customer Care Department within the United States at (800) 762-2974, outside the United States at (317) 572-3993 or fax (317) 572-4002.

Wiley also publishes its books in a variety of electronic formats. Some content that appears in print may not be available in electronic books. For more information about Wiley products, visit our web site at www.wiley.com.

Library of Congress Cataloging-in-Publication Data

Regan, Mardee Haidin.

The bartender's best friend: a complete guide to cocktails, martinis, and mixed drinks / Mardee Haidin Regan. -- Updated and rev.

   p. cm.

Includes bibliographical references and index.

ISBN 978-0-470-44718-5 (pbk.)

1. Cocktails. 2. Bartending. I. Title.

TX951.R368 2010

641.8'74--dc22

                                        2009009331

Book design by Richard Oriolo

Printed in the United States of America

10 9 8 7 6 5 4 3 2 1

This book is for my extraordinary friends and family (in alphabetical order to lessen any and all arguments): Bettina, Bill, Bobby, BooBoo, Brenda, Catherine, Courtney, Debbie, Evelyn, Gary, Gatchie, Howie, Janet, Joe, Judy, Judy, Karl, Kate, Kim, Laura & Tim, Laurie, Liann, Lisa, Lizzie, Marilyn, Mavis, Molly, Nancy, Pam, Paul, Robert, Roseann, Sandra, Stephanie, Susan, Sylvia, Thomas, Tony, Tracy, Vincent, and Winnie.

ACKNOWLEDGMENTS

This book is testament to all its talented and passionate bartender contributors and all bartenders everywhere, but also to us, their customers, who so enjoy their work. Thanks to all and . . . cheers!

CONTENTS

INTRODUCTION

ABOUT THIS BOOK

SEVEN YEARS AGO, WHEN I WROTE the first version of this book, this is part of what I had to say: "Cocktails are fashion—they bespeak the era of their creation. Cocktails are an expression of style, and like music, art, architecture, theater, and design, in many ways they reflect the attitude of the nation. Right now cocktail culture is soaring. No matter where you look—in magazines, newspapers, films, and on television—you see people drinking cocktails.

"Many of our favorite cocktails reflect our mind-set. Some are based on classic combinations, some are casual and irreverent, often verging on downright silly, and many are the result of any number of incredible new ingredients in the marketplace."

Well, wow, who knew just how much things could change in a relatively short time? Of course, the Internet has had an enormous effect: Hundreds of sites are devoted to bibulous mixtures; spirits companies have elaborate Web sites detailing each and every product they produce; entrepreneurs have found the money and the guts to start out small with just one or two fine products and the hope of finding the right audience. And it's working!

Credit also must be given to the ever-increasing global market in our day-to-day lives: Though not every experience of the global economy is necessarily pleasant, the bright side is the unbelievable wealth of people, products, and knowledge that have become easily available to us all.

But most importantly, it's the people who have made the biggest difference. Whereas once just a few names—Dale DeGroff, Salvatore Calabrese, Audrey Saunders, Gary Regan— were the cocktailians who mattered, now a raft of imaginative, highly talented bartenders, bar chefs, restaurant and bar owners, writers, historians, and quirky aficionados have come to the fore. Chances are that no matter where you live, you can seek out and find a bartender who really cares about his or her craft. Best yet, you can taste their talent.

And so we return to the question: Who is the bartender's best friend? And in a purely practical way, the answer stays the same: The best tipper at the bar? Probably. But in fact, it's you and me, the appreciative audience that can support great technique, a friendly smile, and have enthusiasm for our tasting experiences.

But, alas, a most serious note that will never change with time: The bartender's very best friend can often be an experienced, sober driver or the local taxi service. Why? Because as enjoyable and fun as drinking and serving cocktails, wines, and beers can be, the unimpeachable fact is that alcohol affects our bodies and our minds, impairing our judgment and reaction time. Don't drink and drive, and don't let others drink and drive either. What's ultimately most fashionable is being alive to enjoy another day.

BARTENDING BASICS

MAKING A COCKTAIL HAS JUST FOUR requirements. The first three are easy: You need ingredients—the spirits, the juices, the ice, the sodas, the garnishes. You need equipment—a shaker, a strainer, a spoon. And you need something to serve the drink in, be it the finest lead crystal cocktail glass or a paper cup. The fourth requirement, however, is the tough one. You need to understand how to use these elements, and, ideally, you must acquire a grasp of how they intermingle. And therein lies the rub: You can make drinks or you can master drink-making, the craft of bartending. The choice is yours; the basics are outlined here. Mastering the craft requires thought, effort, and—just like getting to Carnegie Hall—practice, practice, practice.

Equipment

Tools and the methods of using them define the quality of the job performed. And just as a carpenter invests in his saws, a chef in his knives, or a painter in his brushes, a bartender needs to have the right equipment on hand to make the job easier and more professional. Once the proper tools are in place, you're good to go. Here's what's needed:

Barspoon: An ingenious long-handled spoon that has an almost teardrop-shaped bowl and a twisted shaft that makes stirring with one hand very easy. Absolutely essential if you want to do it right.

Bar towels: Two kinds—small, absorbent terry-cloth towels that can be used as bar mats to soak up spillage, splashes, and condensation; and tightly woven, flat-weave cotton or linen dishtowels for polishing glasses or grasping wet, chilled wine bottles that are being held in a wine bucket. You'll need several of each.

Blender: A heavy-duty machine capable of rendering ice cubes and other ingredients into slush. Opt for the 32- or 48-ounce container; I prefer a metal to a plastic blending container. Essential for frozen drinks.

Boston shaker: The most important tool for cocktail making—a two-part implement consisting of a mixing glass bottom and a taller, slightly wider, flat-bottomed metal cup. In use, the metal half is upended over the mixing glass; it overreaches the juncture of the two rims and allows the bartender to shake with ease and with no spills or leaks. The cups are "broken" apart. If pouring from the metal half, a Hawthorne strainer is used; if pouring from the mixing glass half, a Julep strainer is used.

Bottle opener: The standard tool for removing bottle caps. A number of different designs are available, but all deliver the same end result: getting that metal cap off the bottle.

Can opener: The handheld kitchen tool that will remove one end of a can; useful for very thick mixtures, such as coconut cream. A handheld model is sufficient for behind the bar.

Champagne stopper: A winged, spring-loaded gizmo that clamps over the lip of a champagne bottle and helps keep the CO_2 (carbon dioxide) inside the bottle where it belongs.

Cheesecloth: Essential for straining solids from steeped mixtures. Remember, always soak cheesecloth with water and wring out well before using it to strain liquid mixtures; if you don't, you'll lose a considerable amount of the liquid ingredient to absorption by the cheesecloth.

Churchkey: A double-duty device: The rounded end is a bottle opener; the pointed end is for piercing cans of liquids, like tomato juice.

Citrus reamer: A manual device for extracting the juice from halved citrus fruits. Some are handheld and must be used over a glass or bowl to collect the juices; others are stationary with a bowl-shaped bottom to collect the juices; still others are large levered devices that sit on the countertop. Electric juicers are also available.

Citrus strippers and zesters: Handy devices that can help cut various widths of citrus zests—from very small, fine curls to $1/4$-inch-wide swaths. In capable hands, a paring knife can be used.

Cocktail napkins and/or coasters: Essential for collecting any condensation or drips when serving a cocktail.

Cocktail picks: Usually small, thin skewers for selecting garnishes for a drink; one end of a cocktail pick might be adorned in some way to make picking it up easier.

Cocktail shaker: The three-part tool made for shaking cocktails. A large bottom cup is topped with a tight-fitting lid, and the lid itself has a built-in strainer and a cap. After shaking, just remove the cap and the strainer will prevent all but the tiniest shards of ice from being poured into the drink. Some more-stylized cocktail shakers have a capped pour spout—like a teapot with a spout cover—with a built-in strainer.

Corkscrew: Absolutely essential for uncorking a wine bottle. Dozens and dozens of designs exist; choose whatever style

Bartending Basics

makes your life easiest. I personally prefer the Screwpull to all others because it does not require upper-arm strength; the cork is removed by continually turning the handle in one direction.

Cutting boards: Necessary for preparing garnishes and avoiding damage to wooden bartops.

Fine-toothed grater: A small, handheld device that can be used for whole nutmegs and for producing fine shreds of citrus zest or fresh ginger.

Foil cutter: A handy gizmo for cleanly cutting away the foil, lead, or plastic capsule that encases the top of a wine bottle.

Funnel: A useful tool for transferring liquids into small-mouthed containers or bottles.

Glass pitcher: An excellent, multipurpose vessel for behind the bar. It will hold water, juices, and mixtures of all kinds for easy pouring when needed.

Ice bucket: Absolutely vital for the home bar—a sizeable container to hold fresh ice for use in preparing and serving cocktails.

Ice crusher: An electric device that breaks large cubes into crushed shards of ice. Be warned: They are noisy in operation. Manual ice crushers, usually with a side handle that must be turned, are very difficult to use. A thick canvas bag and a rubber mallet offer an easy way to crush ice, but for me, at least, it can become arm-numbing and is noisy.

Ice pick: Used to break up large blocks of ice, these usually consist of a wooden handle with a single sharp prong. Some antique ice picks, with multiple prongs, can be found at online auctions, and these are preferable when breaking up large sheets of ice made on baking trays and the like.

Ice scoop: A stainless-steel tool that makes quick work of filling a shaker, mixing glass, or serving glass with ice.

Ice tongs: A tool that provides a stylish but tedious method for adding ice cubes to a vessel; *see* Ice scoop.

Jigger: An hourglass-shaped, most likely metal

device that usually has a 1-ounce measure on its smaller end and a $1^1/_2$-ounce measure on the opposite end. However, jiggers are made in many sizes; check yours to know what volume each end measures. I suggest that beginners search out what I call a tippable measure: It looks like a large tablespoon-size measuring spoon that has a metal rod sticking out from the measure's bowl on opposite sides. You can center it over a mixing glass, pour in the desired measure of ingredient, and just rotate the rod to pour the ingredient into the glass, leaving the measure empty and ready to measure the next ingredient. Nifty.

Knives: Sharp extensions of the bartender's hands. Two sizes of knife are usually required: a paring knife for cutting fruit garnishes and a larger-bladed all-purpose knife that can halve a grapefruit or behead a pineapple.

Measuring cups: For the beginning bartender, a 1-cup liquid measuring cup will aid in checking free-poured measures. Large measuring cups are handy for punch-making and as auxiliary pitchers.

Measuring spoons: Usually used for measuring dry ingredients, such as spices.

Mixing glass: The workhorse tool at any bar: the 16-ounce glass vessel that is used for stirring ingredients over ice.

Muddler: Usually a wooden, pestle-shaped implement that has a flat but bulbous end that is used to crush ingredients together in the bottom of a mixing glass or in a serving glass. My friend Chris Gallagher makes a particularly pleasing one, the PUG! Muddler. Do a Google search to locate retail sources.

Sip-sticks, stirrers, swizzle sticks, straws: Thin, often tubular, sometimes disposable devices used to mix ingredients for a Highball or for sipping through.

Speed pourers: Marvelously handy, removable pour spouts that fit tightly into the neck of most standard bottles and allow the bartender to pick up the bottle and pour immediately. Also, these pourers make it easy for a bartender to free pour often-used ingredients by using a counting system that is discussed under Bartending Techniques (pages 41–42).

Strainers: Two types of bar strainers are essential at every bar: a Hawthorne strainer (at right) is the one with the curly wire around half of its circumference so that it fits snugly inside the metal half of a Boston shaker. A julep strainer is a shallow-bowled, perforated, short-handled spoon that fits neatly inside a mixing glass.

Ingredients

Spirits

Distilled spirits have been with us since the 1100s, when the art of distillation, which had been practiced for centuries at that point, was finally used to distill alcoholic products, such as wine. Initially, because spirits were liquids that could be set on fire, they were known as "ardent spirits," from the Latin *adere*, meaning "to burn," but because they were first used as medicines, they became known as "water of life," and this name is still with us today. France produces eaux-de-vie; Scandinavia makes aquavit, and both of these terms translate to "water of life." Even the Gaelic word *uisga beatha* (Ireland) or *usquebaugh* (Scotland), which was anglicized to "whisk(e)y," mean "water of life." Here are some definitions for the main categories of distilled spirits, along with some explanations of various specific bottlings and the most important distillation terms you should know.

Absente: *See* Absinthe and absinthe substitutes.

Absinthe and absinthe substitutes: Absinthe was outlawed in many countries during the first couple of decades of the twentieth century, and although its popularity waned, it has recently made a big comeback since some spirits companies in the twenty-first century have reformulated their absinthe recipes, often using a variety of wormwood that is not mentioned in the laws that banned the product in the first place. The reason that absinthe was banned was that it was said to be addictive and hallucinogenic because of one ingredient, wormwood, a bitter herb that contains thujone, which has a molecular structure that is strikingly similar to

THC, the active ingredient in marijuana. In all probability, though, it was the high alcohol content of absinthe—most bottlings verged on almost 70 percent alcohol by volume (abv)—that caused absinthe drinkers to act so strangely.

In the United States, where absinthe was made illegal in 1915, we can now find absinthe substitutes—Pernod, Ricard, and Herbsaint—and, glory be, we can once again buy true absinthe that is marketed under specific brand names, such as Pernod, Grande Absente, St. George, Lucid, Kubler, and others.

American brandy: Distilled from a fermented mash of grapes. American distillers have a huge advantage over many other brandy makers: The law does not prescribe which grape varieties must be used, and thus, they can employ whichever grape variety takes their fancy. The result of this leniency creates some truly great American brandies that are loaded with complexity, perhaps because they are made from top-notch grapes.

Apple brandy: Distilled from a fermented mash of apples, apple brandy is usually aged in oak barrels, sometimes for decades, but more usually for three to five years.

Applejack: The regular bottling of Laird's Applejack is a blended apple brandy, but Laird's also produces a 100-proof straight applejack and some great aged apple brandies, too.

Armagnac: A grape brandy made in the Gascony region of France, which is divided into three subregions: Ténarèze, Haut-Armagnac, and Bas-Armagnac. Armagnac must be made only from white grapes, Ugni Blanc (also known as Saint-Émilion), Colombard, and Folle Blanche varieties being the most common. Armagnac is usually aged in Monlezun oak barrels.

Armagnac producers use the following designations to denote the minimum age of the brandy in the bottle:

VS (VERY SPECIAL): two years

VSOP (VERY SPECIAL OLD PALE): five years

XO (EXTRA OLD): six years

HORS D'AGE: 10 years

VINTAGE: made from grapes harvested in the year on the label.

Batavia Arrack: Made from sugarcane in Indonesia and the Netherlands; the yeast used to make this spirit comes in the form of fermented red rice. This spirit is the base for Swedish Punch (or Punsch).

Bourbon: Distilled from a fermented mash that must contain a minimum of 51 percent corn; the other grains used are malted barley and either rye or wheat. Bourbon must be aged in new, charred oak barrels for a minimum of two years, though most bottlings have spent at least four years in the wood. The name *bourbon* comes from the Kentucky county from which whiskey from the area was shipped in the late 1700s. Bourbon can be made legally anywhere in the United States, although, with the exception of one Virginia distillery, at the time of this writing it is all made in Kentucky. Bourbon is the only spirit that was born in the United States; all others originated elsewhere.

Small-batch bourbon usually denotes whiskey that has been selected from a small quantity of barrels that has aged into what the distiller thinks is a whiskey that's superior to his regular bottlings. Keep in mind, though, that each distillery has its own criteria for using this term, which has not been legally defined.

Brandy: Distilled from a fermented mash of fruits, brandies are most commonly grape based, though many made from other fruits are also available.

Brandy de Jerez: A brandy made from a fermented mash of grapes, usually Airén or Palomino varietals, in the Jerez district of Spain. Brandy de Jerez is aged in oak using the solera method, which means that the barrels are stacked on top of each other, usually about 12 barrels high, and newly made brandy is entered into the top layer. Every few months, some brandy is taken from the bottom layer, which contains the oldest brandy, and this is replaced with brandy from the next level up. The procedure is repeated until what started out as young brandy on the top layer has aged its way through the layers and is removed. All the while, newly made brandy is entered at the top layer so that the continuous mingling and aging process can continue. "Solera" bottlings are aged for at least one year, "Solera Reserva" brandies must spend three years in oak, and bottles labeled "Solera Gran Reserva" have to be aged in oak for a minimum of 10 years.

Cachaça: A Brazilian rum that's made from sugarcane and is used most often to make a Caipirinha.

Calvados: A brandy distilled from a fermented mash of apples, although a small percentage of pears are also used, made in the Calvados region of Normandy, France. Calvados is aged in oak casks—mainly Limousin.

Calvados producers use the following designations to denote the minimum age of the brandy in the bottle:

FINE: two years

THREE STARS: two years

VIEUX: three years

RÉSERVE: three years

VO: four years

VSOP: four years

VIELLE RÉSERVE: four years

XO: six years

NAPOLÉON: six years

HORS D'AGE: six years

EXTRA: six years

AGE INCONNU: six years

Canadian whisky: Usually a blended whisky from Canada, which can be flavored legally with a small percentage of other products, such as prune wine and even bourbon.

Cognac: A grape brandy made in the Cognac region of France, which is divided into six subregions: Grande Champagne, Petite Champagne, Borderies, Fins Bois, Bons Bois, and Bois Ordinaires. Cognac, by law, must be made only from white grapes, and 90 percent of the grapes must be Ugni Blanc (also known as Saint-Émilion), Folle Blanche, and/or Colombard. Cognac usually is aged in Limousin oak casks.

Cognac producers use the following designations to denote the minimum age of the brandy in the bottle:

VS (VERY SPECIAL): two years

VSOP (VERY SPECIAL OLD PALE): four years

XO (EXTRA OLD): six years

NAPOLÉON: six years

HORS D'AGE: six years

EXTRA: six years

COGNAC VINTAGE: Made from grapes harvested in the year on the label (rare, but more are cropping up).

Distilled Spirits

From the Latin *dis* or *des*, which implies separation, and *stilla*, meaning "drop," distillation means "to separate, drop by drop." In terms of distilled spirits, this means that a fermented mash, or "soup," of fruits, grains, sugars, or vegetables is entered into a still and heated. Since the alcohol in the mash evaporates at a lower temperature than the water, the steam that rises contains more alcohol than the original mash. This steam is collected, then condensed, and depending on the method of distillation used, it might have to be redistilled until it contains enough alcohol—40 percent minimum—to be called a distilled spirit.

Continuous stills, invented in the late 1700s or early 1800s, are tall chimney-like pieces of equipment fitted with numerous perforated plates situated at regular intervals in the chimney. Steam is introduced to the bottom of the still, while the fermented mash is poured into the top. The steam evaporates the alcohol from the mash as it descends through the perforated plates, and this steam, now laden with alcohol, can be drawn off and condensed at various levels in the still. If the steam is allowed to reach the top of the still, it can contain as much as 95 percent alcohol, but if it is drawn off at lower levels, it will be weaker. Continuous stills, however, are not used to produce spirits that have less than 40 percent alcohol, so redistillation is unnecessary. Continuous stills are used to produce vodka and most other varieties of distilled spirits.

Pot stills, usually onion-shaped copper vessels with a long, tapering chimney extending from the top, are used to make specialty spirits, such as single-malt scotches, certain bourbons, and various brandies. In this kind of still, the fermented mash is usually strained of all solids before being entered, in order to prevent scorching. The still is heated, usually by means of a steam jacket, but sometimes coal and/or wood is still used. The vapors rise up the tapered chimney and are condensed. This product of one distillation doesn't contain enough alcohol to be known as a spirit, so it must then be entered into another pot still, and go through the process again.

Eaux-de-vie: Distilled from a fermented mash of fruits, eaux-de-vie are rarely aged, and are made in, more or less, every country that produces fruit. Most of the best bottlings come from the United States (mainly from California and Oregon), France, Italy, Germany, and Switzerland.

Fruit brandies: The most common fruit brandies found behind American bars contain a small amount of true brandy, and they are sweetened and flavored to be suitable cocktail ingredients.

Gin: Gin was first made in Holland in the 1500s, and English soldiers who fought alongside the Dutch in the Thirty Years' War brought the spirit home, calling it "Dutch Courage" because it had been used to prepare them for battle. The word *gin* comes from the French *genièvre*, which means "juniper."

Basically, gin is a flavored vodka, the main flavoring agent being juniper, but other botanicals, such as angelica, caraway, cardamom, cassia, cinnamon, coriander, fennel, ginger, lemon zest, licorice, and orange zest can also be used. Gin producers don't normally reveal their recipes, and even if they list their ingredients, they rarely tell us what amounts they have used. London Dry gin is crisp and dry, and the words denote a style, not necessarily where the product was made. Plymouth gin is similar in style to some London Dry gins, but it must be made in Plymouth, England. Old Tom gin is a sweetened gin that, at the time of writing, has just been released under the Hayman's label in the United States and in Europe. Genever or Hollands gin is made in Holland, and the aged bottlings—*oude genever*—have a malty sweetness not found in other styles, while the unaged, or *jonge* genevers, are almost vodka-like in character.

Many new styles of gin have been released in the first decade of the twenty-first century, and the number of styles seems to be growing at a delightfully alarming rate.

Grappa: An unaged Italian brandy distilled from grape pomace—the leftover skins, seeds, and other detritus from the wine-making process.

Herbsaint: *See* Absinthe and absinthe substitutes.

Irish whiskey: Irish whiskey, like scotch, can be divided into two distinct categories—single malts and blended whiskeys—although most Irish whiskey is blended. Single-malt Irish whiskey is made in the same way as single-malt scotch (*see* page 15), although peat isn't usually used in the process, and therefore the smokiness evident in scotch isn't found in the vast majority of Irish whiskeys. Blended Irish whiskey is made by blending together single malts with neutral grain whiskeys, in the same way that blended scotch is made.

Kirsch: An unaged brandy distilled from a fermented mash of cherries.

Marc: An unaged French brandy distilled from grape pomace—the leftovers from the wine-making process. Marc is the French equivalent of Italian grappa.

Mash: A "soup" of fruits, grains, sugars, sometimes vegetables, and water that is fermented, by the introduction of yeast, to produce alcohol.

Mezcal: A Mexican spirit that can be made from any of five species of the agave plant, but not from the blue agave that must be used for tequilas. While tequila must be produced in certain designated areas, mezcal can be made anywhere in Mexico. Mezcal is often tinged with a smoky flavor from roasting the agave in clay ovens. Other nuances that can be found in some bottlings are attributable to the fact that much mezcal is distilled only once, hence many impurities remain in the spirit.

Pernod: *See* Absinthe and absinthe substitutes.

Pisco brandy: Made in Chile and other parts of South America, the best pisco comes from Peru, where, by law, it is distilled once in a pot still, and it must leave the still at bottling proof—that's tough to do. Grape-wise, Peruvians can choose to make pisco from only eight specific varietals, four of which are of the aromatic type, and four of which are non-aromatic. The non-aromatic grapes are Negra Corriente, Quebranta, Mollar, and Ubina, and the aromatic varietals are Italia, Muscatel, Torontel (or Torrontes), and Albilla. But they can distill only one variety of grape at a time. Pisco brandy is essential to a Pisco Sour.

Ricard: *See* Absinthe and absinthe substitutes.

Rum: Distilled from a mash of molasses or sugarcane juice, most of the rum consumed in the United States comes from Puerto Rico. However, rum is produced in and imported from almost every Caribbean nation and, indeed, almost every sugar-producing country.

Rums imported from Puerto Rico are required by law to be aged in oak for at least one year. Many rums are aged for far longer, developing into complex, dry spirits suitable for sipping.

Rums are available in light (or white), amber, añejo, and dark varieties, but since every rum-producing nation has its own rules and regulations governing these products, it's impossible to know how long each one of them has been aged in oak unless an age statement appears on the label.

Flavored rums have become very popular in the past decade or so. It's easy to find a variety of flavors, banana, citrus, coconut, lemon, lime and mint, orange, pineapple, raspberry, spiced, vanilla, and wild cherry among them.

Rye whiskey: Made from a fermented mash containing a minimum of 51 percent rye and aged in new charred oak barrels, rye whiskey has made a big comeback among whiskey drinkers. Although some people refer to blended Canadian whiskies as "ryes," they are not; look for the words *straight rye whiskey* on the label.

Scotch whisky: Made in Scotland from a fermented mash of grains, scotch can be divided into two main categories. Single-malt scotch is distilled in pot stills from a fermented mash of malted barley and must spend a minimum of three years in oak barrels before being bottled. Most bottlings, however, spend far longer than that in the wood, and this is usually reflected by an age statement on the label. Each single malt must be the product of just one distillery, the name of which is found on the label of most bottlings. Complicating matters even more, single-malt scotches as a category are often further broken down according to the region in which they are made (*see* box, page 16). Blended malt scotch is a term introduced in the early twenty-first century to describe what used to be known as pure malt scotch in the United States and vatted malt whisky in Europe.

SINGLE-MALT SCOTCHES

Single-malt scotches can be made anywhere in Scotland, but generalizations about specific qualities found in whiskies from various regions can be drawn, even though bottlings vary from one distillery to the next.

Islay (EYE-luh) single malts, such as Ardbeg, Bowmore, and Laphroaig, are from an island just off the western coast of Scotland. Islay malts are usually quite peaty and smoky with notes of iodine, and even with seaweed sometimes being present.

Lowland single malts, such as Auchentoshan, Bladnoch, Glenkinchie, and Littlemill, are usually lighter in character than other bottlings, and they are seldom described as being overly smoky or peaty.

Campbeltown single malts, such as Glen Scotia, Longrow, and Springbank, from the west coast of Scotland, are known for their brininess, and they usually display a certain degree of smokiness, too.

Highland single malts, such as Edradour, Glenmorangie, Knockando, and Oban, vary widely in character, but most often they can be described as being fresh and heathery, with some fruity notes present in certain bottlings.

Speyside single malts, such as Aberlour, The Glenlivet, and The Macallan, come from a subregion of the Highlands that most aficionados claim produces the best of the best whiskies. Speyside bottlings vary tremendously from one to the next, but virtually all of them are very complex, well-knit whiskies, with hints of smoke and peat.

It is made by blending single malts from more than one distillery to achieve a specific flavor profile.

Blended scotch is made by blending single-malt scotch with neutral grain whisky, which can be made from a fermented mash of any grain, although corn is usually predominant and a small amount of malted barley is usually used as well. The amount of single-malt scotch in a blended bottling usually governs its price, so the more expensive blended whiskies tend to be made with a higher percentage of single malt.

The smokiness found in scotch, whether it be single malt or blended, varies from one bottling to the next, but it comes from the barley, which, after germination, is dried over peat fires prior to being introduced into the mash. The amount of time that the malted barley spends over the smoldering peat will govern the amount of smokiness found in the finished product.

Single-barrel whiskey: Most whiskeys, even single-malt scotches, are made by marrying together whiskeys from a number of barrels. In the case of single-barrel whiskey, this is not the case, and these bottlings contain product from just one barrel that the distiller has decided has matured into a superior spirit.

Sloe gin: Not every bottling of sloe gin uses gin as its base, but some, such as Plymouth, do. The spirit is flavored with sloe fruit from blackthorn bushes.

Tennessee whiskey: Distilled from a fermented mash containing a minimum of 51 percent corn, Tennessee whiskey must be made within the state of Tennessee, and it differs from bourbon in that it is filtered through large vats of sugar maple charcoal before it is aged in new charred oak barrels, giving it a sweet sootiness not found in any other whiskeys.

Tequila: Distilled from a fermented mash of blue agave (*Weber tequilana azul*), a member of the amaryllis family that looks like a very large pineapple, tequila is made in Mexico, and it must come from demarcated regions within the states of Jalisco, Nayarit, Guanajuato, Michoacán, or Tamaulipas.

The two basic varieties of tequila are 100 percent blue agave and *mixto*. By law, *mixto* tequila can be made with as little as 51 percent blue agave, with the rest of the product usually being made up of sugar-based products. One-hundred percent agave tequilas are just what they sound like—made only from the blue agave plant; these are most prized by tequila lovers. *Blanco*, or "white," tequilas are not aged at all, but *joven abocado*, meaning "young and smoothed," bottlings, usually known as "gold" tequilas, contain an unspecified percentage of tequila that spent at least two months in oak, and these often also contain a sweetening and/or coloring agent. *Reposado*, or "rested," tequilas spend a minimum of two months in barrels before being bottled, and *añejo*, or "aged," tequilas spend a minimum of 12 months in the wood.

Vodka: This spirit can be made from a fermented mash of almost anything, but it's usually made from grains or potatoes.

Whether vodka originated in Poland or Russia is a matter that will be debated for centuries to come. Vodka contains very few, if any, impurities, and therefore it has little in the way of flavor or aroma. However, individual bottlings do differ, and like any other spirit, some are better than others. As a massive generalization, potato vodkas, made mainly in Poland, although at least one is made in the United States, are a little sweeter than grain-based bottlings.

Flavored vodkas have become very popular in recent years, and some of them are responsible for many of today's newest cocktails and mixed drinks. Almost every flavor under the sun seems to be on the market now; you can choose from apple, berry, bilberry, bison grass, chocolate, cinnamon, citrus, coffee, cranberry, currant, honey, honey and pepper, honey and quince, lemon, lime, orange, peach, pear, pepper, raspberry, sake, strawberry, vanilla, wild apple, wild berry, cucumber, and tomato. Several brands are organic vodkas—another new trend—meant to please the greener characters among us. What fun!

Whisk(e)y: Spelled with the e in Ireland and the United States and without it in Scotland and Canada, whiskey is distilled from a fermented mash of grains that is aged until it develops a style that is recognizable as whiskey. See Scotch Whisky, Canadian Whisky, Bourbon, Rye Whiskey, Tennessee Whiskey, and Irish Whiskey.

Liqueurs

Liqueurs are sweetened, usually diluted spirits that have been flavored by specific botanicals, fruits, herbs, nuts, spices, and products from almost every food group. Sometimes known as cordials in the United States, liqueurs have been with us since at least the 1300s, when monks, seeking to make medicines, flavored distilled spirits with medicinal herbs, and sweetened them, sometimes with honey, to make them more palatable.

Alizé: A passion fruit–flavored, brandy-based liqueur.

Alizé Red Passion: A passion fruit– and cranberry juice– flavored, brandy-based liqueur.

Amaretto: An almond-flavored liqueur that originated in Italy.

Amarula: A South African cream liqueur flavored with marula fruit.

Anisette: A syrupy aniseed-flavored liqueur.

Apricot brandy: An apricot-flavored liqueur containing a percentage of real brandy.

Apry: A brand-name apricot-flavored liqueur.

B&B: Bénédictine mixed with brandy—this delicious liqueur was created at New York's "21" Club shortly after the repeal of Prohibition.

Baileys Irish cream: Made with Irish whiskey and heavy cream, Baileys is one of today's most popular liqueurs.

Bärenjäger: A popular honey-flavored liqueur from Germany.

Becherovka: An herbal liqueur from the Czech Republic with strong anise, cinnamon, and clove notes.

Belle de Brillet: A French pear-flavored liqueur with a cognac base.

Bénédictine: A French herbal liqueur made by Benedictine monks since 1510.

Blackberry brandy: A blackberry-flavored liqueur containing a percentage of real brandy.

Chambord: A French black raspberry–flavored liqueur sweetened with honey and spiced with herbs.

Chartreuse: Made by French Carthusian monks since 1737, this is an herbal liqueur available in both green and yellow bottlings. Alcohol content is high.

Chéri-Suisse: A Swiss chocolate- and cherry-flavored liqueur.

Cherry brandy: A cherry-flavored liqueur not to be confused with kirsch, which is an unsweetened brandy made from cherries.

Cherry Heering: A top-notch brand name of cherry brandy made in Denmark.

Cointreau: A top-notch brand-name orange-flavored liqueur; although the company doesn't market this product as a triple sec, that's exactly what it is. It is perhaps the best triple sec on the market.

Cointreau Noir: A top-notch orange-flavored liqueur blended with cognac.

Crème de banane: A sweet banana-flavored liqueur.

Crème de cacao: A chocolate-flavored liqueur available in both white and dark bottlings—they are similar in flavor.

Crème de cassis: A black currant–flavored liqueur originating in France, though many bottlings are now made in the United States.

Crème de framboise: A raspberry-flavored liqueur from France.

Crème de menthe: A mint-flavored liqueur that comes in both green and white bottlings—they are similar in flavor.

Crème de mûre: A blackberry-flavored liqueur.

Crème de noyaux: An almond-flavored liqueur that contributes the pink color to a Pink Squirrel cocktail—substitute amaretto if you can't find this product.

Crème de violette: A violet-flavored liqueur currently available in the United States under the Rothman & Winter label.

Cuarenta y Tres Licor 43: A Spanish fruit- and herb-based liqueur; the name translates to "forty-three," the number of ingredients used in its production.

Curaçao: A sweet, orange-flavored liqueur, sometimes white, sometimes blue, and sometimes red—all bottlings are similar in flavor.

Danziger Goldwasser: A German liqueur with mainly aniseed and caraway flavors and flakes of real gold. This liqueur has been made since 1598, at which time gold was believed to have healing qualities.

Domaine de Canton: A fabulous ginger-flavored liqueur made with a cognac base and also flavored with vanilla beans, honey, and ginseng.

Drambuie: A honeyed scotch-based liqueur flavored with various herbs and spices. The name comes from the Gaelic *an dram buidheach*, meaning "the drink that satisfies." The recipe was supposedly given to Captain John Mackinnon by Bonnie Prince Charlie in 1746, when Mackinnon sheltered him on the Isle of Skye after his defeat by the English at the Battle of Culloden.

Falernum: A Caribbean liqueur flavored with almonds, cloves, lime, and ginger.

Faretti Biscotti Famosi: A surprisingly good biscotti-flavored liqueur with hints of nuts and oranges.

Frangelico: An Italian hazelnut liqueur spiced with cinnamon, cardamom, citrus zest, and various other botanicals.

Galliano: An Italian liqueur with predominant vanilla and orange notes; it is essential for a Harvey Wallbanger.

Glayva: A scotch-based liqueur that, like Drambuie, is flavored with honey and herbs.

Grand Marnier: An orange-flavored, cognac-based French liqueur, made since 1871 by the Marnier-Lapostolle family. Much of the aged cognac used to make Grand Marnier comes from the best regions of Cognac, and after being infused with orange peels and sweetened with simple syrup, the liqueur is then returned to barrels for further aging.

Cordon Rouge is the bottling of Grand Marnier most familiar to us, but it is also available in Grande Marnier Cuvée du Centenaire, which was issued to celebrate the 100-year anniversary of the liqueur, and Grand Marnier Cuvée du Cent Cinquantenaire, released to commemorate the 150-year anniversary of Lapostolle's company, which has been producing liqueurs since 1827. The Grand Marnier Cuvée du Centenaire is made with 10-year-old cognac, and the Grand Marnier Cuvée du Cent Cinquantenaire uses XO cognacs.

Hpnotiq: A tropical fruit–flavored liqueur with a base of cognac and vodka.

Irish Mist: Based on an ancient formula for heather wine, this Irish whiskey–based liqueur is flavored with honey and spiced with herbs.

Kahlúa: A Mexican coffee-flavored liqueur dating back to the 1930s.

Kirsch: Sometimes called Kirschwasser; an eau-de-vie made from a fermented mash of cherries.

Kümmel: A caraway-flavored liqueur from Holland.

Limoncello: An Italian lemon zest–flavored liqueur that is becoming increasingly popular in the United States. Store it in the freezer.

Mandarine Napoléon: A French cognac-based liqueur with the flavors of tangerine zest.

Maraschino: A cherry liqueur that's essential to the Aviation cocktail. It's nutty and spicy, and one bottling, Luxardo, is highly perfumed. This liqueur in no way tastes like the cherries found at most bars. Maraschino is very popular among twenty-first-century mixologists; it was also a common ingredient in several of the earliest cocktails.

Midori: A honeydew melon–flavored liqueur (*midori* is Japanese for "green") that is very popular in the United States.

Nocello: A walnut-flavored liqueur.

Ouzo: A Greek anise-flavored liqueur.

Peach brandy: A peach-flavored liqueur.

Peach schnapps: A dryish peach-flavored liqueur.

Peppermint schnapps: A peppermint-flavored liqueur, usually drier than crème de menthe.

Pernod: *See* Absinthe and absinthe substitutes.

Pimento Dram: *See* St. Elizabeth Allspice Dram below.

Pimm's No. 1 Cup: A gin-based, fruity herbal liqueur created in London by James Pimm, a restaurateur, in the early 1800s. It's usually served over ice with ginger ale and a slice of cucumber.

Qi: A tea-based liqueur available in two bottlings. The white tea bottling is also flavored with oranges, herbs, and spices, and the black tea bottling employs a cedar-smoked tea, spices, fruits, and honey as flavorings.

Sabra: A liqueur from Israel that's flavored with chocolate and oranges.

Sambuca: An Italian anise-based liqueur, available in white and black bottlings—black sambuca is usually flavored with lemon zest as well as anise.

Southern Comfort: An American fruit-flavored liqueur with predominantly peach notes. Though everyone seems to think this product contains bourbon, it does not.

St. Elizabeth Allspice Dram: Made from a base of rum, this Jamaican liqueur is flavored with allspice, giving it notes of cloves, cinnamon, and nutmeg. Also known as Pimento Dram.

St-Germain: A fabulous elderflower-flavored liqueur from France. Very popular among twenty-first-century mixologists.

Strawberry brandy: A strawberry-flavored liqueur.

Strega: An Italian herbal liqueur made with more than 70 botanicals—the word *strega* means "witch."

Swedish Punch (or Punsch): A smoky Scandinavian liqueur made from a base of Batavia Arrack.

Tia Maria: A Jamaican liqueur made from a base of rum and flavored with coffee.

Triple sec: An orange-flavored liqueur used in many mixed drinks, such as the Margarita.

Tuaca: An Italian herbal liqueur with predominant vanilla notes and a hint of oranges.

Vandermint: A Dutch liqueur flavored with chocolate and mint.

Zen: A green tea–flavored liqueur.

Amaros and Other Products in the "Bitter" Category

Amer Picon: Hard to find in the United States, this is a French apéritif wine with orange/herbal notes.

Aperol: A bitter Italian aperitivo that's similar to Campari, though a little lighter.

Averna: A brand of Italian amaro that has made a big comeback in the twenty-first century.

Campari: A bitter aperitivo from Italy used in cocktails and mixed drinks such as the Negroni. It is notable for its red color and its affinity to orange flavors.

Cynar: An Italian herbal aperitivo made from a base of artichokes.

Fernet-Branca: An herbal Italian amaro that's very popular in Venezuela and among San Francisco's bartenders.

Fernet-Branca Menta: A mint-flavored herbal Italian amaro.

Jägermeister: A German liqueur, somewhat medicinal in flavor, but very popular in the United States. *Jägermeister*, literally translated, means "master of the hunt."

Wines and Wine-Based Ingredients

Champagne (and Other Sparkling Wines)

Effervescent wines are made in all wine-making countries, but the methods used are based on those that originated in the Champagne region of France in the early 1700s. Most wine aficionados today still recognize champagnes made in the delimited region of northeastern France known as the Champagne district as the real thing.

French champagne can be made only from three types of grapes—two black and one white—Pinot Noir, Pinot Meunier, and Chardonnay. The grape juice is separated from the black grape skins before they can impart any color to the wine. Further, real champagne (and the best sparkling wines from elsewhere) must be made using the *méthode champenoise*, a stringent, time-consuming process prescribed by French law. The *méthode champenoise* involves adding sugar and yeast to the wine at the time of bottling; this process results in a secondary fermentation that creates the bubbles in champagne. After the secondary fermentation is complete, the champagne is disgorged; that is, the sediment created by the yeast is removed by immersing the neck of the bottle in a freezing liquid, and the temporary cap and the sediment that clings to it are then removed. Usually, a little sugar that has been dissolved in mature wine (*dosage*) is then added to the bottle before it is once again sealed. All that just to get those wonderful little bubbles into the wine and then keep them inside the bottle until it is opened.

STYLES OF FRENCH CHAMPAGNE

Blanc de blancs: Champagnes made from 100 percent Chardonnay (white) grapes.

Blanc de noir: Champagnes made from Pinot Noir and/or Meunier grapes; both grape varieties are black.

Brut: Literally means "very dry," but in fact these champagnes do bear some sweetness.

Extra brut: Drier than brut.

CHAMPAGNE TIPS

If you really want lots of bubbles in your champagne, scratch the bottom of your champagne glass with the tip of a very sharp, slim knife or a small piece of very fine sandpaper. The carbon dioxide will react to the rough bottom of the glass and your bubbly will be really, well, bubbly.

If you have a bottle of champagne that's been sitting in your fridge for too long and has lost its sparkle, take a raisin, squeeze it a little, and drop it into the bottle. Be ready to drink the champagne right away, though—the bubbles won't last forever.

—from Robert Burke, proprietor, Pot au Feu, Providence, Rhode Island

Sec: Literally means "dry," but these champagnes are usually medium-sweet.

Extra sec: Literally means "extra-dry," but in fact, these champagnes are usually only medium-dry.

Demi-sec: Literally means "half-dry," but these champagnes are actually medium-sweet to sweet.

Doux: Literally means "sweet," and these bottlings are very sweet.

Vintage champagnes: Bottlings containing only wines from the year noted on the label. A champagne is chosen to be a vintage bottling when the wine of one particular year is deemed by the winemaker to be exceptional.

HOW TO SERVE CHAMPAGNE

Champagne should be served at a temperature of about 45°F, so be sure to chill it well. Do not shake or agitate the bottle before opening it. Remove the foil that covers the neck, and then loosen the cage by grasping the small wire loop and untwisting it. Hold the bottle at a 45-degree angle and take care that it isn't in a direct line with Grandma's antique mirror or your best friend's head. Firmly grasp the cork with one hand and hold the base of the bottle with the other. Gently twist the bottle while holding the cork steady until the cork is released. Don't "pop" the cork; ease the bottle away from it.

Slowly pour the champagne into Champagne glasses, ideally flutes, adding small amounts to each glass and allowing the foam to subside before adding more. Swirling is not recommended, but staring at the upward-rising stream of bubbles is a treat.

Dubonnet

An apéritif wine produced in two styles: Dubonnet Rouge and Dubonnet Blanc. Though either product is highly recommendable as an apéritif—serve it over ice with a citrus twist—Dubonnet can be used instead of vermouth in cocktails. Be aware, though, that it is far bolder and fruitier than vermouth, so it adds another dimension to such drinks.

Lillet

A French apéritif wine that is produced in Blanc and Rouge renditions. Use Lillet as you would Dubonnet, or try substituting it for vermouth in cocktail recipes. Lillet is somewhat lighter than Dubonnet.

Madeira

A red wine fortified with grape brandy, Madeira is named for the island where it was born. The aging process for Madeira is unique to the wine industry: The wine is stored in oak casks in buildings built especially for the purpose. Temperatures are kept high—usually between 104°F and 114°F—for about six months. The wine then is transferred to cooler cellars, where it rests for at least a year and a half. Finally, it matures in a solera system, as does sherry (see page 30). When you hear about the destructive properties of heat on wine maturation, remember that Madeira is the exception; the heat it withstands is intentional. Once open, this hearty wine will last indefinitely without spoiling.

STYLES OF MADEIRA AND HOW TO SERVE THEM

Madeira can be made in any of five distinct styles. All, except Rainwater, are named after the variety of grape used to make them:

Sercial: The driest style, Sercial should be served slightly chilled in a small wine glass.

Verdelho: A medium-dry, highly acidic style, Verdelho should also be served slightly chilled in a small wine glass.

Rainwater: A versatile, lighter style of Madeira that is a pale, light blend of other Madeiras. Rainwater should be served chilled, from the refrigerator, in a small wine glass.

Bual: This Madeira is medium-sweet, perfect for after-dinner sipping. Serve it at room temperature in a small wine glass.

Malmsey: The sweetest Madeira, wonderfully fragrant, full-bodied and rich on the palate. Serve it at room temperature in a small wine glass.

Port

Originally a Portuguese wine that was fortified with local grape brandy, port now is produced almost everywhere that table wines are made. The brandy used to fortify the new wine is unaged and added to the wine at a very high proof. Since this increases the alcohol content, fermentation stops, leaving some of the grape sugars unfermented, thus sweetening the wine. After fortification, the port is stored in oak casks. Inexpensive ports may be aged for as little as one year, but many of the better bottlings are kept in casks for as long as 10 and up to 40 years. Vintage port, the only type that is aged in glass after aging in wood, continues to improve after it is bottled. It should be kept at a constant temperature of about 48°F, and the bottle should be stored on its side.

STYLES OF PORT AND HOW TO SERVE THEM

Ports are made in three colors—white, tawny, and ruby—so they're extremely easy to tell apart. Their qualities, however, are as different as their colors. Two other types are also produced: late-bottled vintage port and vintage port; the latter is a collector's item, the other can be drunk right away.

White port: Some are dry and light-bodied, but most are sweeter and medium-bodied, so each bottling must be tasted to see what style it is. White ports are made from white grapes. Usually offered as an apéritif, white port should be served well chilled, in small wine glasses.

HOW TO DECANT VINTAGE PORT

During their aging process, sediment develops in vintage ports. Though harmless, this "crust" is visually and texturally unattractive; therefore, these ports are decanted before they are enjoyed. Several hours or even a day ahead of time, stand the bottle upright—away from the light and where it won't be disturbed—to allow the sediment to settle. The ritualistic way of decanting a fine vintage port is very theatrical: Line a funnel with a double or triple layer of dampened cheesecloth. Place the funnel into the neck of a decanter. Next, holding a candle behind the neck of the port bottle, pour the wine into the funnel, checking the neck to see if any sediment can be seen. Once you see sediment, stop pouring. (If you want to modernize the ritual, use a flashlight.) Once the bottle is opened, don't linger in drinking a vintage port; its charms will dissipate with extended exposure to air.

Ruby port: Normally a young wine that has very often spent less than four years in casks (known as "pipes" in the port business). Wines from a variety of pipes are blended together to produce a sweet, medium- to full-bodied port that represents each individual producer's style. Ruby port should be served at room temperature in small wine glasses; it is also the port of choice for cocktail and drink making. A new Croft bottling called Pink port would fall into this category; I like it chilled.

Tawny port: When inexpensive, tawny port is invariably nothing more than a blend of white and ruby ports. Aged tawny ports, on the other hand, are truly special. Tawny port starts its life as ruby port, and it is the extended aging period that contributes to both the change of the wine's color—from a deep purple to ruby to a tawny brown—and its change in flavor: The longer the port rests in the pipes, the more its sweetness mellows to a complex, fruity nuttiness, until, at around age 30, some ports bear the distinct flavors of dried fruits while retaining a pleasant dry nuttiness. Aged tawny port should be savored at room temperature in small wine glasses.

Late-bottled vintage port: Normally a good-quality port that has aged in wood for over four years but seldom more than six. These are fine wines that are far less expensive than vintage bottlings, but they do not improve in the bottle, and can, therefore, be consumed immediately after purchase. Late-bottled vintage port should be served at room temperature in small wine glasses.

Vintage port: Bottled after spending only two years in port pipes, these are wines that have been declared by a very strict regulatory board to be of the finest quality. Unlike wood-aged bottlings, vintage ports continue to age and improve in the bottle and should be kept for at least 10 years or considerably longer before opening. Many experts claim that to experience a truly great vintage port, a minimum of two decades of bottle aging is necessary. Vintage port should be served at room temperature in small wine glasses.

Punt e Mes

The brand name of an Italian apéritif that is like a bitter, less-sweet version of vermouth.

Saké

Is it a beer or a wine? That's the question. Saké is made from rice, a grain, and therefore should be classified as a beer since, technically, wines are made from fruits. However, the U.S. Bureau of Alcohol, Tobacco, and Firearms classifies saké as a Japanese wine that is made from "other agricultural products." Go figure. In any case, no matter what it is, saké is good. Specific types of rice are used and then fermented to produce the product that will mature in wood casks into saké. Don't think that all sakés are served warm; many of the finer ones are chilled for serving. Look for an increase in imports of high-end sakés that are made with the care and precision of other fine wines—or beers.

Sherry

A Spanish wine that is fortified with brandy and can be produced only in a delimited area of southern Andalucía that encompasses the towns of Sanlúcar de Barrameda, Puerto de Santa María, and Jerez de la Frontera. Originally known in England as Sherry-Sack, and commonly referred to in

Elizabethan times simply as Sack, it is thought that the wine gained its name from the town of Jerez (HAIR-eth), which was eventually corrupted to *sherry*. The *sack* part of the name probably originated from the Spanish word *sacar*, meaning "export." It makes great sense that sherry became a widely exported wine, since the main reason for fortifying wines with brandy was to stabilize them so they could stand up to long voyages at sea.

The sherry-making process is complex: After the wine ferments completely, a process that takes several months, it is pumped into oak casks that are deliberately not filled all the way full. The winemaker then must wait to see if a thin white layer of airborne yeast, known as *flor*, will form on its surface.

When the *flor* forms a thick layer, the wine will become the light, dry, fino style of sherry. If the layer is thinner, the wine will oxidize more than fino because it has greater contact with the air; these wines will darken and become amontillado sherries. When no film appears at all, the wine is destined to become an oloroso sherry. Over the next one to two years, the wines are watched closely and checked for alcohol content. Depending on the *flor* and the experience of the bodega master, unaged grape brandy is added to fortify the wine. Wines that will become olorosos are fortified to a slightly higher alcohol level than those that will become finos. When ready, the wine is transferred to sherry butts—smaller oak casks—which are then shipped to the solera for aging.

The solera aging system is reserved for sherries, Spanish brandies (see page 10), and Madeiras (see page 26). The sherry butts are arranged in tiers—often 10 tiers high—with the oldest sherries on the bottom and the youngest on top. When some of the sherry—never more than half—is drawn off the lowest tier, it is replenished with wine from the tier above it. Thus, by the time a wine reaches the bottom level, it has aged and mingled, always with older sherries in the solera.

STYLES OF SHERRY AND HOW TO SERVE THEM

Fino sherries: Pale, light, and dry, fino sherries should be served chilled, from the refrigerator, in Sherry Copita glasses or on the rocks. They are an excellent apéritif and just right for late-afternoon tapas.

Manzanilla sherries: Cousins of finos, manzanillas are aged in Sanlúcar de Barrameda, a town located on the Mediterranean Sea. They feature an extremely delicate body and a slight saltiness, perhaps due to the location of their aging. Manzanillas should be served chilled, from the refrigerator, in Sherry Copita glasses or on the rocks.

Amontillado sherries: Darker in color and nuttier on the palate than their drier fino cousins, amontillado sherries should be served chilled, from the refrigerator, in Sherry Copita glasses or on the rocks.

Oloroso sherries: These have a deep amber color and a nutty, sweet, full body that fills the mouth. Serve them at room temperature in Sherry Copita glasses.

Cream sherries: Actually a style of oloroso sherry, these, too, are sweet, and have a somewhat creamy texture. Cream sherries should be served at room temperature in Sherry Copita glasses.

Pedro Ximénez sherries: The sweetest of all, these should be served at room temperature in Sherry Copita glasses.

Vermouth

A member of the category known as aromatized wines, vermouths are wines that have been flavored with botanical ingredients—herbs, spices, flowers, roots, seeds, and fruits—and are fortified with brandy. Italy produced the first vermouth in the late 1700s; it was red and sweet and came to be referred to as "Italian." The French produced the first dry, pale-colored vermouth a couple of decades later, and it came to be referred to as "French." These days, vermouths are produced in many, many countries; each bottling, though, has its own character and style. Though some inexpensive vermouths are made by merely introducing essences and flavorings to fortified wine, the best bottlings are manufactured using a far more complicated procedure.

Many companies start out with a wine that has been aged, sometimes for as long as 12 months, and most vermouths—even most red, sweet vermouths—are made from white wine. The wine is then fortified, but only slightly, by the addition of *mistelle*, a mixture of unfermented grape juice and brandy.

Botanicals are then introduced to the wine by any of several methods. Sometimes they are infused into the wine at room temperature; sometimes the wine is heated slightly to speed up infusion time; and sometimes herbs are infused into distilled spirits, such as brandy, that are then added to the wine, fortifying it further.

After the wine has been aromatized, it is sometimes returned to oak casks for further aging. Before bottling, it must undergo a technical stabilizing process that filters out any tartrates.

STYLES OF VERMOUTH

Dry vermouth: Usually made from very light, dry wines, dry vermouths are usually soft, herbal, and crisp. Vital for a Martini.

Sweet vermouth: Sweeter, of course, than dry vermouth, sweet vermouth also bears a slight bitterness due to the higher percentage of quinine used in production, and the herbal accents are often less forthcoming.

Bianco vermouth: Clear in color, like dry vermouth, bianco bottlings are slightly sweeter than their dry cousins and somewhat more herbal.

Rosé vermouth: Similar to bianco vermouth but pale pink in color and dry on the palate.

Carpano Antica Formula: A very distinctive, and highly desirable, style of sweet vermouth with notes of vanilla.

STORING AND SERVING VERMOUTH

Once the bottle is opened, store your vermouth in the refrigerator. And if the bottles you have are more than six months old, replace them, because oxidation will have ruined their sprightly appeal. If you don't use vermouth very often, it might be a good idea to buy the smaller 375-ml bottles.

Serve vermouths straight from the bottle, on ice. The French Kiss cocktail—a 50-50 combination of sweet and dry vermouths—can be an excellent apéritif. Also, when cooking, if a bit of wine is called for, vermouth can add more complexity than most table wines.

Wine

Wine is an entire world of its own, and, indeed, it spans the world, produced on every continent except Antarctica. Bartending involves using all four types of wine: sparkling wine, like champagne and Prosecco; aromatized wines, like vermouth and many apéritifs; fortified wines, like port, sherry, and Madeira; and still wines, like your basic reds, whites, and rosés.

Most cocktail recipes that call for still wines should be made with a good dry white, a dry red, or a dryish rosé. And when your guest or customer requests, say, a white wine, be sure that the wine you're pouring is fresh and tasty and properly presented.

HOW TO SERVE WINE

Though dozens of different sizes and shapes of wine glasses can be found in the market, a good basic wine glass will have a capacity of at least eight ounces, preferably more, and ideally, it will be a stemmed glass. When you pour, do not fill the glass more than halfway full, and handle the glass by the stem only.

White wines should be served chilled, not icy cold; red wines should be at cool room temperature—don't keep them next to the radiator.

HOW TO TASTE WINE

Tasting wine requires your whole body. Start by looking at the wine; note its color, texture, and clarity. Smell the wine; stick your nose well into the glass and take a deep breath. Next, swirl the wine in the glass and smell it again; new aromas might present themselves. Now, taste the wine; take a mouthful, not just a sip, and swish it around your mouth so that it comes in contact with all of your taste buds. Take note of every quality—its feel, its texture, its flavor, its acidity. Finally, swallow the wine. Does it linger in the mouth? Does it have any effect on your throat? Consider the experience. Did it taste like it smelled? Did it look full-bodied but feel and taste thin in the mouth? Would you like to drink more of it?

Screw caps—and they're becoming increasingly popular—aside, many people are intimidated by the act of pulling a cork from a wine bottle. You shouldn't be—if you have a good corkscrew and know how to use it. (I'll repeat my personal recommendation, the Screwpull.) First, wipe off the bottle with a clean cloth. Stand it on a flat surface and use a small knife or a foil cutter to remove the top of the plastic, foil, or lead capsule that covers the cork. Cut just below the lip of the bottle. Next, position the worm of your corkscrew slightly off-center and begin turning it firmly to burrow the worm into the cork—because the worm is a spiral, starting it off-center will result in its being centered in the cork. Use levers, elbow grease, or whatever mechanism your corkscrew offers to extract the cork from the bottle. Finally—and this is important—use a clean cloth to wipe the interior and exterior lip of the bottle before pouring from it.

Beer

Like wine, beer is an entire world of its own, the product of grains, hops, water, and yeasts that promote fermentation. The category divides into two parts: lagers, which are brewed using yeasts that ferment on the bottom of a tank, and ales, which are brewed using top-fermenting yeasts. Lagers are low in alcohol, light in body, and the most popular style of beer in the United States; styles include light lagers, bocks, pilsners, smoked beers (rauchbiers), and malt liquors. Ales, generally higher in alcohol, heavier in body, and more robust in flavor, include many styles: stout, porter, wheat beers, and pale ales, as well as numerous others.

Mixers

Mixers require little explanation; most are complete the way you buy them. One exception is simple syrup, which you will see throughout the recipes in this book. I ardently recommend that you make your own—it's very simple—and keep it on hand in the refrigerator; its shelf life is practically infinite. Having simple syrup on hand and using it in place of granulated sugar and water in recipes ensures a better blending of flavors and a better texture in the drink.

Beef bouillon	Lemon juice (fresh)
Clamato juice	Lemon-lime soda (diet and regular)
Club soda	
Coconut cream	Lime juice (fresh)
Cola (diet and regular)	Lime juice cordial, such as Rose's
Cranberry juice	
Fruit nectars (peach, pear, apricot)	Milk
	Mineral water (still)
Ginger ale	Orange juice
Ginger beer	Pineapple juice
Grapefruit juice	Simple syrup (recipe follows)
Grenadine	Tomato juice
Half-and-half	Tonic water
Heavy cream	Whipped cream

Simple Syrup

MAKES 4 CUPS (1 QUART)

3 cups water
3 cups granulated sugar

Heat the water in a saucepan set over moderately high heat. When it begins to simmer, add the sugar and stir until it dissolves. Do not let the mixture boil. Remove the pan from the heat and set aside to cool to room temperature. Pour the simple syrup through a funnel into an empty, clean, 1-liter liquor bottle and cap tightly. Store in the refrigerator.

Condiments and Flavorings

Allspice (ground)

Angostura bitters

Apples

Bananas

Berries

Black pepper

Candies

Celery seeds

Cinnamon (sticks and
ground)

Cloves

Cocktail onions

Cocoa powder
(unsweetened)

Coffee beans

Cucumbers

Eggs

Falernum syrup

Fresh mint

Gingerroot

Grapefruits

Horseradish

Lemons

Limes

Maraschino cherries

Nutmeg

Old Bay Seasoning

Olives (cocktail, anchovy-
stuffed, almond-stuffed)

Orange bitters

Orange flower water

Oranges

Orgeat syrup

Peach bitters

Peychaud's bitters

Rose water

Salt (kosher or sea)

Sugar (granulated, superfine,
and confectioners'; cubes
or lumps)

Tabasco sauce

Worcestershire sauce

Infusions, Tinctures, Elixirs, and Flavored Syrups

Today's bartenders and bar chefs love to play; they just can't seem to leave anything alone. As a result, you will find recipes that call for infusions of all kinds—fruits, teas, spices, and more—homemade tinctures, syrups, and unlikely-seeming purées. Most are easy to do but must be prepared ahead of time. Indeed, an avid cocktailian could have a dozen different flavored simple syrups in the refrigerator at once. Use your judgment, but, please give at least some of them a try. You might want to halve the recipe if that's possible for home bar use.

Glassware

Let's face it: Drinking a Mint Julep out of an antique, sterling silver, ice-coated Julep cup is an experience everyone should have—at least once. But then, sipping a Julep from a plastic cup will do quite nicely, thank you, if you happen to be sitting in a box seat at Churchill Downs on the first Saturday in May, just aching for the Kentucky Derby to begin its run. Indeed, whenever we have the opportunity to drink from fine glassware, we should, as it's marvelous. But we can't expect the corner bar to share such finery with us; they use what's appropriate and affordable, and clean (we ardently hope). Don't think about running out to buy a whole wardrobe of cocktail glasses; they're easily collected one or two or six at a time. And depending on your drinking and entertaining habits, you might not need certain special-purpose glasses at all.

Here's a roundup of what's typically stocked at a bar. Whatever glass you use, do yourself a favor: Fill the glass with water and then pour it into a measuring cup for liquids so you know the glass's capacity. Then you can adjust your recipe to suit the glass. Also, if you are having cocktails near a pool or on a beach, use plastic or paper drinkware. Broken glass is just too dangerous in those locales.

beer glass,
16 to 20 ounces

Champagne flute
glass, 6 to 9 ounces

beer mug,
12 to 20 ounces

Champagne Saucer
glass, 6 to 9 ounces

Pilsner glass,
10 to 20 ounces

Sherry Copita glass,
4 to 6 ounces

all-purpose
wine goblet,
8 to 14 ounces

sherry glass,
4 to 6 ounces

white wine glass,
8 to 14 ounces

cocktail glass,
4 to 12 ounces

red wine glass,
8 to 14 ounces

Collins glass,
8 to 14 ounces

Champagne tulip glass,
6 to 9 ounces

cordial glass,
1 to 3 ounces

Highball glass,
8 to 10 ounces

Hurricane glass,
16 to 20 ounces

Irish Coffee glass,
8 to 10 ounces

jigger glass,
2 to 3 ounces

Rocks (old-fashioned)
glass, 5 to 6 ounces

large Rocks
(Double Old-Fashioned)
glass, 8 to 10 ounces

Pony glass,
2 to 3 ounces

Pousse-Café glass,
3 to 4 ounces

Brandy snifter

punch cup,
6 to 8 ounces

shot glass,
1 to 3 ounces

Sour glass,
4 to 6 ounces

Zombie glass,
12 to 20 ounces

Basic Garnishes

Whenever you think that garnishes are just extras or fancy flourishes, take a look at the Gibson, a cocktail that is a Naked Martini until it is defined by its pearl onion garnish. Garnishes are not mere optional extras. Many, many cocktails don't have specific garnishes; you may add one, of course, if you choose to, but its qualities should complement the drink, not merely fancy it up. When a twist is called for, I am instantly furious if the bartender merely waves a piece of citrus zest over my glass and drops it in. If I want the benefit of the oils from the zest, I must fish it out myself, rub the outside of it around the lip of the glass, and then twist it for its almost invisible little spritz of oils on top of my drink. The difference between a Scotch and Soda with a twist dropped in and one that's properly made is remarkable.

If you know beforehand that you'll be preparing a variety of drinks, it's a good idea to prepare at least the basics—twists, wedges, and wheels—ahead of time. Don't, however, let them dry out once cut. Fold several sheets of paper towels and soak with cold water. Place on top of the cut fruit and refrigerate until needed.

One last general hint: Wash and dry all fruit that is used with its peel intact for a garnish. You don't know where it's been!

Citrus wedges: Top and tail each fruit. Cut lengthwise into two equal halves. Cut each half into no more than four wedges—there's nothing worse than a citrus wedge with no oomph to it.

Citrus twists: Cut off one end of the fruit to create a flat base. Stand the fruit upright on a cutting board. Working from the top toward the bottom of the fruit and using a paring knife, cut vertical $1/2$-inch-wide strips of peel. You want the colorful outer peel and just enough of the inner white pith to keep the twist sturdy enough to twist without breaking. Continue cutting twists; the remaining fruit can be squeezed for its fresh juice.

Citrus wheels: Top and tail each fruit. Place the fruit on its side and, using a large knife, thinly slice into uniform rounds; discard the end pieces if they are not attractive. If the wheel will be perched on the lip of the glass, make a single cut from the outer edge to the center of each wheel.

Citrus slices: Though these look like wheels cut in half, that's not the proper way to cut them. Top and tail each fruit. Cut lengthwise into two equal halves. Place each half, cut side down, on a cutting board and cut into uniform slices. If the slice is meant to perch over the rim of the glass, make a single cut from the center of each wheel up to, but not through, the peel.

Fruit spirals: Citrus spirals are essential for all drinks in the Crusta category. Though citrus spirals are most often called for, several fruits lend themselves to spiral cutting—especially apples and pears. Spirals are very pretty, but unless you're a genius with a knife, they might take some practice to master. Using a paring knife or a citrus zester and starting toward the blossom or stem end of the fruit, cut into the peel and keep cutting around the circumference, spiraling round and round toward the opposite end of the fruit. Ideally, you'll end up with a continuous, springy coil of fruit peel. Usually, the entire spiral is used in a cocktail (although some of your mistakes can be attractive hung over the lip of a glass). Remember, practice makes perfect—I suggest using apples for starters and working up to citrus.

Bartending Techniques

Pouring with a Jigger

Many bartenders prefer to know for sure that they are being precise when measuring ingredients for a cocktail, and these people use jiggers to guide them. This is a stylistic difference between free-pourers and the people who use jiggers. Neither one is right or wrong.

Learning to Free Pour

The most important—and liberating—technique worth learning is how to pick up a bottle and free pour a shot of liquor. The method is simple; all it requires is practice and consistency. Here's how to learn to free pour:

Fill an empty liquor bottle with water; insert a speed pourer into the neck of the bottle. Have ready a $1^1/_2$-ounce jigger and an empty mixing glass. Now, pick up the bottle, grasping it so that your thumb or index finger is wrapped over the base of the speed pourer and the others are tightly wrapped around the top of the neck of the bottle. Upend the bottle over the jigger and start silently counting in your head until the jigger is full. Pour out the water and continue the process, finding your own count for pouring $1^1/_2$ ounces of liquid. Remember, you must always count at the same speed for your measurement to be consistent.

When you think you have mastered your count, pour your $1^1/_2$-ounce measure directly into the empty mixing glass, and then pour the water from the mixing glass into a jigger to check that your measurement is correct. Once you are confident that you can pour a $1^1/_2$-ounce measure by using the counting method, you should be able to pour other measurements— 1 ounce, 2 ounces, etc.—simply by adjusting your count appropriately.

Chilling a Glass

If possible, store the glassware you think you'll need in the refrigerator or freezer. If there's no room, glass chilling should be done before you start preparing the cocktail so that there's enough time for it to get cold. I suggest doing this in a sink. Fill the glass with ice and enough water to overflow the glass; let it sit in the sink while you mix the drink. Pick up the glass of ice and water by the stem, if there is one. Jiggle the glass so the water overflows again; pour out the ice and water. Hold the glass upside down and shake to get rid of any remaining drops.

Coating the Rim of a Serving Glass with a Dry Ingredient

I'm more or less "my way or the highway" about this topic, since the sugar, salt, cocoa powder, or chocolate sprinkles are ingredients that you consume while sipping your drink.

Indeed, a Sidecar without its sugar-coated rim is too tart, and a Chocolate Martini is only half as good and less than half as pretty without its cocoa powder rim. Technique is everything here; following are detailed instructions for how to do it the right way.

We've all experienced it: You order a Margarita. The bartender moistens the rim of the glass with a wedge of lime and then inverts the glass into a shallow bowl or tray of coarse salt. The salt forms a thickish crust where the glass was moistened. The bartender then prepares the drink, pours it into the glass, and sets it in front of you. Yuk! Where oh where does any recipe for a Margarita include a half-teaspoon or more of salt in the drink? Nowhere. Does no one realize that after running a wedge of lime around the circumference of the glass, both the inside and outside edges are being moistened, and that by then upending the rim in salt, both the inside and outside of the glass's rim will be thickly coated with salt? Pour the liquid in the glass and all that salt on the inside of the glass melts into the drink.

Here is the very best way to coat the rim of a glass for serving. Use it with salt on the rim of Margarita or Salty Dog cocktails, use it with sugar for your Sidecars and Lemon Drops, and use it with cocoa powder for the rim of your Chocolate Martinis.

Please note: Glasses can be rimmed ahead of time; in fact, it gives the coating time to air-dry a bit before use. If you know you'll be serving, say, a Lemon Drop to all guests upon their arrival at a party, prepare the glasses in advance so they're ready to use when you need them.

Using a wedge of fruit or a bit of paper towel dipped in one of the liquid ingredients of the cocktail you're making, moisten the exterior of the rim of the serving glass. Grasp the glass from its base or stem and hold it sideways, parallel to the floor, over a sink or trash basket. Pour the coating ingredient—sugar, salt, cocoa powder, and so forth—into a salt shaker or onto a small plate, and sprinkle it onto the moistened edge of the glass, rotating the glass as you go, until it is lightly but evenly coated with the ingredient, and letting any excess fall into the sink. It's that simple.

Drink-Making Techniques

Bartending is all about verbs, and verbs provide a type of shorthand for describing the techniques of making a cocktail. The key verbs in bartending are: *build, stir, shake, blend,* and *layer.* Three further action verbs can crop up from time to time: *float, muddle,* and *flame.* If you listen to bartenders discussing a new recipe, you might hear, "Build, Highball, lemon wedge," or "Shake, strain, cocktail, float." The first of these describes, probably, a Highball, a drink that is made in the glass you will serve it in. The second drink referred to above would involve shaking some of the ingredients together, straining them into a cocktail glass, and then floating another ingredient on top. Here are the techniques that should be mastered by everyone who wants to think of himself or herself as a bartender.

Building

Building a drink most usually refers to making a Highball—a drink that is made in the glass in which it is served. A Highball glass is filled with ice, the liquor is poured in, and the mixer is added on top. If a citrus garnish such as a lemon or lime wedge is to be added, the juice is squeezed into the drink after the mixer. When that's done, the bartender must stir the drink with a sip-stick to combine the ingredients. However, if the drink is, say, a Scotch and Soda with a twist of lemon peel, the bartender would stir the liquids together first and then rim the edge of the glass with the oils and express the oils over the top. In any case, the sip-stick remains in the glass so the drinker can stir more, if desired, or sip through it.

Stirring

The technique used in classic Martini making applies to all cocktails that are made from clear ingredients—no eggs, milk, cream, or fruit juices allowed. Basically, if you can see through each ingredient, you will be stirring the drink. The mixing glass should be two-thirds full of ice. The ingredients are poured in and the barspoon is used to stir the ingredients together and, most critically, chill them with the ice for 20 to 30 seconds. The amount of water that is melted during this stirring is vital to the overall balance of the drink. This is the best reason not to use spirits that have been stored in the freezer; the cold temperature of the chilled ingredient will lessen ice meltage during stirring, and the drink's balance will be affected. Though a barspoon can be used like any spoon for stirring, the twisted shaft offers its user an easier and more stylish technique. Place your thumb on one side of the shaft and the first two fingers on the opposite side. Slide your thumb back and forth along the shaft, pushing against the two fingers on the opposite side; the spoon will agitate the ice in an up-and-down movement.

Stirred drinks must be strained into a chilled glass or onto fresh ice in the serving glass. Use a Julep strainer, fitted at a slant into the mixing glass, to strain the liquid from the ice.

Shaking

My personal favorite method—I love truly cold cocktails, and shaking often produces tiny shards of ice so small that they sneak through the perforations of a strainer. Cocktails are shaken when they contain fruit juices, milk, cream, eggs, horseradish, or other thickish ingredients. You will use either a three-part cocktail shaker or a Boston shaker, the favored choice of most professional bartenders.

To shake a cocktail in a cocktail shaker: Fill the bottom cup two-thirds full of ice. Pour in the ingredients; set the top in place and check that it is tightly closed. Grasp the shaker where the top and bottom parts meet, raise the shaker to the side of your head, curl your index finger over the top to prevent it from flying off, and begin shaking vigorously. (I like to do a little dance while I shake; however, this silliness is not mandatory.) Continue shaking for 10 to 20 seconds. Remove the cover and strain the cocktail into the chilled or ice-filled glass.

To shake a cocktail using a Boston shaker: Fill the glass half of the shaker two-thirds full of ice. Add the ingredients. Invert the metal half of the shaker over the glass and rap it firmly on its flat bottom to unite the two parts. Lift up the shaker and invert it, metal cup end down. Grasp the shaker—

the bottom in one hand, the top in the other—lift it to the side of your head, and shake vigorously (while dancing?) for 10 to 20 seconds. Complete your shaking with the metal cup on the bottom and the glass half on top.

To "break" the metal cone from the glass part, strike the metal half of the shaker with the heel of your hand at the juncture where the cups meet. Lift off the mixing glass and set it aside. Fit a Hawthorne strainer within the mouth of the metal cup. Holding it in place with your index finger, strain the cocktail into the chilled or ice-filled glass.

Dry Shaking or Mime Shaking

If you are making a cocktail that contains the white of an egg, it's best to shake it without ice for 5 to 10 seconds. After that, add the ice and shake vigorously for a further 10 to 20 seconds. The dry shaking, or mime shaking—so called because the shaker makes no noise when you shake without ice, and it looks like you're miming—emulsifies the egg white, and the resultant drink has a far silkier texture.

Blending

An electric blender is required to make frozen drinks. If the amount of ice is not stated in the recipe, fill the container no more than half full. Add the ingredients; cover. Set the container in place and blend, pulsing if necessary, until all of the ingredients are puréed and the ice is crushed. After a few seconds you will hear the noise of the blender change; stop the blender and stir the ingredients. Cover and blend some more. Repeat as needed to prevent lumps.

Muddling

Muddling requires a muddler (see Equipment, page 7) and a sturdy glass; don't use your finest hand-blown crystal for a drink that requires muddling. The ingredients—usually fruit slices, herbs, sugar, bitters, and/or water—are placed in the bottom of a glass. The flat end of the wooden muddler is used to press the juices from the fruit and break up the fruit or sugar while mashing it together with any liquid. Muddling brings out the qualities of fruits because it presses oils from the peel as well as juice from the flesh.

Floating

Floating an ingredient is usually the last act before serving the cocktail. Often high-proof rum or a liqueur is floated on a drink that has been stirred or shaken, strained, and poured. Floated ingredients are meant to stand alone on top of the drink; you don't want to mix them in. Pour them gently over the back of a barspoon.

Flaming

First, last, and always, be careful when igniting alcohol. Do it away from bottles of liquor, your face and hair, or hanging party decorations. Sometimes a floated ingredient, say 151-proof rum, is ignited because its high alcohol content ensures a quick ignition. Sometimes the oil expressed from a citrus peel is ignited for the burst of flavor it produces, for the marvelous aroma that can result, or purely for the pyrotechnical show that results. Remember that smothering a fire is the most effective way to extinguish it, so the wise bartender will keep a saucer and a moist bar towel handy.

Layering

The classic layered drink is the Pousse-Café, a rainbow-hued sweet drink that calls for a number of liqueurs but requires they be poured one atop the other without mixing. Layering works because different liquids have different specific densities, and as long as you pour the densest liquid as the bottom layer and then top it with a succession of second-densest, third-densest, and so on, the ingredients will float perfectly. But there, too, is the problem: Because we have such a profusion of different brands and flavors of liqueurs available today, the specific density of each product differs—one company's crème de menthe will be more dense or less dense than another's. (Basically, the ones with the highest sugar content will have the highest specific densities.) Thus, though you will find lists of ingredients, usually from densest to least dense, I suggest you judge for yourself based on the thickness of the ingredients you want to use. And though some recipes tell you to layer the specific ingredients they contain, you'll find that often it simply doesn't work or that the ingredient will layer properly when it's cold but not at room temperature.

If you do want to layer liqueurs, slowly, gently, and carefully pour each layer over the back of a barspoon so that it glides atop the layer below.

THE HOME BAR

THERE ARE NO RULES WHEN it comes to setting up a home bar; there are just lots and lots of things to think about. If you have a finished basement that's sitting there empty, you can put together a real bar, providing you have the cash, of course. But if you're living in a studio apartment with five other people, your "bar" will likely be a drawer and a little shelf space next to the cereal—if you're lucky. My best advice, then, when it comes to setting up your home bar, is to read this chapter and make notes about what you need to buy that you will actually drink or use, keeping in mind what you have room for and what you have cash for. After you've considered everything, you should end up with the essentials for your particular needs and desires.

Stocking a Home Bar

Even if none of your friends drink gin, you really should keep one bottle on hand if you want to have a properly stocked home bar. If many of your friends drink gin, then think about stocking two or three different brands. Here's a list of everything you should at least consider having in stock if you want to be known as a well-prepared home bartender.

Spirits

Absinthe: It's so very twenty-first century.

Applejack: Optional but desirable.

Blended whisky: Optional at my house, but maybe not at yours.

Bourbon

Campari: Optional but desirable.

Cognac

Gin

Irish whiskey

Rum: Light rum is a must; amber, dark, and añejo are optional.

Rye whiskey (straight)

Scotch: Blended scotch is a must; single-malt scotch is somewhat optional unless you have to have it.

Tennessee whiskey: Could you really have a bar without a bottle of Jack Daniel's?

Tequila: White, aka Blanco, Plata, or silver is a must; reposado and añejo are optional, and at my house, gold tequila is barred.

Vodka: Plain vodka is a must. A few flavored vodkas are optional but desirable; if you want to make Cosmos, you'll need a citrus vodka.

Liqueurs

Consider which cocktails and mixed drinks your crowd likes before deciding on your final list. Here are some likely suspects:

Amaretto

Baileys Irish cream: Refrigerate after opening.

Chambord

Cherry Heering: For a good Singapore Sling.

Cointreau or other triple sec

Crème de cacao: White, at least. No, get both.

Crème de cassis

Crème de menthe: Both white and green.

Crème de violette: If you want to make Aviations, you'll need this.

Domaine de Canton ginger liqueur: Optional, but oh, so very good.

Drambuie

Grand Marnier

Hpnotiq

Kahlúa

Limoncello

Maraschino liqueur

Peach schnapps

Pimm's

Sambuca

Southern Comfort: Optional for me, but very popular with others.

St-Germain Elderflower liqueur: Optional, but fabulous.

Amaros and Other Products in the "Bitter" Category

Aperol: Sort of Campari light.

Campari: For your Negronis.

Fernet-Branca: You *must* have Fernet-Branca.

Jägermeister: See Fernet-Branca.

Wines

Many of these wines are optional, so you should consider which cocktails and mixed drinks you'll be making on a regular basis, and whether or not you'll actually open a bottle of, say, port or sherry if you buy it.

Dry vermouth: Refrigerate after opening.

Sweet vermouth: Refrigerate after opening.

Port and/or sherry: Refrigerate dry sherries after opening.

Dry white wine: Chardonnay and/or Sauvignon Blanc— refrigerate before opening.

Dry red wine: Consider Merlot, Côtes du Rhône, Cabernet Sauvignon, Pinot Noir.

Beer

American lager	Nonalcoholic beer
Craft-brewed pale ale	Stout
Low-calorie beer	

Mixers

Bottled water	Lemon-lime soda
Club soda or seltzer	Milk, half-and-half, or heavy cream
Cola	Simple syrup (see page 35)
Diet cola	Tonic water
Ginger ale	

Fruit juices

Cranberry	Orange
Grapefruit	Pineapple
Lemon	Tomato
Lime	

Condiments, etc.

Angostura bitters

Celery seeds or celery salt

Cocktail olives: Refrigerate after opening.

Cocktail onions: Refrigerate after opening.

Grenadine

Horseradish: Refrigerate after opening.

Lime juice cordial: Refrigerate after opening.

Maraschino cherries: Refrigerate after opening.

Orange bitters

Peychaud's bitters

Salt and pepper

Sugar: Granulated and superfine.

Sugar cubes or lumps

Tabasco sauce

Worcestershire sauce

Equipment

Barspoon

Boston shaker or cocktail shaker

Bottle opener

Churchkey

Citrus reamer

Coasters or cocktail napkins

Cocktail picks or toothpicks

Cocktail stirrers or sip-sticks

Corkscrew

Cutting board

Fine-holed grater, for nutmeg, fresh ginger, citrus zests

Hawthorne strainer, if using a Boston shaker

Ice bucket with tongs

Jigger

Julep strainer

Mixing glass

Paring knife

Straws

The Cocktail Party Bar

Some people are party givers; others can't imagine throwing a party. Here's my thinking: For a dinner party, holiday meal, or special celebration where I will serve a meal, my limit is 12 for a sit-down and maybe up to 20 for a serve-yourself buffet or barbecue. On the other hand, one of the greatest hosts I ever met, the very stylish Lee Bailey, taught me a secret many moons ago: Have a cocktail party—all you need to serve is nuts. And that's just what he did—with great élan, mixed cocktail nuts in bail-handled shiny paint cans direct from the nut supplier—at the many parties I attended chez Bailey.

Well, I'm a big copycat. That's just what I do, too. The best aspect of cocktail parties is that you can invite dozens—hundreds, even—of people, and though you'll run yourself ragged getting everything ready on party day, you'll be free to enjoy your guests, your cocktails, and the crowd.

Now, don't get crazy about this party; you can limit its difficulty. Indeed, I hereby give you permission to be different: You do not have to have a full open bar. You can make it, say, a Cosmopolitan party, where the only alcoholic drink served will be the Cosmopolitan. Or you could pick, say, three cocktails, such as one made with vodka, one made with tequila, and perhaps a bourbon-based drink, and that way you should have something to suit a wide range of people. You could have a vodka party that features iced vodka, flavored vodkas, and no other liquor. You can have a punch party if you want to do absolutely everything ahead of time. In fact, making a tasty nonalcoholic punch that individual drinkers can spike for themselves is an excellent ploy for a get-together that can include children and adults.

My best tips for large-scale party giving are these:

- have large trash cans handy;
- have lots and lots of cocktail napkins around;
- don't run out of ice;
- serve nuts—or equally simple-to-put-out-and-replenish store-bought snacks;
- hire a bartender, if possible;
- don't let anyone overdo it;
- appoint designated drivers and have a taxi-service number handy;
- pray for good weather.

The drinks that follow include classics, old favorites, contemporary favorites, and some popular, trendy drinks that may or may not last. Listings are alphabetical by title, from A to Z, to make finding them easy.

DRINKS A TO Z

PLEASE NOTE: The bartenders, chefs, cocktailians, and mixologists credited for specific recipes in this chapter might no longer work at the bars, clubs, and restaurants mentioned. They worked there, though, when the drink was created.

A.B.C.

Let's start at the very beginning.

> **2 ounces scotch**
> **1/2 ounce apricot brandy**
> **1/2 ounce sweet vermouth**

Pour all of the ingredients into a mixing glass two-thirds full of ice cubes. Stir well. Strain into a chilled Cocktail glass.

Abbey Cocktail

A recipe from the 1930s—still going strong.

> **2 ounces gin**
> **1 ounce Lillet Blanc**
> **1 ounce fresh orange juice**
> **2 dashes of orange bitters**

Pour all of the ingredients into a shaker two-thirds full of ice cubes. Shake well. Strain into a chilled Cocktail glass.

Absinthe Cocktail

Absinthe was illegal in the United States and many other countries for almost 100 years, but in the early twenty-first century, it came back to us!

> **2 ounces absinthe**
> **1 ounce cold water**
> **2 dashes of anisette**
> **Dash of Angostura bitters**

Pour all of the ingredients into a mixing glass two-thirds full of ice cubes. Stir well. Strain into a chilled Cocktail glass.

Absinthe Drip

The ritual of making this drink is well worth the effort.

> **1 sugar cube**
> **1¹/₂ ounces absinthe**
> **Water**

Place an absinthe spoon or tea strainer over a wineglass. Place the sugar cube over the perforations. Pour in the absinthe, letting it drip over the sugar cube. Add water to taste, pouring it slowly over the sugar cube, until the sugar dissolves and the mixture turns cloudy.

Absolut Sex

Some men have been known to fall asleep immediately after having one of these.

> **1 ounce Absolut Kurant vodka**
> **1 ounce Midori melon liqueur**
> **1 ounce cranberry juice**
> **Splash of lemon-lime soda**

Pour the vodka, melon liqueur, and cranberry juice into a shaker two-thirds full of ice cubes. Shake well. Strain into a chilled Cocktail glass or serve on the rocks. Add the splash of soda on top.

Acapulco Cocktail

This is almost like a rum-based Margarita.

> **2 ounces light rum**
> **¹/₂ ounce triple sec**
> **¹/₂ ounce lime juice cordial, such as Rose's**
> **¹/₂ ounce simple syrup (page 35)**

Pour all of the ingredients into a shaker two-thirds full of ice cubes. Shake well. Strain into a chilled Cocktail glass.

A Day at the Beach

The perfect sweet drink for summertime sipping.

1 ounce Malibu rum

$1/2$ ounce amaretto

4 ounces orange juice

$1/2$ ounce grenadine

Wedge of fresh pineapple and a fresh strawberry, for garnishes

Pour the rum, amaretto, and orange juice into a shaker two-thirds full of ice cubes. Shake well. Strain into a chilled Highball glass. Drizzle the grenadine on top. Garnish with the pineapple wedge and strawberry.

Adios Motherfucker (AMF)

In other words, bye-bye.

$1/2$ ounce vodka

$1/2$ ounce rum

$1/2$ ounce tequila

$1/2$ ounce gin

$1/2$ ounce blue curaçao

1 ounce fresh lemon juice

$1/2$ ounce simple syrup (page 35)

2 ounces lemon-lime soda

Pour all of the ingredients into an ice-filled Collins glass. Stir gently.

Affinity Cocktail

I have an affinity for this one.

1 ounce scotch

1 ounce sweet vermouth

1 ounce dry vermouth

2 dashes of Angostura bitters

Pour all of the ingredients into a mixing glass two-thirds full of ice cubes. Stir well. Strain into a chilled Cocktail glass.

Afternoon Delight Martini

Something to sip while listening to the Starland Vocal Band.

    2 ounces vanilla vodka

    1 ounce white chocolate liqueur

    1 ounce Cointreau

    Maraschino cherry and a Nilla Wafer cookie, for garnishes

Pour all the ingredients into a shaker two-thirds full of ice cubes. Shake well. Strain into a chilled Cocktail glass. Garnish with the cherry; serve the cookie alongside.

Alabama Slammer

A tasty, sweet drink—no matter where you drink it, in Alabama or in the slammer.

    1 ounce amaretto

    1 ounce Southern Comfort

    1 ounce sloe gin

    1 ounce fresh orange juice

Pour all of the ingredients into a shaker two-thirds full of ice cubes. Shake well. Strain into an ice-filled Rocks glass.

Alana

Adapted from a recipe by Marie-Louise Bignall, Kabaret's Prophecy, United Kingdom.

    2 kumquats, halved lengthwise

    4 blood orange segments

    1³/₄ ounces Belvedere Cytrus vodka

    ¹/₂ ounce Bottlegreen Apple & Elderflower Cordial

    ¹/₄ ounce Creole Shrubb liqueur

Muddle the kumquats and 3 of the blood orange segments in a mixing glass. Add ice cubes, the vodka, cordial, and Shrubb liqueur. Shake and strain into a crushed ice–filled Old-Fashioned glass. Garnish with the remaining blood orange segment.

Alaska

They say this drink is favored by gnomes from Nome. Wouldn't Juneau?

> 1¹/₂ ounces gin
>
> ¹/₂ ounce yellow Chartreuse

Pour both ingredients into a mixing glass two-thirds full of crushed ice. Stir well. Strain into a chilled Cocktail glass.

Alexander

The paterfamilias of the Brandy Alexander.

> 2 ounces gin
>
> 1 ounce white crème de cacao
>
> 1 ounce light cream
>
> Freshly grated nutmeg, for garnish

Pour all the ingredients into a shaker two-thirds full of ice cubes. Shake well. Strain into a chilled Cocktail glass. Sprinkle lightly with the nutmeg.

Alfonso Cocktail

Make this one with dry champagne or sparkling wine.

> 1 sugar cube
>
> 2 dashes of Angostura bitters
>
> ¹/₂ ounce Dubonnet Rouge
>
> 5 ounces champagne or other sparkling wine

Drop the sugar cube into a Champagne flute and dash the cube with the bitters. Pour the Dubonnet and champagne into the glass. Don't stir: You'll lose the bubbles.

Algonquin

Named for the hotel on West 43rd Street in Manhattan, not the tribe.

> 2 ounces blended Canadian whisky
>
> ¹/₂ ounce dry vermouth
>
> 1 ounce pineapple juice

Pour all of the ingredients into a shaker two-thirds full of ice cubes. Shake well. Strain into a chilled Cocktail glass.

Allies Cocktail

This drink was around in 1930, so it's not a tribute to the victors of WWII.

>   1 ounce gin
>   1 ounce dry vermouth
>   1/4 ounce kümmel

Pour all of the ingredients into a mixing glass two-thirds full of ice cubes. Stir well. Strain into a chilled Cocktail glass.

Almond Saffron Daisy

Created by Claire Smith, winner of the U.K. Battle of the Giants Cocktail Competition, 2001; Global Communication Manager for Belvedere and Chopin vodkas, 2007.

>   1 1/2 ounces Belvedere Cytrus vodka
>   1/2 pinch saffron threads
>   1/2 ounce fresh lemon juice
>   1/2 ounce almond syrup
>   1/2 egg white
>   Saffron thread, for garnish

Pour all of the ingredients into a shaker two-thirds full of ice cubes. Shake very well. Strain into a chilled Cocktail glass. Add the garnish.

Almost All Grape

Adapted from a recipe by Frank Caiafa, bar manager at New York City's Peacock Alley in the Waldorf-Astoria hotel.

>   1 ripe apricot, peeled, pitted, and cut into cubes
>   1 wedge fresh peach, peeled
>   2 1/2 ounces Cîroc vodka
>   1 ounce Domaine La Suffrene Bandol Rosé wine
>   1/2 ounce Inniskillin Vidal Icewine
>   Orange twist, for garnish

Combine the apricot and peach in an empty cocktail shaker and muddle well. Add ice cubes, the vodka, and both wines; shake for about 15 seconds. Strain into a chilled Cocktail glass. Add the orange twist.

(Almost) Blow My Skull Off

Created by Gary Regan, circa 1999.

> **2 ounces cognac**
> **1/2 ounce peach schnapps**
> **1/2 ounce Jägermeister**

Pour all of the ingredients into a mixing glass two-thirds full of ice cubes. Stir well. Strain into a chilled Cocktail glass.

Amanda's Challenge

Created by Amanda Washington, bartender at Rye, San Francisco, 2007.

> **1 3/4 ounces Redbreast Irish whiskey**
> **3/4 ounce dry vermouth**
> **3/4 ounce sweet vermouth**
> **3/4 ounce B&B**
> **3 dashes of Peychaud's bitters**

Pour all of the ingredients into a mixing glass two-thirds full of ice cubes. Stir well. Strain into a chilled Cocktail glass.

Amaretto Sour

> **2 ounces amaretto**
> **1 ounce fresh lemon juice**
> **Maraschino cherry, for garnish**

Pour both ingredients into a shaker two-thirds full of ice cubes. Shake well. Strain into a chilled Sour glass. Garnish with the cherry.

American Beauty

Just a little something to fix up before stepping into a tubful of hot water and rose petals.

> **3/4 ounce brandy**
> **3/4 ounce dry vermouth**
> **Dash of white crème de menthe**
> **3/4 ounce orange juice**
> **3/4 ounce grenadine**

Pour all of the ingredients into a shaker two-thirds full of ice cubes. Shake well. Strain into a chilled Cocktail glass.

American Dream

This shooter might just give you a sugar rush.

> **1/4 ounce Kahlúa**
> **1/4 ounce amaretto**
> **1/4 ounce Frangelico**
> **1/4 ounce dark crème de cacao**

Pour all of the ingredients into a mixing glass two-thirds full of ice cubes. Stir well. Strain into a chilled Pony glass.

American Flag

Think about serving this layered drink on the Fourth of July.

> **3/4 ounce grenadine**
> **3/4 ounce white crème de cacao**
> **3/4 ounce blue curaçao**

Pour the grenadine into a Sherry glass. Gently float the white crème de cacao on top. Pour the blue curaçao on top to make the third layer.

Americano

If you love Campari, you'll love this cocktail. *Cin-cin!*

> **1 1/2 ounces Campari**
> **1 1/2 ounces sweet vermouth**
> **Club soda**
> **Orange slice, for garnish**

Pour the Campari and vermouth into an ice-filled Highball glass. Stir well. Fill the glass with club soda. Garnish with the orange slice.

Ana Mandara's Beach Street Fog Cutter

Adapted from a recipe by Bradley Plymale, beverage manager, Cham Bar, Ana Mandara, San Francisco.

> **1/2 cup chopped peeled cucumber**
> **2 ounces Southern Comfort**
> **1/2 ounce triple sec**

$^1/_4$ ounce Midori melon liqueur

$^1/_2$ ounce fresh lemon juice

$^1/_2$ ounce fresh lime juice

$^1/_2$ ounce simple syrup (page 35)

Spicy ginger beer

Cucumber wheel, for garnish

Place the cucumber into an empty mixing glass and muddle well. Add ice cubes, the Southern Comfort, triple sec, Midori, citrus juices, and simple syrup. Shake for about 15 seconds. Strain into an ice-filled Collins glass, top with ginger beer, and add the cucumber wheel.

An-Apple-a-Day

Created by Audrey Saunders, aka "Libation Goddess," New York City, 2000.

1 ounce Gordon's gin

1 ounce Pucker apple liqueur

$^1/_4$ ounce maraschino liqueur

$^3/_4$ ounce fresh lime juice

$^1/_2$ ounce fresh grapefruit juice

$^1/_2$ ounce simple syrup (page 35)

Maraschino cherry, for garnish

Pour all of the ingredients into a shaker two-thirds full of ice cubes. Shake well. Strain into an ice-filled Highball glass. Add the cherry.

Andrea's Drink

Adapted from a recipe by Tony Abou-Ganim, 2004. Created for Andrea Immer Robinson.

6 tangerine segments

2 ounces Lillet Blanc

1 ounce Belvedere Pomarancza (orange) vodka

Lime twist, for garnish

Muddle the tangerine segments in an empty shaker. Add ice cubes, the Lillet, and the vodka. Shake and strain into a chilled Cocktail glass. Add the lime twist.

Añejo Highball

Created by master mixologist Dale DeGroff, New York City.

1¹/₂ ounces añejo rum

¹/₂ ounce white curaçao

¹/₂ ounce fresh lime juice

2 dashes of Angostura bitters

4 to 5 ounces ginger beer

Lime wheel and orange slice, for garnishes

Pour all of the ingredients into an ice-filled Collins glass. Stir well. Add the lime wheel and orange slice.

The Angelina

Created for Angelina Jolie by Yvan D. Lemoine, New York City, 2008.

HIBISCUS VERMOUTH

4 hibiscus tea bags

1 750-ml bottle Martini & Rossi Bianco vermouth

COCKTAIL

2¹/₂ ounces Chopin vodka

1¹/₂ ounces hibiscus vermouth

1¹/₂ ounces pomegranate juice

Splash of champagne or other sparkling wine

Fresh cherry, for garnish

HIBISCUS VERMOUTH: Drop the tea bags into the bottle of vermouth. Cover and shake well; set aside to infuse overnight. Remove the tea bags or strain the infused vermouth into a clean bottle.

COCKTAIL: Combine the vodka, hibiscus vermouth, and juice in a shaker two-thirds full of ice cubes. Shake well. Strain into a chilled Cocktail glass and top with the champagne. Add the cherry.

The Angel's Share

Adapted from a recipe by the wonderful Jacques Bezuidenhout, Harry Denton's Starlight Room, San Francisco.

> $1/8$ ounce Chartreuse V.E.P. liqueur, for coating the glass
> $1^1/4$ ounces Remy Martin Louis XIII cognac
> $3/4$ ounce Charbay Nostalgie Black Walnut liqueur
> $1/2$ ounce Porto Rocha 20-year Tawny

Pour the Chartreuse into a Brandy snifter and tilt, rotating the glass, to coat the interior of the glass with the liqueur. Discard any excess liqueur. Carefully ignite the liqueur coating the interior of the glass with a match; allow it to burn for a few seconds, and then extinguish the flame by placing a saucer on top of the glass. Pour in the remaining ingredients, and stir briefly to mix.

Angel's Tit

Believe it or not, this one has been around since at least the 1930s.

> 2 ounces dark crème de cacao
> Dollop of whipped cream
> Maraschino cherry, for garnish

Pour the crème de cacao into a small Pousse-Café glass or Sherry glass. Top with the whipped cream. Garnish with the cherry.

Antifreeze

This drink can also be served as a shooter—it was taught to me by Stuffy Shmitt, a bartender and musician in New York City.

> $1/2$ ounce vodka
> $1/2$ ounce blue curaçao
> $1/2$ ounce Bacardi 151-proof rum
> $1/2$ ounce peppermint schnapps

Pour all of the ingredients into a mixing glass two-thirds full of ice cubes. Stir well. Strain into a chilled Rocks glass.

Apocalypse

Now!

1 ounce white crème de menthe
1 ounce peppermint schnapps
³/₄ ounce vodka
³/₄ ounce Southern Comfort
¹/₂ ounce Kahlúa
¹/₂ ounce bourbon
2 to 4 ounces hot chocolate
Whipped cream, for garnish

Pour the crème de menthe, schnapps, vodka, Southern Comfort, Kahlúa, and bourbon into a large coffee mug. Fill with the hot chocolate. Garnish with the whipped cream.

Apple & Cinnamon Joy

This is a great variation on the Apple Martini.

1 ounce apple schnapps
¹/₄ ounce Goldschlager

Pour the schnapps into a Pony glass. Drizzle the Goldschlager on top. Stir twice.

Apple Blossom

1 ounce brandy
2 ounces apple juice
¹/₄ ounce fresh lemon juice
Splash of vodka

Pour all of the ingredients into a shaker two-thirds full of ice cubes. Shake well. Strain into an ice-filled Rocks glass.

Apple Brandy Cocktail

You can use applejack if you have no apple brandy.

2 ounces apple brandy
¹/₂ ounce fresh lemon juice
¹/₂ ounce grenadine

Pour all of the ingredients into a shaker two-thirds full of ice cubes. Shake well. Strain into a chilled Cocktail glass.

Apple Knocker

Adapted from a recipe from the Ugly Mug, Cape May, New Jersey.

MAKES 4 SERVINGS

12 ounces apple cider
Grated zest of 1 orange
2 cinnamon sticks, broken into pieces
4 whole cloves
6 ounces Laird's Applejack

Combine the cider, zest, cinnamon, and cloves in a nonreactive saucepan over moderate heat. Bring to a simmer. Reduce the heat to low, cover the pan, and let steep for 20 minutes. Strain the mixture, dividing it among 4 mugs. Add $1^1/_2$ ounces of the applejack to each mug.

Apple Martini

Without a doubt, the hottest drink of 2000 and still going strong.

1 ounce vodka
1 ounce sour apple schnapps
1 ounce apple juice
Thin slices of Granny Smith apple, for garnish

Pour all of the ingredients into a shaker two-thirds full of ice cubes. Shake well. Strain into a chilled Cocktail glass. Garnish with the apple slices.

Apple Pie à la Mode

Adapted from a recipe from Dylan Prime, New York City.

$1/_2$ ounce Quarenta y Tres Licor 43
1 ounce heavy cream
1 ounce apple schnapps
1 ounce vodka
1 ounce maple syrup

Shake the Licor 43 and the cream over ice; reserve. Pour all of the remaining ingredients into another shaker two-thirds full of ice cubes. Shake well. Strain into a chilled Cocktail glass. Carefully pour the liqueur–heavy cream mixture over the back of a barspoon so that it floats on top of the drink.

Apple Sidecar

Adapted from a recipe by Ryan Magarian, Restaurant Zoe, Seattle, Washington.

> **Superfine sugar and a tangerine wedge, for rimming the glass**
>
> **$1^1/_2$ ounces vodka**
>
> **$1/_2$ ounce Clear Creek apple brandy**
>
> **1 ounce fresh lemon juice**
>
> **1 ounce simple syrup (page 35)**
>
> **$1/_2$ ounce fresh tangerine juice**

Prepare a Cocktail glass. Pour all of the remaining ingredients into a shaker two-thirds full of ice cubes. Shake well. Strain into the prepared glass.

Appleberry Punch

MAKES TWENTY 4-OUNCE SERVINGS

> **1 quart unsweetened apple cider**
>
> **1 quart cranberry juice**
>
> **5 whole cloves**
>
> **2 small (3-inch) cinnamon sticks, broken**
>
> **1 teaspoon freshly grated nutmeg**
>
> **1 large block of ice, for serving**
>
> **8 ounces Van Gogh Wild Appel vodka**
>
> **20 orange wheels, for garnish**

Pour the apple cider and cranberry juice into a large nonreactive pot over high heat. Add the cloves, cinnamon sticks, and nutmeg, and bring the mixture to a boil. Reduce the heat to low, cover, and simmer for 20 minutes.

Strain the mixture through a double layer of dampened cheesecloth; discard the solids. Set aside to cool to room temperature, about $1^1/_2$ hours.

Cover and refrigerate for at least 2 hours and up to 5 days.

Place the block of ice into a punch bowl. Add the chilled punch and the vodka. Float the orange wheels on top.

The Applejack Rabbit

Adapted from a recipe by Julien Gualdoni, head bartender, The Player, London, circa 2004.

Granulated sugar and ground cinnamon, mixed well, for rimming the glass

3 ounces calvados

2 ounces maple syrup

$1^1/_2$ ounces fresh orange juice

$1^1/_2$ ounces fresh lemon juice

Rim a Cocktail glass with the sugar mixture. Pour all of the remaining ingredients into a shaker two-thirds full of ice cubes. Shake well. Strain into the prepared glass.

Apples & Oranges Martini

$1^1/_2$ ounces Van Gogh Wild Appel vodka

1 ounce triple sec

$1/_2$ ounce orange juice

$1/_2$ ounce apple juice

Apple slice and orange slice, for garnishes

Pour all of the ingredients into a shaker two-thirds full of ice cubes. Shake well. Strain into a chilled Cocktail glass. Garnish with the apple slice and orange slice.

Apricot Sour

One of the most popular cocktails from the swinging 1970s.

2 ounces apricot brandy

$3/_4$ ounce fresh lemon juice

$1/_2$ ounce simple syrup (page 35)

Orange wheel and maraschino cherry, for garnishes

Pour all of the ingredients into a shaker two-thirds full of ice cubes; shake well. Strain into a chilled Sour glass. Add the orange wheel and cherry.

Apricot Vesper Martini

1¹/₂ ounces gin

1¹/₂ ounces vodka

³/₄ ounce apricot brandy

Pour all of the ingredients into a shaker two-thirds full of ice cubes. Shake well. Strain into a chilled Cocktail glass.

Arabesque

Created at La Griglia, Houston, Texas.

5 strawberries, hulled

1 ounce citrus vodka

1 ounce Campari

1 ounce champagne or other sparkling wine

In a blender, combine the strawberries, vodka, and Campari with a few ice cubes. Pour into a Champagne flute and top with the champagne.

Arawak Cocktail

Created at Trotters, Port of Spain, Trinidad.

2 ounces blended whisky

¹/₂ ounce dry vermouth

¹/₄ ounce pineapple juice

Dash of tamarind juice

2 dashes of Angostura bitters

Pineapple cube, for garnish

Pour all of the ingredients into a shaker two-thirds full of ice cubes. Shake well. Strain into a chilled Cocktail glass. Add the pineapple cube.

Armagnac Cloud

Adapted from a recipe by Jeff Dorau, Gaby Restaurant, Sofitel, New York City, 2003.

Ground cinnamon, for rimming the glass

1¹/₄ ounces armagnac

1 ounce Baileys Irish cream liqueur

3/4 ounce Kahlúa
1/2 ounce heavy cream
Cinnamon stick and a mint leaf, for garnishes

Prepare a Cocktail glass. Pour the armagnac, liqueurs, and cream into a shaker two-thirds full of ice cubes. Shake well. Strain into the prepared glass. Add the cinnamon stick and mint leaf.

The Armagnac Newton

Adapted from a recipe by chef-owner Sam DeMarco and bartender Lisa Tine, District restaurant, New York City.

At District restaurant, this is served with a drizzle of fig purée and a caramelized blue cheese–stuffed fig. You might want to go with the apple slice I suggest.

1¹/2 ounces Castarède armagnac
1/2 ounce triple sec
1/2 ounce Rose's lime juice
1/2 ounce fresh lemon juice
Splash of simple syrup (page 35)
Thin apple slice, for garnish

Pour all of the ingredients into a shaker two-thirds full of ice cubes. Shake well. Strain into a chilled Cocktail glass. Add the apple slice.

Arnaud's Swan Cocktail

Adapted from a recipe by Gary Regan and me for Arnaud's restaurant, New Orleans, 2003.

2 ounces cognac
3/4 ounce Frangelico
1/2 ounce fresh lemon juice
Maraschino cherry, for garnish

Pour all of the ingredients into a shaker two-thirds full of ice cubes. Shake well. Strain into a chilled Champagne flute. Add the cherry.

Artillery Punch

MAKES TWENTY-FOUR 6-OUNCE SERVINGS

1 750-ml bottle straight rye whiskey

1 750-ml bottle red wine

1 quart chilled strong tea

12 ounces dark rum

6 ounces gin

6 ounces brandy

1 ounce Bénédictine

12 ounces orange juice

8 ounces fresh lemon juice

6 ounces simple syrup (page 35)

1 large block of ice, for serving

Lemon wheels, for garnish

Pour all of the ingredients, except for the ice and lemon wheels, into a large pot or bowl. Stir well, cover, and refrigerate for at least 4 hours.

Place the block of ice in the center of a punch bowl. Pour in the punch; float the lemon wheels on top.

Astor Champagne Cocktail

Created by Gary Regan for the Astor Center, New York City, 2008.

1/2 ounce Campari

1/2 ounce Luxardo maraschino liqueur

Chilled champagne

Lemon twist, for garnish

Build in a chilled Champagne flute. Add the lemon twist.

Astor Martini

From Astor Place, South Beach, Florida.

4 ounces Ketel One vodka

1 ounce Campari

2 ounces grapefruit juice

Pour all of the ingredients into a shaker two-thirds full of ice cubes. Shake well. Strain into a very large chilled Cocktail glass.

Attaboy

From the Savoy Hotel, London.

> **2 ounces gin**
>
> **1 ounce sweet vermouth**
>
> **¹/₄ ounce grenadine**

Pour all of the ingredients into a mixing glass two-thirds full of ice cubes. Stir well. Strain into a chilled Cocktail glass.

Austrian Martini

Created by Gary Regan, 2006.

> **2 ounces Tanqueray gin**
>
> **1 ounce Noilly Prat dry vermouth**
>
> **¹/₂ ounce Zirbenz Stone Pine liqueur**
>
> **Lemon twist, for garnish**

Pour all of the ingredients into a mixing glass two-thirds full of ice cubes. Stir for about 30 seconds; strain into a chilled Cocktail glass. Carefully flame the twist and drop it into the drink.

Autumn Apple

Adapted from a recipe by Scott Beattie, bar manager at Cyrus, Healdsburg, California, 2006.

At Cyrus, this drink is garnished with a baked Pink Lady apple chip that's sprinkled with cinnamon. You can substitute a lemon twist for ease of preparation.

> **1 ounce Germain-Robin apple brandy**
>
> **1 ounce Gravenstein apple juice**
>
> **1 ounce Sonoma Sparkler Apple Cider or Martinelli's Sparkling Cider**
>
> **¹/₂ ounce fresh lemon juice**
>
> **¹/₂ ounce ginger simple syrup, or ¹/₂ ounce simple syrup (page 35) and a dash of ginger juice**
>
> **1 lemon twist, for garnish**

Pour all of the ingredients into a shaker two-thirds full of ice cubes. Shake for about 15 seconds. Strain into a chilled Cocktail glass. Add the lemon twist.

DRINKS A TO Z

Aviation Cocktail

A pre-Prohibition classic.

>   **2 ounces gin**
>   **$1/2$ ounce maraschino liqueur**
>   **$1/2$ ounce crème de violette**
>   **$1/2$ ounce fresh lemon juice**

Pour all of the ingredients into a shaker two-thirds full of ice cubes. Shake well. Strain into a chilled Cocktail glass.

Aviator

Adapted from a recipe by Jay Crabb, bartender at Martini Monkey Bar & Lounge, San Jose International Airport.

>   **$1^1/2$ ounces Van Gogh gin**
>   **$1/4$ ounce Luxardo maraschino liqueur**
>   **3 dashes of orange bitters**
>   **1 ounce fresh lemon juice**
>   **$1/2$ ounce simple syrup (page 35)**
>   **$1/2$ ounce Marie Brizard crème de cassis**
>   **Orange twist, for garnish**

Pour the gin, maraschino, bitters, lemon juice, and simple syrup into a shaker two-thirds full of ice cubes. Shake well. Strain into a chilled Cocktail glass. Pour the crème de cassis down the side of the glass so that it settles at the bottom. Carefully flame the twist and drop it into the drink.

AWOL

An excellent shooter created by Lane Zellman, New Orleans, 1993.

>   **$1/2$ ounce Midori melon liqueur**
>   **$1/2$ ounce chilled pineapple juice**
>   **$1/2$ ounce vodka**
>   **$1/2$ ounce 151-proof rum**

Layer all of the ingredients in a Pousse-Café glass. Carefully ignite the rum and allow it to burn for only 7 to 10 seconds. Extinguish the flame by blowing it out or covering the top with the stem of another glass. Drink slowly, in one luxurious swallow.

The Aztec's Mark

Adapted from a recipe by Neyah White, Nopa, San Francisco, 2007.

1¹/₄ ounces Maker's Mark bourbon
¹/₂ ounce dark crème de cacao
¹/₄ ounce Bénédictine
2 drops of Tabasco sauce
Orange twist, for garnish

Pour all of the ingredients into a mixing glass two-thirds full of ice cubes. Stir well. Strain into a chilled Cocktail glass. Add the orange twist.

B & B

Created at The "21" Club, New York City, shortly after the repeal of Prohibition.

1 ounce brandy
³/₄ ounce Bénédictine

Pour both ingredients into a Brandy snifter. Swirl to blend.

Bacardi Cocktail

Much like a Daiquiri, but this one gets its rosy color from the grenadine.

2 ounces Bacardi light rum
1 ounce fresh lime juice
¹/₂ ounce grenadine

Pour all of the ingredients into a shaker two-thirds full of ice cubes. Shake well. Strain into a chilled Cocktail glass.

BACARDI COCKTAIL

Watch what you're pouring when you make a Bacardi Cocktail—in 1936 a New York bar owner was taken to court for using a rum other than Bacardi. Bacardi won the case, and the New York State Supreme Court upheld the decision.

Bahama Mama

A favorite tropical drink on Paradise Island.

$^1/_4$ ounce Kahlúa

$^1/_2$ ounce dark rum

$^1/_2$ ounce coconut liqueur

$^1/_2$ ounce Bacardi 151-proof rum

1 ounce fresh lemon juice

4 ounces pineapple juice

Pour all of the ingredients into a shaker two-thirds full of ice cubes. Shake well. Strain into an ice-filled Collins glass.

Bajan Breeze

Adapted from a recipe by Jonny Raglin, bartender, Absinthe Brasserie & Bar, San Francisco.

$1^1/_2$ ounces Foursquare spiced rum

$^1/_2$ ounce fresh lime juice

$^1/_4$ ounce simple syrup (page 35)

2 dashes of Angostura bitters

3 ounces nonalcoholic sparkling cider

Pour the rum, lime juice, simple syrup, and bitters into a shaker two-thirds full of ice cubes. Shake well. Strain into an ice-filled Collins glass and top with the cider.

Bald Pussy

$^3/_4$ ounce Midori melon liqueur

$^1/_2$ ounce lime vodka

$^1/_2$ ounce vodka

$^1/_2$ ounce triple sec

$^3/_4$ ounce blueberry schnapps

Splash of fresh lime juice

Splash of lemon-lime soda

Fill a Collins glass with ice. Pour in all of the ingredients and stir to distribute.

Baltimore Bracer Cocktail

2 ounces brandy

³/₄ ounce anisette

1 egg white

Pour all of the ingredients into a shaker two-thirds full of ice cubes. Shake very well. Strain into a chilled Cocktail glass.

Bamboo Cocktail

The apéritif that's said to be a panda's favorite.

2 ounces dry sherry

2 ounces dry vermouth

2 dashes of Angostura bitters

Pour all of the ingredients into a mixing glass two-thirds full of ice cubes. Stir well. Strain into a chilled Cocktail glass.

Banana Cream Pie

1 ounce crème de banane

1 ounce white crème de cacao

1 ounce vodka

1 ounce half-and-half

Pour all of the ingredients into a shaker two-thirds full of ice cubes. Shake well. Strain into a chilled Cocktail glass.

Banana Daiquiri

When using fresh bananas in cocktails such as this, riper is always better.

1¹/₂ ounces light rum

¹/₂ ounce simple syrup (page 35)

1 small ripe banana, cut up

1¹/₂ ounces fresh lime juice

Place 1 cup of ice cubes in a blender. Add all of the ingredients. Blend at low speed to break up the ice. Increase the speed to high and blend until thick. Pour the drink into a wine goblet or other large glass.

Banana Daiquiri Jelly Shots

Created by Gary Regan, 2002.

> 1 ounce fresh lime juice
>
> 1 ounce simple syrup (page 35)
>
> 1 ounce water
>
> 1 (¹/₄-ounce) package unflavored gelatin
>
> 3 ounces rum
>
> 3 ounces banana liqueur
>
> Food coloring (optional)

Pour the lime juice, simple syrup, and water into a small glass measuring cup, and sprinkle the gelatin on top. Let soften for 1 minute. Microwave the mixture on high for 30 seconds. Stir thoroughly to ensure that all of the gelatin has dissolved. Add the rum, banana liqueur, and food coloring, if desired; stir well. Pour the mixture into a shallow pan or mold. Refrigerate until set, preferably overnight.

Banana Split Martini

Adapted from a recipe by Christie Hartmann and Gage Tschyevkosky, Wolfgang Puck's Grand Café, Denver, Colorado.

> Strawberry and chocolate syrups, for drizzling inside the glass
>
> 2 ounces Grey Goose vodka
>
> 2 ounces Godiva White Chocolate liqueur
>
> 1 ounce crème de banane
>
> Banana slice and a strawberry pirouette cookie, for garnishes

Drizzle a large, chilled Cocktail glass with a bit of the strawberry and chocolate syrups. Pour the vodka, chocolate liqueur, and crème de banane into a shaker two-thirds full of ice cubes. Shake well. Strain into the Cocktail glass. Add the garnishes.

Barcelona

Adapted from a recipe by Dale DeGroff for the James Beard House when the Olympic Games were held in Barcelona, 1992.

> ³/₄ ounce Spanish brandy
>
> ³/₄ ounce Dry Sack sherry
>
> ³/₄ ounce fresh orange juice

³/₄ ounce heavy cream

1 ounce simple syrup (page 35)

Splash of Cointreau

Ground cinnamon, for garnish

Place 1 cup of ice cubes in a blender. Add the brandy, sherry, orange juice, cream, and simple syrup; blend until well mixed at low speed to break up the ice. Increase the speed to high and blend until thick. Pour into a Sherry glass. Float the Cointreau on top, and garnish with a light dusting of cinnamon.

Basque Martini

Adapted from a recipe by Sarah Duncan, bartender, Ilunna Basque restaurant, San Francisco, circa 2004.

1¹/₂ ounces Baines Pacharán

1¹/₂ ounces crème de banane

2 ounces pineapple juice

1 ounce fresh lime juice

Pour all of the ingredients into a shaker two-thirds full of ice cubes. Shake well. Strain into a chilled Cocktail glass.

Batida Mango

Batidas are Brazil's answer to frozen fruit Daiquiris.

2 ounces cachaça

¹/₂ ripe mango, cut into chunks

1 teaspoon granulated sugar

In a blender, combine the cachaça, mango, sugar, and 1 cup of ice cubes. Blend well. Pour into a chilled wine goblet.

Bay Breeze

It's a common mistake to make this drink with vodka, but rum was the original base spirit.

2 ounces light rum

3 ounces cranberry juice

1 ounce pineapple juice

Pour all of the ingredients into a Highball glass filled with ice cubes. Stir briefly.

Beachcomber

A drink favored by "Trader Vic" Bergeron.

Superfine sugar and a lime wedge, for rimming the glass
2 ounces light rum
1/4 ounce maraschino liqueur
1/4 ounce cherry brandy
1/2 ounce fresh lime juice

Use the sugar and lime wedge to coat the exterior rim of a Cocktail glass. Pour all of the remaining ingredients into a shaker two-thirds full of ice cubes. Shake well. Strain into the sugar-rimmed glass.

Beadlestone Cocktail

2 ounces scotch
1 ounce dry vermouth
Dash of Angostura bitters

Pour all of the ingredients into a mixing glass two-thirds full of ice cubes. Stir well. Strain into a chilled Cocktail glass.

Beam Me Up Scotty

1/2 ounce Kahlúa
1/2 ounce crème de banane
1/2 ounce Baileys Irish cream liqueur

Layer in order in a Pony glass.

Beauchamp Cocktail

Created by Gary Regan and Amanda Washington, bartender at Rye, San Francisco, 2007.

2 slices peeled kiwi
1 ounce B&B
2 1/2 ounces Bombay Sapphire gin
1/4 ounce fresh lemon juice
1/4 ounce simple syrup (page 35)
Lemon twist, for garnish

In an empty shaker, muddle the kiwi with the B&B. Add the gin, lemon juice, and simple syrup. Shake well. Strain into a chilled Cocktail glass. Add the twist.

Beauty Spot Cocktail

1 ounce gin
$1/2$ ounce dry vermouth
$1/2$ ounce sweet vermouth
$1/4$ ounce orange juice
1 egg white
Dash of grenadine

Pour the gin, both vermouths, and orange juice into a shaker two-thirds full of ice cubes; add the egg white. Shake very well. Strain into a chilled Cocktail glass. Drop the grenadine on top.

Bedford

Adapted from a recipe by Del Pedro, Grange Hall, New York City.

2 ounces straight rye whiskey
$2/3$ ounce Dubonnet Rouge
1 teaspoon Cointreau
2 dashes of orange bitters
Orange twist, for garnish

Pour all of the ingredients into a mixing glass two-thirds full of ice cubes. Stir well. Strain into a chilled Cocktail glass. Add the twist.

The Beezer Cocktail

Adapted from a recipe by William "Chili Bill" Eichinger, bartender at Finnegan's Wake, San Francisco.

2 ounces bourbon (high-proof recommended)
$1/2$ ounce B&B
2 dashes of Fee Brothers peach bitters
Maraschino cherry, for garnish (optional)

Pour all of the ingredients into a mixing glass two-thirds full of ice cubes. Stir well. Strain into a chilled Cocktail glass. Add the cherry.

Bellini

When in Venice, do as everyone else does: Go to Harry's Bar and sip on one or two of these classic cocktails.

MAKES 4 TO 6 SERVINGS

> 1 to 2 ripe white peaches, pitted (leave the peel on), flesh cut into cubes
> 1/4 to 1/2 ounce fresh lemon juice
> 1/4 ounce simple syrup (page 35)
> 1 750-ml bottle Prosecco

In a blender, combine the peach cubes, lemon juice, and simple syrup; blend well. Spoon about 1/4 cup of the purée into each chilled Champagne flute. Gently pour in the Prosecco. If you have to stir, do so gently.

Bellini Martini

If you don't have peach nectar on hand, leave it out; the schnapps will do the job.

> 2 ounces vodka
> 3/4 ounce peach schnapps
> 3/4 ounce peach nectar
> Lemon twist, for garnish

Pour all of the ingredients into a shaker two-thirds full of ice cubes. Shake well. Strain into a chilled Cocktail glass. Add the twist.

Bénédictine Chapel Martini

From the Purple Martini, Denver, Colorado.

> 3 ounces gin
> Splash of Bénédictine
> Splash of sweet vermouth
> Splash of dry vermouth

Pour all of the ingredients into a mixing glass two-thirds full of ice cubes. Stir well. Strain into a chilled Cocktail glass.

The Bengali Gimlet

Adapted from a recipe by Jonny Raglin, head bartender, Absinthe Brasserie & Bar, San Francisco, 2007.

The Curried Nectar requires advance preparation; it's a goodie to have waiting in the refrigerator.

> $1/4$ **fresh kaffir lime leaf**
>
> $1^1/2$ **ounces Tanqueray Rangpur gin**
>
> $1/2$ **ounce fresh lemon juice**
>
> $1/4$ **ounce fresh lime juice**
>
> $3/4$ **ounce curried nectar (see recipe below)**
>
> **Lemon wedge, for garnish**

Tear the lime leaf and drop it into a shaker two-thirds full of ice cubes. Add the gin, juices, and nectar. Shake well. Strain into a chilled Cocktail glass. Add the lemon wedge.

CURRIED NECTAR
MAKES ABOUT 2 CUPS

> $1^1/4$ **cups hot water**
>
> $1/4$ **cup cumin seeds**
>
> $1/4$ **cup coriander seeds**
>
> $1/4$ **cup allspice berries**
>
> **2 tablespoons black peppercorns**
>
> **2 tablespoons white peppercorns**
>
> **1 teaspoon turmeric powder**
>
> **2 dried Thai chiles**
>
> **1 cup granulated sugar**

Combine the water, seeds, berries, peppercorns, turmeric, and chiles in a heavy nonstick saucepan set over moderately high heat. Bring to a boil and boil for about 10 minutes. Slowly add the sugar, stirring constantly until it dissolves. Reduce the heat to low and simmer, stirring occasionally, for 20 minutes. Set aside to cool for about 1 hour. Strain through a double layer of dampened cheesecloth into a glass jar. Refrigerate for up to 2 weeks.

Bennett Cocktail

It's possible that this was named for James Gordon Bennett, a newspaper baron who used to announce his arrival in a restaurant by yanking the tablecloths from all the tables he passed. A fun date, no?

2 ounces gin
1/2 ounce fresh lime juice
1/4 ounce simple syrup (page 35)
Dash of orange bitters

Pour all of the ingredients into a shaker two-thirds full of ice cubes. Shake well. Strain into a chilled Cocktail glass.

Bermuda Rose Cocktail

Drink this only if wearing dark pink shorts.

2 ounces gin
1/2 ounce apricot brandy
1/2 ounce sweet vermouth
Dash of grenadine

Pour all of the ingredients into a mixing glass two-thirds full of ice cubes. Stir well. Strain into a chilled Cocktail glass.

Betsy Ross

Something to sip while sewing or on Independence Day.

3 ounces brandy
1 ounce ruby port
1/2 ounce white curaçao
Dash of Angostura bitters

Pour all of the ingredients into a mixing glass two-thirds full of ice cubes. Stir well. Strain into a chilled Cocktail glass.

Between the Sheets

If you know where or how this drink's name originated, please let me know—it's a mystery to me, but the drink was popular in London during the 1920s.

1 ounce brandy

1 ounce light rum

1 ounce triple sec

$^1/_2$ ounce fresh lemon juice

$^1/_2$ ounce simple syrup (page 35)

Pour all of the ingredients into a shaker two-thirds full of ice cubes. Shake well. Strain into a chilled Cocktail glass.

B-52

Layer this beautifully in three stripes or drink it as a shooter.

$^3/_4$ ounce Kahlúa

$^3/_4$ ounce Baileys Irish cream liqueur

$^3/_4$ ounce Grand Marnier

Pour the Kahlúa into a Pousse-Café glass. Float the Irish cream liqueur on top, and gently pour the Grand Marnier on top of that.

Big Pine Key Cocktail

Adapted from a recipe by Robert (Bobbo) Semmes, a cocktail aficionado from South Carolina.

$1^1/_2$ ounces gin

1 ounce Cointreau

$^3/_4$ ounce fresh lime juice

Orange twist, for garnish

Pour all of the ingredients into a shaker two-thirds full of ice cubes. Shake well. Strain into a chilled Cocktail glass. Add the twist.

Bijou Cocktail

This one's a jewel.

$1^1/_2$ ounces gin

$^1/_2$ ounce sweet vermouth

$^1/_4$ ounce green Chartreuse

2 dashes of orange bitters

Pour all of the ingredients into a mixing glass two-thirds full of ice cubes. Stir well. Strain into a chilled Cocktail glass.

Bishop Punch

Here's a drink that's called a punch but is made in individual servings—like a Planter's Punch. Go figure.

> 1 ounce fresh lemon juice
> 1 ounce orange juice
> $1/2$ ounce simple syrup (page 35)
> 4 ounces red wine
> Orange slice, for garnish

Pour the citrus juices and simple syrup into a shaker two-thirds full of ice cubes. Shake well. Strain into a chilled wine goblet. Pour in the wine; stir briefly. Add the orange slice.

Bistro Sidecar

Adapted from a recipe by Chef Kathy Casey, Kathy Casey Food Studios, Seattle, Washington.

> Superfine sugar and a lemon wedge, for rimming the glass
> $1^1/2$ ounces brandy
> $1/2$ ounce Tuaca
> $1/2$ ounce Frangelico
> $1/2$ ounce fresh tangerine juice
> $1/4$ ounce fresh lemon juice
> $1/4$ ounce simple syrup (page 35)
> Roasted hazelnut, for garnish

Prepare a Cocktail glass. Pour all of the ingredients into a shaker two-thirds full of ice cubes. Shake well. Strain into the sugar-rimmed glass. Drop the hazelnut into the drink.

Bitches Brew

Created by Daniel Eun, PDT, New York City, who took first place in the 2008 Rhum Clément Cocktail Challenge in New York City.

> 1 ounce Clément Première Canne rum
> 1 ounce Pampero Aniversario
> 1 ounce fresh lime juice
> $1/2$ ounce St. Elizabeth Allspice Dram
> $1/2$ ounce demerara syrup (simple syrup using demerara sugar) (page 35)
> 1 egg

Combine all of the ingredients in an empty shaker. Dry-shake to emulsify. Add ice cubes and shake very well. Strain into a Champagne flute.

Bitter-Sweet

The bitters really bring this drink together, and if you are a fan of Angostura, feel free to add an extra dash or two.

1 ounce sweet vermouth
1 ounce dry vermouth
2 dashes of Angostura bitters
Lemon twist, for garnish

Pour all of the ingredients into a mixing glass two-thirds full of ice cubes. Stir well. Strain into a chilled Cocktail glass. Garnish with the twist.

Black & Tan

Though traditionally the stout and amber ale are mixed together in the glass, a more recent trend is to layer the stout on top of the ale. I'm going traditional on this; you can do what you want.

8 ounces Irish stout
8 ounces amber ale

Carefully pour the stout and the ale into a 16-ounce beer glass.

Black & White Cocktail

3¹/₂ ounces chilled strong coffee
1¹/₂ ounces brandy
¹/₂ ounce white crème de cacao
Dollop of whipped cream
Chocolate sprinkles, for garnish

Pour the coffee, brandy, and crème de cacao into a chilled Champagne flute. Top with the whipped cream and a flurry of chocolate sprinkles.

Black Devil

Black olives are seldom used in mixed drinks, but they taste wonderful after sipping this dry rum Martini.

2 ounces light rum

1/2 ounce dry vermouth

Brined black olive, pitted, for garnish

Pour both ingredients into a mixing glass two-thirds full of ice cubes. Stir well. Strain into a chilled Cocktail glass. Add the olive.

The Black-Eyed Susan

The Black-Eyed Susan was created at Pimlico and is that horse track's answer to Churchill Downs's Mint Juleps. So if you go see the Preakness, be sure to try one.

1 ounce vodka

1 ounce Mount Gay Eclipse rum

3/4 ounce Cointreau

1 1/2 ounces fresh orange juice

1 1/2 ounces pineapple juice

Maraschino cherry, orange wheel, pineapple cube, and lime wedge, for garnishes

Build in a Collins glass filled with crushed ice. Add the garnishes.

Note: It's imperative to squeeze the juice from the lime wedge into the drink.

Black Feather

"He stuck a feather in his cap . . ."

Adapted from a recipe by Robert Hess (aka "DrinkBoy"), Seattle.

2 ounces brandy

1 ounce dry vermouth

1/2 ounce Cointreau

Angostura bitters, to taste

Orange twist, for garnish

Pour all of the ingredients into a mixing glass two-thirds full of ice cubes. Stir well. Strain into a chilled Cocktail glass. Add the twist.

Black Russian

Use less Kahlúa for a drier drink. Yum.

2 ounces vodka
1¹/₂ ounces Kahlúa

Pour the vodka and Kahlúa into an ice-filled Rocks glass. Stir to distribute.

Black Seal Cocktail

Adapted from a recipe by "DrinkBoy" Robert Hess, 2000.

2 ounces Goslings Black Seal rum
1 ounce fresh lime juice
Splash of Falernum liqueur
Lime twist, for garnish

Pour all of the ingredients into a shaker two-thirds full of ice cubes. Shake well. Strain into a chilled Cocktail glass. Add the twist.

Black Velvet

A stately drink that is said to have been created after the death of Prince Albert, Queen Victoria's beloved consort, so that "even the champagne could be in mourning," but it's impossible to verify that.

8 ounces chilled Irish stout
8 ounces chilled not-too-dry champagne or other sparkling wine

Carefully pour the stout and champagne into a chilled 16-ounce beer glass.

Black Velveteen

This is a less expensive version of the Black Velvet and it works very well indeed.

8 ounces chilled Irish stout
8 ounces chilled hard cider

Carefully pour the stout and cider into a chilled 16-ounce beer glass.

Blackthorne

2 ounces Irish whiskey

3/4 ounce sweet vermouth

2 dashes of Pernod

2 dashes of Angostura bitters

Lemon twist, for garnish

Pour the whiskey, vermouth, Pernod, and bitters into a mixing glass two-thirds full of ice cubes. Stir well. Strain into a chilled Cocktail glass. Add the twist.

Blarney Stone

Named for the famous "wishing stone" at Blarney Castle, which is believed to have been broken from the Scottish Stone of Scone. Scottish kings were crowned over the stone because it was believed to have special powers. This drink has special powers of its own.

2 ounces Irish whiskey

1/4 ounce white curaçao

1/4 ounce absinthe

Dash of maraschino liqueur

Lemon twist, for garnish

Pour all of the ingredients into a mixing glass two-thirds full of ice cubes. Stir well. Strain into a chilled Cocktail glass. Add the twist.

Blood and Sand

You should try this drink even if you don't care for scotch—it's a rich, fruity treat.

1 ounce blended scotch

1 ounce orange juice

1 ounce cherry brandy

1 ounce sweet vermouth

Pour all of the ingredients into a shaker two-thirds full of ice cubes. Shake well. Strain into a chilled Cocktail glass.

Blood Orange

Created by John Simmons, Petaluma, New York City, 1995.

2 ounces Stolichnaya Ohranj vodka
1 1/2 ounces Campari
Blood orange slice or wedge, for garnish

Pour both ingredients into a mixing glass two-thirds full of ice cubes. Stir well. Strain into a chilled Cocktail glass. Add the blood orange garnish.

Bloodhound Cocktail

2 ounces gin
1/2 ounce dry vermouth
1/2 ounce sweet vermouth
1/4 ounce strawberry liqueur

Pour all of the ingredients into a mixing glass two-thirds full of ice cubes. Stir well. Strain into a chilled Cocktail glass.

Bloody Bull

2 ounces vodka
2 ounces tomato juice
2 ounces beef bouillon
1/4 ounce fresh lemon juice
Pinch of ground black pepper
Pinch of celery salt
3 dashes of Worcestershire sauce
Dash of hot sauce
Lemon wedge, for garnish

Pour the vodka, tomato juice, beef bouillon, and lemon juice into a shaker two-thirds full of ice cubes. Add the pepper, celery salt, Worcestershire, and hot sauce. Shake well. Strain into an ice-filled Highball glass. Add the lemon wedge.

Bloody Caesar

2 ounces vodka

4 ounces Clamato juice

1/4 ounce fresh lemon juice

Pinch of ground black pepper

Pinch of celery salt

Dash of hot sauce (optional)

Lemon wedge, for garnish

Pour the vodka, Clamato juice, and lemon juice into a shaker two-thirds full of ice cubes. Add the pepper, celery salt, and hot sauce. Shake well. Strain into an ice-filled Highball glass. Add the lemon wedge.

Bloody Maria

See **Bloody Mary**; substitute tequila for the vodka.

Bloody Mary

This classic drink has a long history that began in Paris and moved to New York City, where it was renamed the Red Snapper, then went back to its original moniker. It has been greatly improved over the years and has become universally popular. Note that this one uses lemon juice, which produces a much better cocktail than lime juice.

2 ounces vodka

4 ounces tomato juice

1/2 ounce fresh lemon juice

1/4 teaspoon freshly milled black pepper

Pinch of salt

1/4 teaspoon ground cumin

2 dashes of Worcestershire sauce

2 dashes of hot sauce

Lemon wedge, for garnish

Pour the vodka, tomato juice, and lemon juice into a shaker two-thirds full of ice cubes; add the pepper, salt, cumin, Worcestershire, and hot sauce. Shake well. Strain into an ice-filled Highball glass. Add the lemon wedge.

The Bloody Mary Martini

Adapted from a recipe by Kurt Gutenbrunner, chef-owner of Wallsé, New York City.

1¹/₂ ounces pepper vodka

1 ounce vodka

2 ounces tomato water (see recipe below)

Pinch of celery seeds

Lemon twist, for garnish

Pour all of the ingredients into a shaker two-thirds full of ice cubes. Shake well. Strain into a chilled Cocktail glass. Add the twist.

TOMATO WATER

Simply pureé some ripe tomatoes and place them in a fine-mesh sieve lined with a double layer of dampened cheesecloth. Place the sieve on top of a bowl or large measuring jug, and allow the tomato water to drain into the bowl. (If you are in a hurry, make the cheesecloth containing the tomato pureé into a pouch, and squeeze out the water.)

Bloomsbury

Adapted from a recipe by "DrinkBoy" Robert Hess, 2003.

2 ounces Tanqueray No. Ten gin

¹/₂ ounce Quarenta y Tres Licor 43

¹/₂ ounce Lillet Blanc

2 dashes of Peychaud's bitters

Lemon twist, for garnish

Pour all of the ingredients into a mixing glass two-thirds full of ice cubes. Stir well. Strain into a chilled Cocktail glass. Add the twist.

Blow Job

This shot should be drunk without using your hands. Pick up the Pony glass between your lips and tilt your head back.

1/2 ounce butterscotch schnapps

1/2 ounce Irish cream liqueur

Whipped cream

In a Pony glass, layer the butterscotch schnapps with the Irish cream. Spray the whipped cream on top, mounding it about 2 inches high.

Blue Blazer

This Blazer dates to before 1862—must be threadbare by now. If you try this at home, be verrrry careful.

2 ounces scotch

1 1/2 ounces hot water

1/2 ounce simple syrup (page 35)

Lemon twist, for garnish

Pour the scotch and the hot water into an Irish Coffee glass or a metal tankard and ignite it carefully with a match. Carefully pour the flaming liquid into a second Irish Coffee glass or metal tankard and repeat this process, pouring it back and forth between the glasses 3 or 4 times. Add the simple syrup; stir briefly. Add the twist.

Blue Café

Adapted from a recipe by William Conklin, Los Angeles.

1 ounce Bombay Sapphire gin

1 1/2 ounces blueberry schnapps

1 ounce fresh lemon juice

1/2 ounce simple syrup (page 35)

Splash of blue curaçao

3 fresh blueberries, for garnish

Pour all of the ingredients into a shaker two-thirds full of ice cubes. Shake well. Strain into a chilled Cocktail glass. Add the blueberries.

Blue Devil

Adapted from a recipe by Dale DeGroff, 2003.

1¹/₂ ounces Hpnotiq liqueur

1 ounce Martini & Rossi dry vermouth

¹/₂ ounce Ardbeg 10-year-old single-malt scotch

Pour the Hpnotiq and vermouth into an ice-filled Old-Fashioned glass and stir briefly. Float the Ardbeg on top.

Blue-Eyed Blonde

This is a favorite shooter among Trinidadians.

¹/₂ ounce Frangelico

¹/₂ ounce crème de banane

¹/₂ ounce blue curaçao

Layer in the order given into a Pousse-Café or Pony glass.

Blue Kamikaze

2 ounces vodka

³/₄ ounce blue curaçao

³/₄ ounce fresh lime juice

Pour all of the ingredients into a shaker two-thirds full of ice cubes. Shake well. Strain into a chilled Cocktail glass.

Blue Mountain Bronx

2 ounces Appleton Estate V/X rum

¹/₄ ounce sweet vermouth

¹/₄ ounce dry vermouth

1 ounce orange juice

3 dashes of Angostura bitters

Pour all of the ingredients into a shaker two-thirds full of ice cubes. Shake well. Strain into a chilled Cocktail glass.

Blue Train Cocktail

Could this be named for the gorgeous turn-of-the-twentieth-century restaurant in Paris?

> **2 ounces gin**
> **$1/_2$ ounce blue curaçao**
> **$1/_2$ ounce fresh lemon juice**

Pour all of the ingredients into a shaker two-thirds full of ice cubes. Shake well. Strain into a chilled Cocktail glass.

B9 Martini

From Butterfield 9, Washington, D.C.

> **$1^1/_2$ ounces Grey Goose orange vodka**
> **$1/_2$ ounce peach schnapps**
> **Chilled champagne or other sparkling wine**

Pour the vodka and peach schnapps into a mixing glass two-thirds full of ice cubes. Stir well. Strain into a chilled Cocktail glass. Add a splash of the champagne.

Bobbo's Bride Straight-Up

Adapted from a recipe by Laurel Semmes, somewhere in South Carolina.

> **1 ounce gin**
> **1 ounce vodka**
> **$1/_2$ ounce peach schnapps**
> **$1/_2$ ounce Campari**
> **Peach slice, for garnish**

Pour all of the ingredients into a mixing glass two-thirds full of ice cubes. Stir well. Strain into a chilled Cocktail glass. Add the peach slice.

Bobby Burns

This cocktail is probably named for the eighteenth-century Scottish poet Robert Burns, whose works include the incomprehensible lyrics to "Auld Lang Syne."

2 ounces blended scotch

1 ounce sweet vermouth

1/4 ounce Bénédictine

Pour all of the ingredients into a mixing glass two-thirds full of ice cubes. Stir well. Strain into a chilled Cocktail glass.

The Bobtail Nag

Adapted from a recipe by Jonny Raglin, Absinthe Brasserie & Bar, San Francisco, circa 2005.

1 1/2 ounces Michter's straight rye whiskey

1/2 to 1 ounce Cocchi Barolo Chinato wine

3 dashes of mint bitters

Lemon twist, for garnish

Pour all of the ingredients into a mixing glass two-thirds full of ice cubes. Stir well. Strain into a chilled Cocktail glass. Add the twist.

Bocce Ball

2 ounces amaretto

4 ounces orange juice

Orange wheel, for garnish

Pour both ingredients into an ice-filled Highball glass. Stir briefly; add the orange wheel.

Boilermaker

This is a shooter followed by a chaser.

2 ounces whiskey

10 ounces beer

Pour each ingredient into its own glass. Toss back the whiskey and chase it with the beer.

Bolero

2 ounces dark rum

¹/₂ ounce brandy

¹/₂ ounce fresh lime juice

¹/₂ ounce orange juice

¹/₂ ounce simple syrup (page 35)

Pour all of the ingredients into a shaker two-thirds full of ice cubes. Shake well. Strain into a chilled Cocktail glass.

Bolo's Pomegranate Sangria

Created by chef Bobby Flay, Bolo, New York City.

MAKES ABOUT EIGHT 6-OUNCE SERVINGS

1 750-ml bottle dry red wine

8 ounces American brandy

8 ounces simple syrup (page 35)

4 ounces orange juice

6 ounces pomegranate molasses or pomegranate juice

2 oranges, sliced into thin wheels

3 green apples, cored and cut into thin slices

2 lemons, sliced into thin wheels

Combine all of the ingredients in a large pot or bowl. Stir to blend. Cover and let sit, refrigerated, for at least 2 hours and up to 2 days. Serve in ice-filled wine goblets.

Bolo's White Peach Sangria

Created by chef Bobby Flay, Bolo, New York City.

MAKES ABOUT EIGHT 6-OUNCE SERVINGS

1 750-ml bottle Pinot Grigio

8 ounces American brandy

8 ounces simple syrup (page 35)

4 ounces orange juice

6 ounces white peach purée

4 peaches, pitted and sliced

3 green apples, cored and cut into thin slices

2 lemons, sliced into thin wheels

Combine all of the ingredients in a large pot or bowl. Stir to blend. Cover and let sit, refrigerated, for at least 2 hours and up to 2 days. Serve in ice-filled wine goblets.

Bonnie Ginger

Adapted from a recipe by Dale DeGroff, circa 2004.

$^1/_2$ ounce Velvet Falernum liqueur

1 small piece of fresh ginger

2 ounces single-malt scotch

Lemon wedge, for garnish

In an Old-Fashioned glass, gently muddle together the Falernum and fresh ginger. Add ice cubes and the scotch; stir briefly. Squeeze the lemon wedge into the drink to release the juice, and drop the wedge into the glass. Stir again, and serve.

Bootlegger

Adapted from a recipe created at the Martini House, St. Helena, Napa Valley, California.

$1^1/_2$ ounces Charbay vodka

$^1/_2$ ounce Junipero gin

Splash of Lillet Blanc

Lemon twist and a cocktail olive, for garnishes

Pour all of the ingredients into a mixing glass two-thirds full of ice cubes. Stir well. Strain into a chilled Cocktail glass. Add the lemon twist and olive.

Bosom Caresser

Surprisingly, given its racy name, this drink dates to the late 1800s.

2 ounces brandy

1 ounce white curaçao

Dash of grenadine

1 egg yolk

Pour all of the ingredients into a shaker two-thirds full of ice cubes. Shake very well. Strain into a chilled Cocktail glass.

The Boston Cream Martini

Adapted from a recipe by Russ Hovermale, Buzz restaurant, Boston.

Chocolate Magic Shell (an ice-cream topping sold at many supermarkets), for rimming the glass

2¹/₂ ounces Grey Goose vodka

¹/₂ ounce Baileys Irish cream liqueur

Dash of vanilla extract

Place a Cocktail glass in the freezer until very cold. Coat the interior rim of the glass with the Magic Shell; refreeze. Pour all of the remaining ingredients into a shaker two-thirds full of ice cubes. Shake well. Strain into the prepared glass.

Bourbon & Branch

The recipe that answers the question "What is 'branch water,' anyway?"

2¹/₂ ounces bourbon

4 to 5 ounces still spring water

Pour both of the ingredients into an ice-filled Highball glass. Stir briefly.

Bourbon & Cranberry Cobbler

Adapted from a recipe by Audrey Saunders, Bemelmans Bar, New York City, circa 2003.

1 ounce fresh cranberry sauce

3 orange slices

3 dashes of Angostura bitters

¹/₄ ounce pomegranate molasses

2 ounces Maker's Mark bourbon

¹/₂ ounce Punt e Mes

¹/₂ ounce Berentzen Apfelkorn apple schnapps

Place the cranberry sauce, orange slices, bitters, and pomegranate molasses in an empty shaker. Muddle well. Add ice cubes and the remaining ingredients. Shake very well. Strain into a chilled Cocktail glass.

Bourbon Ball

Adapted from a recipe by Joy Perrine, Jack's Lounge, Louisville, Kentucky, circa 2003.

1 ounce Woodford Reserve bourbon

1 ounce dark crème de cacao

1 ounce Tuaca

Fresh strawberry, for garnish

Pour all of the ingredients into a mixing glass two-thirds full of ice cubes. Stir well. Strain into a chilled Cocktail glass. Add the strawberry.

Bourbon Milk Punch

Milk punches are very popular in New Orleans, "The Big Easy."

2 ounces bourbon

$1/2$ ounce dark crème de cacao

4 ounces milk

Dash of vanilla extract

Dash of ground cinnamon

Freshly grated nutmeg, for garnish

Pour the bourbon, crème de cacao, milk, and vanilla into a shaker two-thirds full of ice cubes; add the cinnamon. Shake well. Strain into an ice-filled Rocks glass. Sprinkle with the nutmeg.

Bourbon-Mint Iced Tea

Adapted from a recipe by Audrey Saunders, 2002.

$1/2$ ounce fresh lemon juice

$3/4$ ounce simple syrup (page 35)

$1/4$ ounce Fernet-Branca Menta liqueur

$3/4$ ounce Maker's Mark bourbon

5 ounces cold brewed tea

Lemon wheel and a mint sprig, for garnishes

Pour the lemon juice, simple syrup, liqueur, and bourbon into a shaker two-thirds full of ice cubes. Shake well. Strain into a large ice-filled glass. Add the tea and stir; add the lemon wheel and mint sprig.

Bourbon Old-Fashioned

1 sugar cube

3 dashes of Angostura bitters

1 orange slice

1 lemon wedge

1 maraschino cherry

2$^{1}/_{2}$ ounces bourbon

In a Double Old-Fashioned glass, muddle the sugar cube, bitters, orange slice, lemon wedge, and maraschino cherry. Fill the glass with ice cubes. Add the bourbon; stir well.

Bourbon Rickey

2$^{1}/_{2}$ ounces bourbon

1 ounce fresh lime juice

5 to 6 ounces club soda

Lime wedge, for garnish

Pour the bourbon and lime juice into an ice-filled Highball glass. Add the club soda; stir briefly. Squeeze the lime wedge into the drink and add it to the glass.

Brain Damage

1 ounce Jägermeister

$^{3}/_{4}$ ounce gin

$^{1}/_{2}$ ounce vodka

Pour all of the ingredients into a mixing glass two-thirds full of ice cubes. Stir well. Strain into a chilled Pony glass.

Brain Hemorrhage

Prepared properly, this drink looks like an internal organ. Check with your neurosurgeon before drinking.

2 ounces peach schnapps

$^{1}/_{2}$ ounce Baileys Irish cream liqueur

Splash of grenadine

Pour the peach schnapps into a Sherry or Pony glass. Slowly pour in the Irish cream; do not mix—the cream will clump together and settle at the bottom of the schnapps all by itself. Pour the grenadine on top.

Brain Tumor

Another awful-looking drink that tastes good to those with a sweet tooth.

2 ounces Baileys Irish cream liqueur
$1/2$ ounce Chambord raspberry liqueur

Pour the Irish cream into an ice-filled Pony glass. Carefully drizzle the Chambord over the top so that it resembles veins of blood.

Brandied Eggnog

MAKES EIGHT 6-OUNCE SERVINGS

4 eggs
6 ounces brandy
2 ounces Grand Marnier
1 teaspoon vanilla extract
$1/2$ teaspoon ground cinnamon
$1/2$ teaspoon ground allspice
$1/4$ teaspoon ground cloves
1 quart whole milk
Freshly grated nutmeg, for garnish

Break the eggs into a bowl and whisk until frothy. Add the brandy, Grand Marnier, vanilla, cinnamon, allspice, and cloves. Slowly whisk in the milk until the eggnog is thoroughly mixed. Ladle or pour into Irish Coffee glasses; add a sprinkle of nutmeg to each serving.

Brandy Alexander

It's possible that this drink popped up on the other side of the Atlantic while Americans were suffering through the dry days of Prohibition.

2 ounces brandy
1 ounce dark crème de cacao
1 ounce heavy cream
Freshly grated nutmeg, for garnish

Pour the brandy, crème de cacao, and heavy cream into a shaker two-thirds full of ice cubes. Shake well. Strain into a chilled Cocktail glass. Sprinkle the nutmeg on top.

Brandy Crusta

The original Crusta, this drink has been around since the mid-1800s.

> **Superfine sugar and a lemon wedge, for rimming the glass**
> **Lemon peel spiral (page 41)**
> **2 ounces brandy**
> **$1/2$ ounce white curaçao**
> **$1/2$ ounce fresh lemon juice**

Rim a Sour glass using the sugar and lemon wedge. Place the lemon peel spiral into the glass so that it lines almost the entire interior.

Pour the brandy, curaçao, and lemon juice into a shaker two-thirds full of ice cubes. Shake well. Strain into the glass.

Brandy Milk Punch

If you've never had a milk punch, run, don't walk—they are delicious.

> **2 ounces brandy**
> **1 ounce white crème de cacao**
> **4 ounces milk**
> **Freshly grated nutmeg, for garnish**

Pour the brandy, crème de cacao, and milk into a shaker two-thirds full of ice cubes. Shake well. Strain the mixture into an ice-filled Collins glass. Sprinkle the nutmeg on top.

Brandy Smash

The Brandy Smash is the original Smash.

> **6 fresh mint leaves**
> **$3/4$ ounce simple syrup (page 35)**
> **$2 1/2$ ounces brandy**
> **Mint sprig, for garnish**

Place the mint leaves in the bottom of a Rocks glass; add the simple syrup and muddle well. Fill the glass with crushed ice. Pour in the brandy; stir briefly. Add the mint sprig.

Brandy Sour

2 ounces brandy
3/4 ounce fresh lemon juice
1/2 ounce simple syrup (page 35)
Orange wheel and maraschino cherry, for garnishes

Pour the brandy, lemon juice, and simple syrup into a shaker two-thirds full of ice cubes. Shake well. Strain the drink into a chilled Sour glass. Add the orange wheel and cherry.

Brass Monkey

"It would freeze the tail off a brass monkey."
　　—Before the Mast, *C. A. Abbey, 1857*

4 ounces orange juice
1 ounce vodka
3/4 ounce light rum
Splash of Galliano

Pour the orange juice, vodka, and rum into an ice-filled Collins glass; stir to blend. Float the Galliano on top.

Brave Bull

This drink was immensely popular during the 1970s, perhaps because the combination of tequila and Kahlúa is a match made in heaven.

2 ounces white tequila
1/2 ounce Kahlúa

Pour both ingredients into an ice-filled Rocks glass; stir briefly.

Breakfast Martini

Adapted from a recipe by Salvatore Calabrese, Salvatore @ 50, London.

1 3/4 ounces Bombay gin
1/2 ounce Cointreau
1/2 ounce fresh lemon juice
1 1/2 teaspoons Wilkin & Sons orange marmalade
Shredded orange peel, for garnish

Pour all of the ingredients into a shaker two-thirds full of ice cubes. Shake very well to blend in the marmalade. Strain into a chilled Cocktail glass. Add the orange peel.

Bronx Cocktail

This drink was reportedly created at the old Waldorf-Astoria when the hotel was on the site where the Empire State Building now stands. The bartender who first made it, Johnnie Solon, had visited the Bronx Zoo just prior to inventing this cocktail. He said he had heard that his customers saw strange animals after having too many drinks, so it seemed appropriate to him.

2 ounces gin
1 ounce fresh orange juice
$1/4$ ounce dry vermouth
$1/4$ ounce sweet vermouth

Pour all of the ingredients into a shaker two-thirds full of ice cubes. Shake well. Strain into a chilled Cocktail glass. Hang a plastic monkey off the edge.

Brooke Shields

An excellent choice for the designated driver.

1 ounce orange juice
$1/2$ ounce fresh lemon juice
$1/4$ ounce fresh lime juice
6 ounces ginger ale
Dash of grenadine
Maraschino cherry, for garnish

Pour the citrus juices into a shaker two-thirds full of ice cubes. Shake well. Strain into an ice-filled Collins glass. Add the ginger ale and grenadine; stir briefly. Add the cherry.

Brown Cow Special

3 ounces Kahlúa
10 to 12 ounces milk
Splash of chocolate syrup

Combine the Kahlúa and milk in a Hurricane glass half-filled with ice. Stir well. Drizzle the chocolate syrup on top.

Brunch Punch

Preparing brunch tends to be a busy time for the host, so serving a premade punch is an excellent idea.

MAKES ABOUT TWENTY-FOUR 6-OUNCE SERVINGS

8 ounces vodka

8 ounces peach schnapps

4 ounces Chambord raspberry liqueur

1/2 gallon orange juice

2 liters ginger ale or lemon-lime soda

1 block of ice

Chill all of the ingredients ahead of time. Mix together in a large punch bowl and add the block of ice.

Buck's Fizz

Named for the Buck's Club, London.

2 ounces fresh orange juice

4 ounces champagne or other sparkling wine

Dash of grenadine

Orange slice, for garnish

Pour the orange juice into a Champagne flute; carefully add the champagne. Drizzle the grenadine on top. Add the orange slice.

Bullshot

I like to use celery seeds instead of celery salt in this drink; if you do, keep in mind that their flavor takes a few seconds to come through.

2 ounces vodka

4 ounces beef bouillon

1/4 ounce fresh lemon juice

Pinch of freshly milled black pepper

Pinch of celery seeds

3 dashes of Worcestershire sauce

Dash of hot sauce

Lemon wedge, for garnish

Pour the vodka, beef bouillon, and lemon juice into a shaker two-thirds full of ice cubes; add the pepper, celery seeds, Worcestershire sauce, and hot sauce. Shake well. Strain into an ice-filled Highball glass. Add the lemon wedge.

The Burnet

Created by Gary Regan, circa 2000.

2¹/₂ ounces Glenmorangie single-malt scotch
¹/₂ ounce Cherry Heering
2 dashes of Angostura bitters
Lemon twist, for garnish

Pour all of the ingredients into a mixing glass two-thirds full of ice cubes. Stir well. Strain into a chilled Cocktail glass. Add the twist.

Burnished Gold

2 ounces brandy
¹/₂ ounce Frangelico

Pour both ingredients into a mixing glass two-thirds full of ice cubes. Stir well. Strain into a chilled Cocktail glass or an ice-filled Old-Fashioned glass.

Buttery Nipple

Nary a clue as to how this one got its name.

³/₄ ounce butterscotch schnapps
³/₄ ounce Baileys Irish cream liqueur

Pour the schnapps into a Pony glass. Layer the Irish cream on top.

Cabaret

This drink used to contain a sweet-vermouth type of wine known as Caperitif, but it's no longer available.

2 ounces gin
¹/₂ ounce sweet vermouth
Dash of absinthe
Dash of Angostura bitters
Lemon twist, for garnish

Pour all of the ingredients into a mixing glass two-thirds full of ice cubes. Stir well. Strain into a chilled Cocktail glass. Add the twist.

The Cable Car

Adapted from a recipe by Tony Abou-Ganim, San Francisco, circa 1998.

Ground cinnamon and granulated sugar, mixed together, for rimming the glass

1¹/₂ ounces Captain Morgan spiced rum

³/₄ ounce white curaçao

1 ounce fresh lemon juice

¹/₂ ounce simple syrup (page 35)

Orange twist, for garnish

Prepare a Cocktail glass; refrigerate to chill. Pour the remaining ingredients into a shaker two-thirds full of ice cubes. Shake well. Strain into the prepared glass. Add the twist.

The Cacharita

Created by Gary Regan for Marty Friedland, Efco Importers, 2001.

1¹/₂ ounces Pitú cachaça

1¹/₂ ounces Cointreau

¹/₂ ounce fresh lime juice

Pour all of the ingredients into a shaker two-thirds full of ice cubes. Shake well. Strain into a chilled Cocktail glass.

Café Brûlot

I'll never forget my first Café Brûlot. It was at Commander's Palace in New Orleans way back when Emeril Lagasse was chef there.

MAKES 2 SERVINGS

3 lemon twists

3 orange twists

4 whole cloves

1 cinnamon stick (about 2 inches long)

1¹/₂ ounces brandy

1 ounce white curaçao

1¹/₂ cups strong, hot coffee

Place the citrus twists, cloves, cinnamon stick, brandy, and curaçao in a nonreactive large saucepan over moderately low heat. Cook until warm but not too hot. Carefully ignite the liquid with a match and allow it to flame for about 10 seconds. Pour in the hot coffee and stir well until the flames subside. Divide the mixture between 2 Irish Coffee glasses.

DRINKS A TO Z

Caipirinha

Brazil has become famous for its national drink that's made with cachaça (kuh-SHAH-suh). If you can't find cachaça, use an inexpensive light rum. Alternately, try a Caipiroska.

$^1/_2$ lime, cut into 4 or 6 wedges
1 tablespoon granulated sugar
2 ounces cachaça

Place the lime wedges and sugar in a heavy Rocks glass and muddle thoroughly to release all of the juice from the limes. Fill the glass with crushed ice. Add the cachaça; stir thoroughly.

Caipiroska

$^1/_2$ lime, cut into 4 to 6 wedges
1 tablespoon granulated sugar
2 ounces vodka

Place the lime wedges and sugar in a heavy Rocks glass and muddle them thoroughly to release all of the juice from the limes. Fill the glass with crushed ice. Add the vodka; stir thoroughly.

Cajun Martini

$2^1/_2$ ounces pepper vodka
$^1/_2$ ounce dry vermouth
Slice of jalapeño pepper, for garnish

Pour both ingredients into a mixing glass two-thirds full of ice cubes. Stir well. Strain into a chilled Cocktail glass. Add the jalapeño.

The Calvados Cocktail

2 ounces calvados
$^1/_2$ ounce Cointreau
$^1/_2$ ounce fresh orange juice
$^1/_2$ ounce fresh lemon juice
Orange bitters, to taste

Pour all of the ingredients into a shaker two-thirds full of ice cubes. Shake well. Strain into a chilled Cocktail glass.

Campari & Grapefruit Juice

2 ounces Campari

4 ounces grapefruit juice

Pour both ingredients into an ice-filled Highball glass; stir briefly.

Campari & Orange Juice

2 ounces Campari

4 ounces orange juice

Pour both ingredients into an ice-filled Highball glass; stir briefly.

Campari Royale

2 ounces Campari

1 ounce Grand Marnier

3 ounces orange juice

Orange wheel, for garnish

Pour all of the ingredients into an ice-filled Highball glass; stir briefly. Add the orange wheel.

Canaletto

I learned how to make this in Venice in the late 1990s, and I find that the sweetness of the Prosecco works magic here.

MAKES 3 TO 4 SERVINGS

1 cup fresh raspberries

1/4 ounce fresh lemon juice

1/4 ounce simple syrup (page 35)

Chilled Prosecco or other sparkling wine

Purée the raspberries, 2 or 3 ice cubes, the lemon juice, and simple syrup in a blender. Divide the mixture equally among 3 or 4 Champagne flutes. Carefully top each drink with Prosecco, slowly stirring the ingredients together. (You might have to do this in stages, waiting for the Prosecco to settle each time.)

Cannonball

Developed by Gary Regan and me for Jameson Irish whiskey, 2002.

2 ounces Jameson Irish whiskey
1 ounce peach schnapps
1/2 ounce Jägermeister

Pour all of the ingredients into a mixing glass two-thirds full of ice cubes. Stir well. Strain into a chilled Cocktail glass.

Canteen

Adapted from a recipe by Joey Guerra, Canteen restaurant, New York City.

2 ounces light rum
2 ounces Southern Comfort
1/4 ounce amaretto
1/4 ounce fresh lime juice
Dash of simple syrup (page 35)

Pour all of the ingredients into a shaker two-thirds full of ice cubes. Shake well. Strain into a chilled Cocktail glass.

Cape Codder

This could be the drink that put cranberry juice on the map at cocktail bars.

2 1/2 ounces vodka
4 to 6 ounces cranberry juice
Lime wedge, for garnish

Pour both ingredients into an ice-filled Highball glass. Stir briefly; add the lime wedge.

Caprice

1¹/₂ ounces gin

¹/₂ ounce dry vermouth

¹/₂ ounce Bénédictine

Dash of orange bitters

Lemon twist and a maraschino cherry, for garnishes

Pour all of the ingredients into a mixing glass two-thirds full of ice cubes. Stir well. Strain into a chilled Cocktail glass. Add the lemon twist and cherry.

Carbonated Piston Slinger

Adapted from a recipe by "Dr. Cocktail" (Ted Haigh), high priest of cocktail history.

1¹/₂ ounces 151-proof Demerara rum

¹/₂ ounce sloe gin

¹/₂ ounce fresh lime juice

Club soda

Lime wedge and a maraschino cherry, for garnishes

Build in an ice-filled Hurricane glass. Fill with club soda and stir well. Add the lime wedge and cherry.

Cardinal

1¹/₂ ounces añejo rum

¹/₂ ounce maraschino liqueur

Dash of triple sec

Dash of grenadine

Pour all of the ingredients into a mixing glass two-thirds full of ice cubes. Stir well. Strain into a chilled Cocktail glass.

Cardinal Punch

If you're serving this to the Monsignor, you can rename the recipe.

MAKES ABOUT TWENTY 6-OUNCE SERVINGS

6 ounces dark rum

4 ounces fresh lemon juice

3 ounces simple syrup (page 35)

2 750-ml bottles dry red wine

1 750-ml bottle champagne or other sparkling wine

8 ounces sweet vermouth

8 ounces brandy

1 large block of ice

Orange wheels, for garnish

Pour 2 ounces of the rum, all of the lemon juice, and all of the simple syrup into a shaker two-thirds full of ice cubes; shake well. Strain into a large punch bowl. Pour in the remaining 4 ounces of rum, the red wine, champagne, vermouth, and brandy; stir well. Add the ice and let chill, stirring from time to time, for at least 30 minutes. Ladle into punch cups; garnish each serving with an orange wheel.

Caribbean Cooler

2^1/$_2$ ounces light rum

4 ounces ginger beer

Lemon twist, for garnish

Pour both ingredients into an ice-filled Collins glass; stir briefly. Add the twist.

Caribbean Cosmopolitan

2^1/$_2$ ounces citrus vodka

^{1}/$_2$ ounce Cointreau

^{1}/$_4$ ounce pineapple juice

^{1}/$_4$ ounce cranberry juice

Maraschino cherry, for garnish

Pour all of the ingredients into a shaker two-thirds full of ice cubes. Shake well. Strain into a chilled Cocktail glass. Add the cherry.

The Bartender's Best Friend

114

Caribbean Martini

1¹/₂ ounces Stolichnaya Vanil vodka

³/₄ ounce Malibu rum

Splash of pineapple juice

Pour all of the ingredients into a shaker two-thirds full of ice cubes. Shake well. Strain into a chilled Cocktail glass.

Caribbean Punch

If serving this in a family situation, omit the rums and spike individual servings for the adults.

MAKES TWENTY-FIVE TO THIRTY 6-OUNCE SERVINGS

1 pineapple, peeled and cored

8 ounces fresh lemon juice

3 ounces simple syrup (page 35)

1 teaspoon freshly grated nutmeg

1 teaspoon ground cinnamon

1 teaspoon ground allspice

1 750-ml bottle light rum

1 750-ml bottle spiced rum

32 ounces pineapple juice

48 ounces orange juice

12 ounces ginger ale

1 large block of ice, for serving

Thinly slice half of the peeled, cored pineapple and set aside. Cut the remaining pineapple half into 1-inch cubes. Place the cubes in a blender and add 4 ounces of the lemon juice, the simple syrup, nutmeg, cinnamon, and allspice. Blend on high speed; pour the mixture into a large punch bowl.

Add the remaining 4 ounces lemon juice, both rums, the pineapple juice, the orange juice, and the ginger ale. Stir well. Add the ice. Float the reserved sliced pineapple on top.

The Caricature Cocktail

Created by Gary Regan for caricaturist Jill DeGroff, 2001.

1¹/₂ ounces gin
¹/₂ ounce sweet vermouth
³/₄ ounce Cointreau
¹/₂ ounce Campari
¹/₂ ounce fresh grapefruit juice
Orange twist, for garnish

Pour all of the ingredients into a shaker two-thirds full of ice cubes. Shake well. Strain into a chilled Cocktail glass. Add the twist.

Carrot Cake

But where's the cream cheese icing?

1 ounce Baileys Irish cream liqueur
1 ounce butterscotch schnapps
¹/₄ ounce Goldschlager or cinnamon schnapps

Pour all of the ingredients into a shaker two-thirds full of ice cubes. Shake well. Strain into a chilled Pony glass.

Caruso

Named for the late opera tenor Enrico Caruso, this drink used to be made with equal amounts of all three ingredients. It works far better this way; it's a drink that will make you sing.

2 ounces gin
¹/₂ ounce dry vermouth
Dash of green crème de menthe

Pour all of the ingredients into a mixing glass two-thirds full of ice cubes. Stir well. Strain into a chilled Cocktail glass.

Casablanca

Ah, Rick. Ah, Ilsa. Ah, Victor Laszlo. Ah, Sam.

2¹/₂ ounces light rum
¹/₂ ounce triple sec

$^1/_2$ ounce maraschino liqueur

$^1/_2$ ounce fresh lime juice

Pour all of the ingredients into a shaker two-thirds full of ice cubes. Shake well. Strain into a chilled Cocktail glass.

Casino Cocktail

$2^1/_2$ ounces gin

$^1/_2$ ounce maraschino liqueur

1 ounce fresh lemon juice

Dash of orange bitters

Pour all of the ingredients into a shaker two-thirds full of ice cubes. Shake well. Strain into a chilled Cocktail glass.

Casino Royale

Adapted from a recipe by Dale DeGroff.

$^1/_2$ ounce gin

1 ounce maraschino liqueur

1 ounce fresh orange juice

$^1/_4$ ounce fresh lemon juice

Champagne or other sparkling wine

Orange peel spiral, for garnish

Pour the gin, liqueur, and juices into a shaker two-thirds full of ice cubes. Shake well. Strain into a chilled Cocktail glass. Top with the champagne and add the orange spiral.

Century Sour

Created by "King Cocktail," Dale DeGroff, New York City, 1998.

1 ounce Alizé passion fruit liqueur

1 ounce Apry apricot liqueur

$^3/_4$ ounce fresh lemon juice

Lemon twist, for garnish

Pour all of the ingredients into a shaker two-thirds full of ice cubes. Shake well. Strain into a chilled Cocktail glass. Add the twist.

CEO Cocktail

Adapted from a recipe by "Dr. Cocktail" (Ted Haigh).

Just for big shots.

2 ounces brandy

1 ounce Lillet Blanc

$1/2$ ounce Chambord raspberry liqueur or crème de cassis

2 dashes of orange bitters

Lemon twist, for garnish

Pour all of the ingredients into a shaker two-thirds full of ice cubes. Shake well. Strain into a chilled Cocktail glass. Add the twist.

Chambord French Martini

Adapted from a recipe from Asia de Cuba, New York City.

1 ounce vodka

$1/2$ ounce Chambord raspberry liqueur

2 ounces pineapple juice

Pour all of the ingredients into a shaker two-thirds full of ice cubes. Shake well. Strain into a chilled Cocktail glass.

Chambord Royale

1 ounce Chambord raspberry liqueur

1 ounce vodka

1 ounce pineapple juice

$1/2$ ounce cranberry juice

Pour all of the ingredients into a shaker two-thirds full of ice cubes. Shake well. Strain into a chilled Cocktail glass.

Champagne Cocktail

One of the all-time favorites, this drink has been made this way for more than 150 years.

1 sugar lump

2 to 3 dashes of Angostura bitters

5 ounces champagne or other sparkling wine

Lemon twist, for garnish

Put the sugar lump and the bitters into a Champagne flute; carefully add the champagne. Add the twist.

Champagne Fizz

1 ounce gin

1 ounce fresh lemon juice

Dash of simple syrup (page 35)

4 ounces chilled champagne or other sparkling wine

Pour the gin, lemon juice, and simple syrup into a shaker two-thirds full of ice cubes; shake well. Strain into a chilled Champagne flute. Carefully pour in the champagne.

Champagne Punch Royale

The night they invented champagne? Ah, yes, I remember it well.

MAKES ABOUT TWENTY-FOUR 6-OUNCE SERVINGS

1 large block or ring of ice with raspberries frozen in it

4 ounces chilled brandy

4 ounces chilled Chambord raspberry liqueur

4 ounces chilled triple sec

3 750-ml bottles chilled champagne or other sparkling wine

16 to 20 ounces chilled club soda

Fresh raspberries, for garnish

Place the ice in the center of a large punch bowl; add the brandy, Chambord, triple sec, champagne, and club soda. Stir briefly. Float the raspberries on top.

Charbay Carnival

Adapted from a recipe by Ryan C. Maybee, owner/sommelier at JP Wine Bar and Coffee House, Kansas City, Missouri.

1¹/₂ ounces Charbay pomegranate vodka

1¹/₂ ounces Alvear amontillado sherry

Splash of fresh lemon juice

Lemon twist, for garnish

Pour all of the ingredients into a shaker two-thirds full of ice cubes. Shake well. Strain into a chilled Cocktail glass. Add the twist.

DRINKS A TO Z

119

The Charlie Chaplin Cocktail

1 ounce apricot brandy

1 ounce sloe gin

1 ounce fresh lime juice

Pour all of the ingredients into a shaker two-thirds full of ice cubes. Shake well. Strain into a chilled Cocktail glass.

Charlotterita

Created by Gary Regan for Charlotte Voisey, 2006.

2^1/$_2$ ounces BarSol pisco acholado brandy

1 ounce Cointreau

^{1}/$_2$ ounce PAMA pomegranate liqueur

^{1}/$_2$ ounce fresh lime juice

Orange twist, for garnish (optional)

Pour all of the ingredients into a shaker two-thirds full of ice cubes. Shake well. Strain into a chilled Champagne flute. Carefully flame the twist, if using, and drop it in.

The Chas Cocktail

Adapted from a recipe by Murray Stenson, Zig Zag Café, Seattle.

1^1/$_4$ ounces bourbon

^{1}/$_8$ ounce amaretto

^{1}/$_8$ ounce Cointreau

^{1}/$_8$ ounce Bénédictine

^{1}/$_8$ ounce white curaçao

Orange twist, for garnish

Pour all of the ingredients into a mixing glass two-thirds full of ice cubes. Stir well. Strain into a chilled Cocktail glass. Add the twist.

The Chatham Cocktail

2 ounces gin

^{1}/$_2$ ounce Domaine de Canton ginger liqueur

^{1}/$_2$ ounce fresh lemon juice

Pour all of the ingredients into a shaker two-thirds full of ice cubes. Shake well. Strain into a chilled Cocktail glass.

The Chaya Candy Apple Cosmo

Adapted from a recipe by Eric Schreiber, bar manager at Chaya Brasserie, San Francisco, circa 2003.

1¹/₂ ounces Van Gogh Wild Appel vodka
¹/₂ ounce Cuarenta y Tres Licor 43
¹/₂ ounce fresh lime juice
¹/₂ ounce cranberry juice

Pour all of the ingredients into a shaker two-thirds full of ice cubes. Shake well. Strain into a chilled Cocktail glass.

The Cherry Blossom Cocktail

Reformulated from Harry Craddock's 1930 recipe.

1 ounce brandy
1 ounce cherry brandy
¹/₂ ounce Cointreau
¹/₂ ounce fresh lemon juice

Pour all of the ingredients into a shaker two-thirds full of ice cubes. Shake well. Strain into a chilled Cocktail glass.

Cherry Blossom Martini

Adapted from a recipe by Joe McCanta, beverage director at S.A.F. Organic Restaurant, Istanbul, Turkey.

1¹/₂ ounces Organic Floc de Gascogne
³/₄ ounce saké
1¹/₂ ounces lychee juice
¹/₄ ounce fresh lime juice
³/₄ ounce organic cherry juice
1 whole lychee, for garnish
2 dried cherries, soaked overnight in lychee wine or a mixture of 1 part brandy and 1 part lychee juice, for garnish

Fill a mixing glass two-thirds full of ice and add all of the ingredients. Stir for approximately 30 seconds, and strain into a chilled Cocktail glass. To garnish, cut the lychee in half and thread onto a skewer or cocktail straw, sandwiching the cherries in between.

DRINKS A TO Z

Cherry Kiss Martini

Created by Jim Hewes, the Round Robin Bar at the Willard InterContinental hotel, Washington, D.C.

1/4 ounce Godiva chocolate liqueur

Maraschino cherry with stem, for garnish

2 ounces Ketel One vodka, chilled in the freezer

Chill a Cocktail glass in the freezer. Pour the chocolate liqueur into the frozen glass and swirl it around to coat the glass. Add the cherry to the glass and pour in the vodka.

Chi Chi

The vodka-based variation on the classic Piña Colada. If you're not fond of rum, give this one a try.

2 1/2 ounces vodka

6 ounces pineapple juice

2 ounces coconut cream, such as Coco Lopez

Pineapple spear and a chunk of fresh coconut, for garnishes

Pour all of the ingredients into a blender two-thirds full of ice cubes; blend thoroughly. Pour the mixture into a large wine goblet; add the pineapple spear and coconut chunk.

Chocolate-Covered Martini

1 maraschino cherry

1 1/2 ounces vodka

1/2 ounce Godiva chocolate liqueur

1/2 ounce vanilla schnapps

Place the cherry in the bottom of a chilled Cocktail glass. Pour the remaining ingredients into a mixing glass two-thirds full of ice cubes. Stir well. Strain into the glass.

Chocolate Martini

A massive success! This was a runaway hit in the late 1990s, and it was reportedly created in Miami.

Unsweetened cocoa powder and white crème de cacao, for rimming the glass

2 ounces vodka

1 ounce white crème de cacao

Hershey's Hug or chocolate chips, for garnish

Prepare a Cocktail glass. Pour the vodka and crème de cacao into a mixing glass two-thirds full of ice cubes. Stir well. Place the Hug or chocolate chips in the bottom of the cocoa-rimmed glass. Strain the Martini into the glass.

Chocolate Peppermint

2 ounces Godiva chocolate liqueur

$1/2$ ounce peppermint schnapps

Pour both ingredients into a mixing glass two-thirds full of ice cubes. Stir well. Strain into a chilled Cocktail glass.

Chocolate-Raspberry Martini

1 ounce Kahlúa

1 ounce Chambord raspberry liqueur

2 ounces heavy cream

Chocolate shavings, for garnish

Fill a Cocktail glass with crushed ice. Pour in the Kahlúa and Chambord. Top with the heavy cream. Sprinkle with the chocolate shavings.

Christina Martini

From Villa Christina, Atlanta, Georgia.

3 ounces Tanqueray Sterling vodka

Splash of DiSaronno amaretto

Splash of blue curaçao

Pour all of the ingredients into a mixing glass two-thirds full of ice cubes. Stir well. Strain into a chilled Cocktail glass.

Cider-Cranberry Rum Punch

Without the rum, this makes a good nonalcoholic punch.

MAKES ABOUT TWENTY-FIVE 6-OUNCE SERVINGS

1/2 gallon unsweetened apple cider

48 ounces cranberry juice

10 whole cloves

4 small (3-inch) cinnamon sticks, broken

1 teaspoon freshly grated nutmeg

1 teaspoon ground allspice

1/2 teaspoon ground cardamom

1 large block of ice, for serving

1 750-ml bottle dark rum, bourbon, or brandy

Lemon slices, for garnish

At least 4 hours or up to 1 week before the party, pour the apple cider and cranberry juice into a large, nonreactive stockpot. Set the pot over high heat, add all of the spices, and bring the mixture to a boil. Reduce the heat to low, cover, and simmer for 30 minutes.

Strain the mixture through a strainer lined with a double layer of dampened cheesecloth; discard the solids. Set aside to cool to room temperature, about 2 hours.

Pour the punch back into the bottles that held the cranberry and apple juices and refrigerate.

About 30 minutes before your guests arrive, place the block of ice into the punch bowl. Add the chilled punch. You can add the liquor at this point, or set the bottle next to the punch bowl so guests can decide for themselves. Float the lemon slices on top of the punch.

Cinco de Mayo

Created to celebrate the May 5, 1862, victory of the Mexican army over the French at the Battle of Puebla.

2 1/2 ounces añejo or white tequila

1 ounce fresh lime juice

1/2 ounce grenadine

Pour all of the ingredients into a shaker two-thirds full of ice cubes. Shake well. Strain into a chilled Cocktail glass.

Cinderella

3 ounces orange juice

3 ounces peach nectar

Dash of grenadine

Splash of club soda

Pour the orange juice, peach nectar, and grenadine into an ice-filled Collins glass. Stir briefly; top with the club soda.

The Claiborne Cocktail

Created by Philip Greene for the B&B 70th Anniversary Master Mixologist Showcase, March 25, 2008.

1 ounce B&B liqueur

1 ounce Maker's Mark bourbon

³/₄ ounce Martini & Rossi sweet vermouth

2 to 3 dashes of Peychaud's bitters

2 to 3 dashes of Angostura bitters

Lemon twist, for garnish

Pour all of the ingredients into a mixing glass two-thirds full of ice cubes. Stir well. Strain into an ice-filled Rocks glass. Add the twist.

The Claridge Cocktail

Adapted from Harry Craddock's 1930 recipe.

1 ounce gin

1 ounce dry vermouth

¹/₂ ounce Cointreau

¹/₂ ounce apricot brandy

Pour all of the ingredients into a mixing glass two-thirds full of ice cubes. Stir well. Strain into a chilled Cocktail glass.

The Classic Cocktail

Adapted from Harry Craddock's 1930 recipe.

> Superfine sugar, for rimming the glass
>
> 1¹/₂ ounces brandy
>
> ¹/₂ ounce Cointreau
>
> ¹/₂ ounce maraschino liqueur
>
> ¹/₂ ounce fresh lemon juice

Chill a Cocktail glass and prepare the rim with the sugar. Pour the remaining ingredients into a shaker two-thirds full of ice cubes. Shake well. Strain into the prepared glass.

Clermont Kiss

Adapted from a recipe by Sean Bigley, the Fontana Bar, Bellagio, Las Vegas.

> Superfine sugar, for rimming the glass
>
> 10 fresh mint leaves
>
> ¹/₂ ounce Fee Brothers Peach Syrup
>
> 1¹/₄ ounces Knob Creek bourbon
>
> ³/₄ ounce Apry apricot liqueur
>
> ³/₄ ounce fresh lemon juice
>
> ³/₄ ounce simple syrup (page 35)
>
> Mint sprig, for garnish

Prepare a Cocktail glass. Muddle the mint leaves with the peach syrup in an empty shaker. Add ice cubes and all of the remaining ingredients. Shake well. Strain into the prepared glass. Add the garnish.

Climax

> ¹/₂ ounce amaretto
>
> ¹/₂ ounce white crème de cacao
>
> ¹/₂ ounce triple sec
>
> ¹/₂ ounce vodka
>
> ¹/₂ ounce crème de banane
>
> 1 ounce half-and-half

Pour all of the ingredients into a shaker two-thirds full of ice cubes. Shake well. Strain into a chilled Cocktail glass.

Closing Bell Cocktail

Developed by Gary Regan and me for Jameson Irish whiskey, 2002.

2 ounces Jameson Irish whiskey
$1/2$ ounce amaretto
$1/2$ ounce triple sec
Maraschino cherry, for garnish

Pour all of the ingredients into a mixing glass two-thirds full of ice cubes. Stir well. Strain into a chilled Cocktail glass and garnish with the cherry.

Cloud Rouge

Adapted from a recipe by Richard Shipman, Picholine, New York City.

2 ounces armagnac
$1/2$ ounce Drambuie
Dash of grenadine

Build in an ice-filled Old-Fashioned glass. Stir briefly.

Clover Club Cocktail

Reportedly created prior to Prohibition at the Philadelphia club of the same name, the original recipe contained raspberry syrup, not grenadine.

2 ounces gin
$1/2$ ounce fresh lemon juice
$1/2$ ounce grenadine
1 egg white

Pour all of the ingredients into a shaker two-thirds full of ice cubes. Shake very well. Strain into a chilled Cocktail glass.

The Coco Cocktail

Adapted from a recipe by Cory Hill, bar manager at Brasserie 8½, New York City.

> 2 ounces pisco brandy
>
> 1 ounce chocolate liqueur, such as Godiva, Mozart, or Vermeer
>
> 1 ounce chilled espresso
>
> Lemon twist, for garnish

Pour all of the ingredients into a shaker two-thirds full of ice cubes. Shake well. Strain into a chilled Cocktail glass. Add the twist.

Coco Loco

A drink for fans of Harry Nilsson.

> 1 whole coconut
>
> 1 ounce white tequila
>
> 1 ounce light rum
>
> 1 ounce gin
>
> 1/2 ounce grenadine
>
> Lime slice, for garnish

Cut a 3-inch hole in the top of the coconut; leave the coconut water inside. Add the tequila, rum, gin, grenadine, and several ice cubes. Stir well. Garnish with the slice of lime (you put the lime in the coconut!); serve with a long straw.

(If you prefer to drink this in a glass, drill 2 holes in the coconut and drain the water into a mixing glass over several ice cubes. Add the tequila, rum, gin, and grenadine; stir well. Strain into a wine goblet or Highball glass and add the lime.)

Cognac Coulis

MAKES TWO 5-OUNCE SERVINGS

> 2 ripe kiwis, peeled and sliced
>
> 6 large ripe strawberries, hulled
>
> 3 ounces cognac
>
> 1 ounce Grand Marnier

Reserve 2 slices of the kiwi for garnish. Place the remaining kiwi, the strawberries, 5 large ice cubes, and the cognac in a blender; purée until smooth. Divide the mixture between 2 Cocktail glasses. Drizzle half of the Grand Marnier over each drink; garnish each with a slice of kiwi.

Colorado Bulldog

Believe it or not, Kahlúa and cola make a great combo for people with a sweet tooth.

> **1 ounce vodka**
> **1 ounce Kahlúa**
> **2 ounces milk**
> **Splash of cola**

Pour the vodka, Kahlúa, and milk into a shaker two-thirds full of ice cubes. Shake well. Strain into an ice-filled Rocks glass. Add the cola.

Compass Box Cocktail

Adapted from a recipe by beer writer and author Stephen Beaumont.

> **1 ounce Compass Box Peat Monster blended malt scotch whisky**
> **3 ounces Imperial stout**
> **3 dashes of Angostura bitters**
> **Maraschino cherry, for garnish**

Pour all of the ingredients into a mixing glass two-thirds full of ice cubes. Stir well. Strain into a chilled Cocktail glass. Add the cherry.

Continental Stinger

> **2^1/$_2$ ounces Metaxa brandy**
> **^{1}/$_2$ ounce Galliano**
> **Lemon twist, for garnish**

Pour both ingredients into a mixing glass two-thirds full of ice cubes. Stir well. Strain into a chilled Cocktail glass. Add the twist.

The Cool Cucumber

Adapted from a recipe created by Shell Thomas for Bong Su Restaurant & Lounge, San Francisco.

3 fresh cucumber slices
1¹/₂ ounces Plymouth gin
1 ounce fresh orange juice
Dash of Campari
Dash of simple syrup (page 35)
Cucumber slice or spear, for garnish

Muddle the cucumber slices in the bottom of an empty shaker. Add ice cubes and all of the remaining ingredients. Shake well. Strain into a chilled Cocktail glass and add the cucumber.

The Copper Swan Cocktail

Created by Gary Regan, circa 2000.

2¹/₂ ounces Highland Park single-malt scotch
³/₄ ounce apricot brandy
Lemon twist, for garnish

Pour both ingredients into a mixing glass two-thirds full of ice cubes. Stir well. Strain into an ice-filled Rocks glass. Add the garnish.

Cornell Cocktail

Said to be most popular at Cornell's renowned School of Hotel Administration.

2 ounces gin
¹/₂ ounce maraschino liqueur
¹/₂ ounce fresh lemon juice
1 egg white

Pour all of the ingredients into a shaker two-thirds full of ice cubes. Shake very well. Strain into a chilled Cocktail glass.

Cornwall Negroni

Created by Phillip Ward, Pegu Club, New York City, 2005.

2 ounces Beefeater gin
1/2 ounce Campari
1/2 ounce Punt e Mes
1/2 ounce sweet vermouth
2 dashes of orange bitters
Orange twist, for garnish

Pour all of the ingredients into a mixing glass two-thirds full of ice cubes. Stir well. Strain into a chilled Cocktail glass. Add the twist.

Coronation

1 ounce gin
1 ounce dry vermouth
1 ounce Dubonnet Blanc

Pour all of the ingredients into a mixing glass two-thirds full of ice cubes. Stir well. Strain into a chilled Cocktail glass.

Corpse Reviver #1

Corpse Revivers were popular in Victorian England and were actually a category of drinks with nothing in common except that all were strong and all were a spirituous way to, well, revive your spirits.

2 ounces brandy
1 ounce sweet vermouth
1 ounce applejack

Pour all of the ingredients into a mixing glass two-thirds full of ice cubes. Stir well. Strain into a chilled Cocktail glass.

Corpse Reviver #2

Completely different from the previous recipe, but, no doubt, sure to revive you.

1 ounce gin
1 ounce triple sec
1 ounce Lillet Blanc
1 ounce fresh lemon juice
Dash of absinthe

Pour all of the ingredients into a shaker two-thirds full of ice cubes. Shake well. Strain into a chilled Cocktail glass.

Corpse Reviver #3

Are you feeling better yet?

1 ounce cognac
1 ounce Campari
1 ounce triple sec
$1/2$ ounce fresh lemon juice

Pour all of the ingredients into a shaker two-thirds full of ice cubes. Shake well. Strain into a chilled Cocktail glass.

Corpse Reviver #4

This Corpse Reviver, like some others that were popular in the 1800s, actually fits into two categories: It's a Pousse-Café since it is a layered drink, and it's also a Shooter, since it is meant to be consumed in one go.

$3/4$ ounce Frangelico
$3/4$ ounce maraschino liqueur
$3/4$ ounce green Chartreuse

Pour the ingredients, in the order given, over the back of a spoon into a Pousse-Café glass, floating one on top of the other.

The Correct Cocktail

Created by Gary Regan, 2008.

> 1¹/₂ ounces Right gin
> ¹/₂ ounce Domaine de Canton ginger liqueur
> ¹/₂ ounce Cointreau
> ¹/₂ ounce fresh lemon juice
> 2 dashes of Regans' Orange Bitters No. 6
> Lemon twist, for garnish

Pour all of the ingredients into a shaker two-thirds full of ice cubes. Shake well. Strain into a chilled Champagne flute. Add the twist.

Cosmopolitan

For my money, the hottest drink in the USA, the drink that became a overnight classic in the 1990s.

> 2 ounces citrus vodka
> 1 ounce Cointreau
> ¹/₂ ounce cranberry juice
> ¹/₂ ounce fresh lime juice

Pour all of the ingredients into a shaker two-thirds full of ice cubes. Shake well. Strain into a chilled Cocktail glass.

Country Cocktail

Adapted from a recipe by Dale DeGroff in 2003.

> Kosher salt mixed with dried thyme, for rimming the glass
> 1¹/₂ ounces Tanqueray gin
> ¹/₂ ounce Velvet Falernum liqueur
> ¹/₂ ounce simple syrup (page 35)
> ³/₄ ounce fresh lime juice
> ¹/₂ ounce Berentzen Apfelkorn apple schnapps
> Wide slice of English cucumber peel and a thin wheel of
>   English cucumber, for garnishes

Prepare a Cocktail glass. Pour all of the ingredients into a shaker two-thirds full of ice cubes. Shake well. Strain into the prepared glass. Add the cucumber garnishes.

Crazzmopolitan

Adapted from a recipe by beverage specialist George Delgado.

1¹/₂ ounces Boru Crazzberry vodka

¹/₂ ounce Cointreau

1 ounce cranberry juice

¹/₂ ounce fresh lime juice

Fresh raspberry, for garnish

Pour all of the ingredients into a shaker two-thirds full of ice cubes. Shake well. Strain into a chilled Cocktail glass. Add the raspberry.

The Creamery

Created by Patrick O'Sullivan, bartender, Seppi's, New York City, circa 2004.

1¹/₂ ounces Jameson Irish whiskey

1 ounce Kahlúa

¹/₂ ounce crème de banane

1 ounce heavy cream

Pour all of the ingredients into a shaker two-thirds full of ice cubes. Shake well. Strain into a chilled Cocktail glass.

Creamsicle

Takes you back, doesn't it? This one's for the daytime.

1¹/₂ ounces vanilla schnapps

1¹/₂ ounces milk

3 ounces orange juice

Pour all of the ingredients into a shaker two-thirds full of ice cubes. Shake well. Strain into an ice-filled Rocks glass.

Creamsicle Martini

And this one's for the nighttime.

1 ounce Stolichnaya Vanil vodka

¹/₂ ounce Cointreau

1 ounce orange juice

¹/₂ ounce simple syrup (page 35)

Pour all of the ingredients into a shaker two-thirds full of ice cubes. Shake well. Strain into a chilled Cocktail glass.

Crème de Menthe Frappé

2 ounces green crème de menthe

3 straws, each cut to measure about 3 inches long

Fill a chilled Sour glass or Champagne Saucer glass with crushed ice until it forms a dome that rises in the center of the glass. Drizzle the crème de menthe over the ice. Sip from the straws.

Creole

A Southern relative of the Bullshot.

2 ounces light rum

2 ounces beef bouillon

$1/2$ ounce fresh lemon juice

2 dashes of hot sauce

Pinch of salt

Pinch of ground black pepper

Pour the rum, bouillon, and lemon juice into a shaker two-thirds full of ice cubes; add the hot sauce, salt, and pepper. Shake well. Strain into an ice-filled Rocks glass.

The Creole Lady

Adapted from a recipe by Neyah White, Nopa, San Francisco, 2008.

$1^1/4$ ounces gin (Martin Miller's Westbourne Strength is good here)

$3/4$ ounce Creole Shrubb liqueur

$1/2$ ounce fresh lemon juice

$3/4$ ounce egg white

Pour all of the ingredients into a shaker two-thirds full of ice cubes. Shake very well. Strain into a chilled Cocktail glass.

Crimson Cosmo

Adapted from Luna Park, San Francisco.

4 ounces fresh pomegranate juice

3 ounces vodka

2 ounces Cointreau

Pomegranate seeds, for garnish (optional)

Pour all of the ingredients into a shaker two-thirds full of ice. Shake vigorously. Strain into a very large chilled Cocktail glass. Garnish with several pomegranate seeds, if desired.

Crimson Martini

A recent addition to many Martini menus, this drink is extremely popular with Campari lovers.

2 ounces gin

$1/2$ ounce dry vermouth

$1/4$ ounce Campari

Orange wheel, for garnish

Pour all of the ingredients into a mixing glass two-thirds full of ice cubes. Stir well. Strain into a chilled Cocktail glass. Add the orange wheel.

Cristina

Created by Gary Regan, 2005.

2 ounces Nocino Della Cristina liqueur

$1/2$ ounce Belvedere Cytrus vodka

Pour both ingredients into a mixing glass two-thirds full of ice. Stir well. Strain into a chilled Cocktail glass.

Crown of Roses

Created by Gary Regan, 2005.

1 ounce Crown Royal

$1/2$ ounce amaretto

1 ounce pineapple juice

$1/4$ ounce cranberry juice

3 dashes of Angostura bitters

Maraschino cherry, for garnish

Pour all of the ingredients into a shaker two-thirds full of ice cubes. Shake well. Strain into a chilled Cocktail glass. Add the cherry.

The Crux Cocktail

Adapted from a recipe in Jones' Complete Barguide.

> **³/₄ ounce brandy**
> **³/₄ ounce Dubonnet Rouge**
> **³/₄ ounce Cointreau**
> **³/₄ ounce fresh lemon juice**

Pour all of the ingredients into a shaker two-thirds full of ice cubes. Shake well. Strain into a chilled Cocktail glass.

Cuba Libre

The trick to a great Cuba Libre lies in the lime juice. Remember, it's not just a simple rum and cola with a lime wedge garnish; it's more, much more. This recipe is terrific.

> **2¹/₂ ounces light rum**
> **1 ounce fresh lime juice**
> **3 ounces cola**
> **Lime wedge, for garnish**

Pour the rum and lime juice into a shaker two-thirds full of ice cubes. Shake well and strain into an ice-filled Collins glass. Add the cola; stir briefly. Add the lime wedge.

Cuban Cocktail

Many cocktails made their way to the United States from Cuba during Prohibition. This is merely a sweet Daiquiri, which also originated in Cuba.

> **2 ounces light rum**
> **¹/₂ ounce fresh lime juice**
> **¹/₂ ounce simple syrup (page 35)**

Pour all of the ingredients into a shaker two-thirds full of ice cubes. Shake well. Strain into a chilled Cocktail glass.

Cubeltini

Adapted from a recipe by Leodil Ramirez, Trina Lounge, Fort Lauderdale.

> **3 cucumber slices**
> **6 mint leaves**
> **1 ounce simple syrup (page 35)**
> **2 ounces Belvedere vodka**
> **1 ounce fresh lime juice**
> **Fresh mint sprig, for garnish**

Muddle the cucumber, mint, and simple syrup in an empty shaker. Add ice cubes, the vodka, and the lime juice. Shake well. Strain into a chilled Cocktail glass. Add the mint sprig.

The Cucumber 75

Adapted from a recipe from Restaurants Unlimited, Seattle.

> **2 ounces Tanqueray No. Ten gin**
> **$^1/_2$ ounce Cointreau**
> **$^3/_4$ ounce fresh lemon juice**
> **$^1/_2$ ounce simple syrup (page 35)**
> **4 very thin cucumber slices**
> **Champagne**
> **Lemon twist, for garnish**

Pour the gin, Cointreau, lemon juice, and simple syrup into a shaker two-thirds full of ice cubes. Add 3 of the cucumber slices; shake well. Strain into a large chilled Cocktail glass. Top with the champagne. Add the remaining cucumber slice and the twist.

Curari Cocktail

Adapted from a recipe by Ted Haigh, author of Vintage Spirits and Forgotten Cocktails.

> **2 ounces straight rye whiskey**
> **$^3/_4$ ounce ruby port**
> **$^3/_4$ ounce Amaro Cora**
> **2 dashes of Regans' Orange Bitters No. 6**
> **Maraschino cherry, for garnish**

Pour all of the ingredients into a shaker two-thirds full of ice cubes. Shake well. Strain into a chilled Cocktail glass. Add the cherry.

The Cuzco Cocktail

Adapted from a recipe by Julie Reiner, Flatiron Lounge, New York City, 2006.

> **Kirschwasser, to rinse the glass**
> **2 ounces Peruvian pisco brandy**
> **$3/4$ ounce Aperol**
> **$1/2$ ounce fresh lemon juice**
> **$1/2$ ounce grapefruit juice**
> **$3/4$ ounce simple syrup (page 35)**
> **Grapefruit twist, for garnish**

Pour a little Kirschwasser into a Highball glass, and swirl the glass to coat the interior. Fill the glass with ice cubes. Pour all of the remaining ingredients into a shaker two-thirds full of ice cubes. Shake well. Strain into the prepared glass. Add the twist.

Cuzco Mojito

Adapted from a recipe by Ian Nal, beverage director at Zengo Restaurant, Washington, D.C.

> **3 peeled cucumber wedges ($1/2$-inch pieces)**
> **4 mint leaves**
> **2 lime wheels**
> **1 teaspoon granulated sugar**
> **$1^1/2$ ounces Bacardi light rum**
> **Splash of club soda**
> **Cucumber slice, for garnish**

Muddle together the cucumber, mint, lime wheels, and sugar in an empty shaker. Add the rum and ice cubes. Shake well. Strain into an ice-filled Collins glass, and top off with the club soda. Add the cucumber.

Cytrus Ballade

Adapted from a recipe by Marcovaldo Dionysos, Enrico's, San Francisco.

1 ounce fresh Meyer lemon juice
1 ounce fresh tangerine juice
1 ounce honey syrup
6 mint leaves
2 slices fresh ginger
1^1/2 ounces Belvedere Cytrus vodka
Ginger beer
**Fresh mint sprig and shaved lemon and tangerine zests,
for garnishes**

Muddle the juices, honey syrup, mint leaves, and ginger in an empty shaker. Add ice cubes and the vodka. Shake well. Strain into a Collins glass filled with crushed ice. Top with ginger beer and stir. Add the mint and zests.

Daiquiri

The Daiquiri dates to the late 1800s, when the Spanish-American War was raging in Cuba. Reportedly, two Americans who were working in Cuba at the time created the drink by mixing the local light rum with sugar and fresh lime juice. They needed to drink the lime juice for their health, and the sugar and the local rum helped it go down nicely. Perhaps they were merely making a drink that pleased them, or maybe they thought that the combination of alcohol, fresh lime juice, and sugar would keep mosquitoes away.

2 ounces light rum
1 ounce fresh lime juice
^{1}/2 ounce simple syrup (page 35)
Lime wedge, for garnish

Pour all of the ingredients into a shaker two-thirds full of ice cubes. Shake well. Strain into a crushed ice–filled Rocks glass. Squeeze the lime wedge on top.

DAM, aka The Reluctant Tabby Cat

Created by Gary Regan for the Museum of the American Cocktail's
(MOTAC) World Cocktail Day, 2007, New York City.

> 1¹/₄ ounces Dubonnet Rouge
> ¹/₂ ounce Pallini Limoncello
> ¹/₄ ounce Laphroaig 10-year-old single-malt scotch
> Lemon twist, for garnish

Pour all of the ingredients into a shaker two-thirds full of
ice cubes. Shake well. Strain into a chilled wine goblet. Add
the twist.

Dark and Stormy

This is a very popular drink in Bermuda and one of the few
Highballs that calls for a specific brand of liquor. The Dark and
Stormy is enormously refreshing when escaping the heat is the
goal of the day.

> 2¹/₂ ounces Gosling's Black Seal rum
> 5 ounces ginger beer
> Lime wedge, for garnish

Pour both ingredients into an ice-filled Highball glass. Stir briefly;
add the lime wedge.

DB-llini

Adapted from a recipe by Xavier Herit, head bartender, Daniel,
New York City.

> 1 ounce Grand Marnier
> ¹/₂ ounce peach purée (see recipe below)
> ¹/₂ ounce fresh orange juice
> 2 ounces chilled champagne
> Splash of grenadine

Pour the Grand Marnier, peach purée, and orange juice into a
shaker two-thirds full of ice cubes. Shake well. Strain into a
chilled Champagne flute. Add the champagne and the grenadine.

PEACH PURÉE

In a blender, purée the flesh, including the skin, of 1 white
peach with 2 to 3 ice cubes and ¹/₂ teaspoon fresh lemon juice.

Deadly Sin

Adapted from a recipe by Rafael Ballesteros, somewhere in Spain.

2 ounces scotch or bourbon
1/3 ounce sweet vermouth
1/4 ounce maraschino liqueur
Dash of orange bitters
Orange twist, for garnish

Pour all of the ingredients into a mixing glass two-thirds full of ice cubes. Stir well. Strain into a chilled Cocktail glass. Add the twist.

Death at Dusk

Adapted from a recipe by Neyah White, head bartender, Nopa, San Francisco, 2008.

1/2 ounce crème de violette
5 ounces chilled sparkling wine
1/2 ounce absinthe
Brandied cherry, for garnish

Pour the crème de violette and the sparkling wine into a Champagne flute. Float the absinthe on top. Sink the brandied cherry.

Death in the Afternoon

Named for one of Ernest Hemingway's novels; no doubt he drank this during his years in Paris.

1 ounce absinthe
5 ounces champagne or other sparkling wine

Pour the absinthe into a Champagne flute. Add the champagne.

Deauville Cocktail

1 ounce brandy
1 ounce applejack
1 ounce triple sec
1 ounce fresh lemon juice

Pour all of the ingredients into a shaker two-thirds full of ice cubes. Shake well. Strain into a chilled Cocktail glass.

Debonair Cocktail

A wonderful cocktail that's made with single-malt scotch.

2 ounces Oban or Springbank single-malt scotch

1 ounce Domaine de Canton ginger liqueur

Lemon twist, for garnish

Pour both ingredients into a mixing glass two-thirds full of ice cubes. Stir well. Strain into a chilled Cocktail glass. Add the twist.

The Debonnaire

Adapted from a recipe by Mathew Silverstein, head bartender at Zoe Restaurant, New York City, circa 2005.

4 ounces Dubonnet Rouge

1 ounce Germain-Robin Fine Alambic brandy

¹/₄ ounce crème de cassis

¹/₂ orange wheel, for garnish

Pour all of the ingredients into a mixing glass two-thirds full of ice cubes. Stir well. Strain into a chilled Cocktail glass. Add the orange wheel.

Delicious Cocktail

Adapted from a recipe by Ryan Magarian, Restaurant Zoe, Seattle.

Superfine sugar, for rimming the glass

2 ounces Tanqueray No. Ten gin

1 ounce fresh lime juice

1 ounce simple syrup (page 35)

5 fresh mint sprigs, dusted with confectioners' sugar, for garnish

Prepare a Cocktail glass. Pour all of the ingredients into a shaker two-thirds full of ice cubes. Shake well. Strain into the prepared glass. Add the mint sprigs.

Delmarva Cocktail

Adapted from a recipe by Ted Haigh, aka "Dr. Cocktail," Los Angeles.

2 ounces straight rye whiskey
1/2 ounce dry vermouth
1/2 ounce white crème de menthe
1/2 ounce fresh lemon juice
Fresh mint leaf, for garnish

Pour all of the ingredients into a shaker two-thirds full of ice cubes. Shake well. Strain into a chilled Cocktail glass. Add the mint leaf.

Delmonico

Reportedly created at Delmonico's bar in New York City, sometime prior to 1917.

1 1/2 ounces gin
1 1/2 ounces dry vermouth
Dash of orange bitters
2 orange twists, for garnish

Pour all of the ingredients into a mixing glass two-thirds full of ice cubes. Stir well. Strain into a chilled Cocktail glass. Add the twists.

Dempsey Cocktail

Named for Jack Dempsey, the famed boxer who won the heavyweight boxing title in 1919.

1 1/2 ounces gin
1 1/2 ounces applejack
1/4 ounce absinthe
1/4 ounce grenadine

Pour all of the ingredients into a mixing glass two-thirds full of ice cubes. Stir well. Strain into a chilled Cocktail glass.

Derby

2 ounces bourbon
$1/4$ ounce Bénédictine
Dash of Angostura bitters
Lemon twist, for garnish

Pour all of the ingredients into a mixing glass two-thirds full of ice cubes. Stir well. Strain into a chilled Cocktail glass. Add the twist.

The Devious Cocktail

Created by Gary Regan, 2006.

2 ounces Deviation dessert wine
1 ounce armagnac
Fresh lemon juice, to taste (go easy)
Lemon twist, for garnish

Pour all of the ingredients into a shaker two-thirds full of ice cubes. Shake well. Strain into a chilled Cocktail glass. Add the twist.

Diplomat

An oh-so-tactful cocktail.

$1^1/2$ ounces dry vermouth
$1/2$ ounce sweet vermouth
Dash of maraschino liqueur
Lemon twist and a maraschino cherry, for garnishes

Pour all of the ingredients into a mixing glass two-thirds full of ice cubes. Stir well. Strain into a chilled Cocktail glass. Add the twist and the cherry.

Dirty Girl Scout

Did she fall in the mud?

1 ounce Baileys Irish cream liqueur

1 ounce Kahlúa

1 ounce vodka

Dash of white crème de menthe

Pour all of the ingredients into a shaker two-thirds full of ice cubes. Shake well. Strain into an ice-filled Rocks glass.

Dirty Martini

Feel free to play with the proportions here, but don't get carried away with the olive juice—too much can be just plain awful.

2¹/₂ ounces gin or vodka

¹/₄ ounce dry vermouth

¹/₄ ounce green olive juice (straight out of the jar)

Stuffed green olive, for garnish

Pour all of the ingredients into a mixing glass two-thirds full of ice cubes. Stir well. Strain into a chilled Cocktail glass. Add the olive.

Dirty Mother

2 ounces Kahlúa

1 ounce light cream

Pour both ingredients into a shaker two-thirds full of ice cubes. Shake well. Strain into an ice-filled Rocks glass.

Distill My Heart

Created by Gary Regan, 2005. Named for Distill My Heart, a racehorse.

2 ounces Woodford Reserve bourbon

1 ounce Tuaca

1 ounce fresh lemon juice

2 dashes of Angostura bitters

Maraschino cherry, for garnish

Pour all of the ingredients into a shaker two-thirds full of ice cubes. Shake well. Strain into a chilled Cocktail glass. Add the cherry.

Doctor's Highball

Adapted from a recipe by "Dr. Cocktail" (Ted Haigh), eminent cocktail historian.

2 ounces applejack or calvados
1 teaspoon superfine sugar
Club soda
4 dashes of peach bitters
Green apple slice, for garnish

Pour the applejack and sugar into an ice-filled Highball glass. Fill with the club soda; add the bitters. Stir briefly. Add the apple slice.

Dog's Nose

This drink dates back to the days of Charles Dickens.

12 ounces porter or stout
2 teaspoons brown sugar
2 ounces gin
Freshly grated nutmeg, for garnish

Pour the beer into a large sturdy glass and heat it in a microwave for about 1 minute. Add the brown sugar and gin and stir lightly. Grate the nutmeg on top.

The Dominick

Adapted from a recipe by Brandon Boudet, chef-owner of Dominick's, West Hollywood.

2 ounces Wild Turkey bourbon
1 ounce San Pellegrino Chinotto soda
Maraschino cherry, for garnish

Pour both ingredients into a mixing glass two-thirds full of ice cubes. Stir well. Strain into a chilled Cocktail glass. Add the cherry.

Donata

Created by Gary Regan, 2006.

2 ounces scotch
³/₄ ounce Galliano
¹/₂ ounce fresh lemon juice
Lemon twist, for garnish

Pour all of the ingredients into a shaker two-thirds full of ice cubes. Shake well. Strain into a chilled Cocktail glass. Add the twist.

Done for the Day

Developed by Gary Regan and me for Jameson Irish whiskey, 2002.

2 ounces Jameson Irish whiskey
1 ounce white crème de cacao
¹/₂ ounce fresh lemon juice
Unwrapped Hershey's Kiss, for garnish

Pour all of the ingredients into a shaker two-thirds full of ice cubes. Shake well. Strain into a chilled Cocktail glass. Add the Kiss.

The Double Shot

Adapted from a recipe by Bruce Tanner, James Beard Foundation.

2 ounces Santa Teresa 1796 rum
1¹/₂ ounces Rhum Orange liqueur
¹/₃ ounce fresh lime juice
Dash of Angostura bitters

Pour all of the ingredients into a shaker two-thirds full of ice cubes. Shake well. Strain into a chilled Cocktail glass.

Double Standard Sour

1 ounce blended Canadian whisky
1 ounce gin
¹/₂ ounce fresh lemon juice
Dash of simple syrup (page 35)
Dash of grenadine
Maraschino cherry and a lemon twist, for garnish

Pour all of the ingredients into a shaker two-thirds full of ice cubes. Shake well. Strain into a chilled Sour glass. Add the cherry and the twist.

Dreamy Dorini Smoking Martini

Adapted from a recipe by "Libation Goddess" Audrey Saunders, 2001.

2 ounces Grey Goose vodka
$1/2$ ounce Laphroaig 10-year-old scotch
2 to 3 drops of Pernod
Lemon twist, for garnish

Pour all of the ingredients into a shaker two-thirds full of ice cubes. Shake well. Strain into a chilled Cocktail glass. Add the twist.

Dr Pepper

Who knew that this combination of ingredients could possibly combine to taste so remarkably like Dr Pepper?

7 ounces beer
7 ounces cola
1 ounce amaretto

Pour the beer and cola into a large beer mug. Pour the amaretto into a shot glass. Drop the shot glass into the mug and drink immediately.

Dubliner

From the Ardent Spirits e-letter: Volume 1, Issue 2, March 1999.

2 ounces Bushmills Malt Irish whiskey
$1/2$ ounce sweet vermouth
$1/2$ ounce Grand Marnier
Green maraschino cherry, for garnish

Pour all of the ingredients into a mixing glass two-thirds full of ice cubes. Stir well. Strain into a chilled Cocktail glass. Add the cherry.

Dubonnet Cocktail

Especially yummy before dinner.

1¹/₂ ounces Dubonnet Rouge

1¹/₂ ounces gin

Lemon twist, for garnish

Pour both ingredients into a mixing glass two-thirds full of ice cubes. Stir well. Strain into a chilled Cocktail glass. Add the twist.

Dubonnet Manhattan

A great variation on the Manhattan.

2 ounces bourbon

1 ounce Dubonnet Rouge

2 dashes of orange bitters

Orange wheel, for garnish

Pour all of the ingredients into a mixing glass two-thirds full of ice cubes. Stir well. Strain into a chilled Cocktail glass. Add the orange wheel.

Duplex

Originally made, prior to World War I, with orange bitters, this version calls for maraschino liqueur instead.

1¹/₂ ounces sweet vermouth

1¹/₂ ounces dry vermouth

¹/₄ ounce maraschino liqueur

Pour all of the ingredients into a mixing glass two-thirds full of ice cubes. Stir well. Strain into a chilled Cocktail glass.

Dylan Collins

Adapted from a recipe by John Mautone, Dylan Prime, New York City.

2 ounces Grey Goose Le Citron vodka

2 ounces Pallini Limoncello

1 ounce fresh lemon juice

¹/₂ egg white

Large orange peel

Pour all of the ingredients into a mixing glass two-thirds full of ice cubes. Stir very well. Rub the orange peel all over the interior of a chilled Cocktail glass, leaving it in the bottom. Strain the cocktail into the glass.

The Earl Grey MarTEAni

Adapted from a recipe by Audrey Saunders, Pegu Club, New York City.

Finely grated zest of 1 lemon mixed with 1/2 cup granulated sugar, for rimming the glass

1 1/2 ounces Tanqueray gin infused with Earl Grey tea (see recipe below)

3/4 ounce fresh lemon juice

1 ounce simple syrup (page 35)

1 egg white

Lemon twist, for garnish

Prepare a Cocktail glass. Pour all of the ingredients into a shaker two-thirds full of ice cubes. Shake very well. Strain into the prepared glass. Add the twist.

TEA-INFUSED GIN

Add 1/4 cup of loose Earl Grey tea to a 1-liter bottle of Tanqueray gin. Replace the cap, and shake well. Let steep for 2 hours. Strain through a double layer of dampened cheesecloth; do not press down on the tea leaves. Pour the infused gin back into the bottle and label it.

East India Cocktail

A cocktail that also makes a great party punch.

1 1/2 ounces brandy

1/2 ounce orange juice

1/2 ounce pineapple juice

2 dashes of Angostura bitters

Pour all of the ingredients into a shaker two-thirds full of ice cubes. Shake well. Strain into a chilled Cocktail glass.

The Eclipse Cocktail

This is how the recipe appeared in *The Savoy Cocktail Book*.

> **1/3 Dry Gin**
> **2/3 Sloe Gin**

Put enough grenadine in a cocktail glass to cover a ripe olive. Mix the spirits together and pour gently onto the Grenadine so that it does not mix. Squeeze orange peel on top.

The Eclipse Cocktail Redux

Created by Gary Regan, circa 2006.

> **1 maraschino cherry**
> **3/4 ounce PAMA pomegranate liqueur**
> **1 1/2 ounces gin**
> **1 1/2 ounces sloe gin**
> **Orange twist, for garnish**

Drop the cherry into a chilled Cocktail glass and pour the PAMA into the glass. Stir the gin and sloe gin together over ice, and pour carefully over the PAMA, making sure that the mixture floats on the liqueur. Add the twist.

El Cubano

Adapted from a recipe by Audrey Saunders, New York City.

> **3 lime wedges**
> **6 fresh mint leaves**
> **2 teaspoons granulated sugar**
> **1 1/2 ounces añejo rum**
> **Chilled champagne**
> **Mint sprig, for garnish**

Muddle the lime wedges, mint leaves, and sugar in an empty mixing glass. Add ice cubes and the rum. Stir well. Strain into a chilled Cocktail glass. Top with the champagne; add the mint sprig.

El Floridita

Named for the Havana bar that Papa Hemingway frequented.

1¹/₂ ounces light rum
¹/₂ ounce sweet vermouth
¹/₂ ounce fresh lime juice
Dash of white crème de cacao
Dash of grenadine

Pour all of the ingredients into a shaker two-thirds full of ice cubes. Shake well. Strain into a chilled Cocktail glass.

El Presidente

2 ounces light rum
¹/₂ ounce fresh lime juice
¹/₂ ounce pineapple juice
Dash of grenadine

Pour all of the ingredients into a shaker two-thirds full of ice cubes. Shake well. Strain into an ice-filled Rocks glass.

The Elderflower Blush

Created by Gary Regan and me, 2008.

3 ounces chilled Croft PINK port
4 ounces chilled champagne
¹/₂ ounce St-Germain Elderflower liqueur
2 dashes of Angostura bitters
Lemon twist, for garnish

Pour all of the ingredients into a chilled Champagne flute. Stir briefly. Add the twist.

Elderwilde

Adapted from a recipe by Keith Waldbauer, bartender at Union in Seattle.

2¹/₂ ounces Bombay gin

¹/₂ ounce elderflower syrup

2 dashes of Angostura bitters

Orange twist, for garnish

Pour all of the ingredients into a mixing glass two-thirds full of ice cubes. Stir well. Strain into a chilled Cocktail glass. Add the twist.

Elegant Without Number

Adapted from a recipe by Rafael Ballesteros, Spain.

2 ounces vodka

³/₄ ounces calvados

¹/₂ ounce Grand Marnier

Maraschino cherry, for garnish

Pour all of the ingredients into a mixing glass two-thirds full of ice cubes. Stir well. Strain into a chilled Cocktail glass. Add the cherry.

Elegante Fizz

Created by Gary Regan, 2008.

¹/₂ ounce Milagro tequila

¹/₂ ounce Domaine de Canton ginger liqueur

Chilled champagne or sparkling wine

Build in a Champagne flute.

Esquire

Adapted from a recipe by Phil Broadhead, Jackson, Mississippi.

2¹/₄ ounces bourbon

³/₄ ounce Grand Marnier

1¹/₂ teaspoons fresh orange juice

1 teaspoon fresh lemon juice

2 dashes of Angostura bitters

Lemon twist, for garnish

Pour all of the ingredients into a shaker two-thirds full of ice cubes. Shake well. Strain into a chilled Cocktail glass. Add the twist.

Esquivel Cocktail

Adapted from a recipe by "Dr. Cocktail" (Ted Haigh).

2 ounces light rum
$1/2$ ounce Kahlúa
1 ounce pineapple juice
Angostura bitters, to taste
Orange bitters, to taste
Chilled champagne or other sparkling wine
Orange twist and ground cinnamon, for garnishes

Pour the rum, Kahlúa, pineapple juice, and both bitters into a shaker two-thirds full of ice cubes. Shake well. Strain into a chilled Cocktail glass. Top with a little champagne. Add the twist and cinnamon.

Everybody's Irish

The greenish tint of this drink makes it ideal for sipping on Saint Patrick's Day.

2 ounces Irish whiskey
$1/4$ ounce green Chartreuse
$1/4$ ounce green crème de menthe

Pour all of the ingredients into a mixing glass two-thirds full of ice cubes. Stir well. Strain into a chilled Cocktail glass.

Eve's Seduction Apple Martini

Adapted from a recipe by Matt Knepper, Fifth Floor Bar, Hotel Palomar, San Francisco.

$1 1/2$ ounces Van Gogh Wild Appel vodka
$1/4$ ounce amaretto
$1/4$ ounce fresh lemon juice
$1/4$ ounce fresh lime juice
$1/4$ ounce simple syrup (page 35)
Chilled champagne or other sparkling wine

Pour the vodka, amaretto, juices, and simple syrup into a shaker two-thirds full of ice. Shake well. Strain into a chilled Champagne flute and top with the champagne.

Eye Catcher

Adapted from a recipe by Gary Regan and me, 2003.

1¹/₂ ounces Appleton Estate white rum

³/₄ ounce Hpnotiq liqueur

3 ounces pineapple juice

1¹/₂ ounces coconut cream

Pineapple wedge and a maraschino cherry, for garnishes

Pour all of the ingredients into a blender; add 1 cup of ice. Blend until smooth. Pour into a chilled Rocks glass. Add the pineapple wedge and cherry.

Fallen Angel Cocktail

Adapted from a recipe from Drovers Tap Room, New York City.

1 ounce Bacardi Limón rum

¹/₄ ounce Cointreau

¹/₄ ounce cranberry juice

Chilled champagne

Pour the rum, Cointreau, and cranberry juice into a shaker two-thirds full of ice cubes. Shake well. Strain into a chilled Cocktail glass. Top with a little champagne.

The Faro Dealer

Created by Gary Regan in honor of F. Paul Pacult, 2008.

2 ounces straight rye whiskey

³/₄ ounce Cointreau

¹/₂ ounce fresh lemon juice

2 dashes of Lucid absinthe

Pour all of the ingredients into a shaker two-thirds full of ice cubes. Shake well. Strain into a chilled Cocktail glass.

Fécamp Frappé

Created by LeNell Smothers for the B&B 70th Anniversary Master Mixologist Showcase, March 25, 2008.

¹/₂ ounce egg white

1 ounce B&B liqueur

1/4 ounce Martini & Rossi dry vermouth

1/4 ounce fresh lemon juice

3 dashes of Angostura bitters, for an aromatic garnish

Pour the egg white into an empty shaker and shake to emulsify. Add ice cubes and the B&B, vermouth, and lemon juice. Shake well. Strain into a Cocktail glass filled with crushed ice. Top with the dashes of bitters.

Fernandito

This drink was created in Puerto Rico in the late 1990s.

1¹/₂ ounces spiced rum

1/2 ounce cranberry juice

1/2 ounce fresh orange juice

1/2 ounce fresh lime juice

Lime wedge, for garnish

Pour all of the ingredients into a shaker two-thirds full of ice cubes. Shake well. Strain into a chilled Cocktail glass. Add the lime wedge.

Fifth Avenue

A very Saks-y classic Pousse-Café that was created in the 1920s.

1/2 ounce white crème de cacao

1/2 ounce apricot brandy

1/2 ounce heavy cream

Pour the ingredients, in the order given, over the back of a spoon into a Pousse-Café glass, floating one on top of the other.

50/50 Martini

Historically, this drink represents the Dry Gin Martini as it was served at the beginning of the twentieth century.

1¹/₂ ounces gin

1¹/₂ ounces dry vermouth

2 dashes of orange bitters

Pour all of the ingredients into a mixing glass two-thirds full of ice cubes. Stir well. Strain into a chilled Cocktail glass.

'57 Chevy

Love those tail fins.

- 1¹/₂ ounces Southern Comfort
- 1/2 ounce vodka
- 1/2 ounce Grand Marnier
- 1 ounce pineapple juice

Pour all of the ingredients into a shaker two-thirds full of ice cubes. Shake well. Strain into a chilled Cocktail glass.

The Final Ward

Adapted from a recipe by Phil Ward, head bartender, Death & Co., New York City.

- 3/4 ounce Rittenhouse straight rye whiskey
- 3/4 ounce Luxardo maraschino liqueur
- 3/4 ounce green Chartreuse
- 3/4 ounce fresh lemon juice

Pour all of the ingredients into a shaker two-thirds full of ice cubes. Shake well. Strain into a chilled Cocktail glass.

Fino Martini

One of the earliest variations on the classic Martini, this drink dates to the 1930s.

- 2¹/₂ ounces gin
- 1/4 ounce fino sherry

Pour both ingredients into a mixing glass two-thirds full of ice cubes. Stir well. Strain into a chilled Cocktail glass.

The First Blush

Created by Gary Regan and me in 2008.

- 3 ounces chilled Croft PINK port
- 4 ounces chilled champagne
- 1/2 ounce Cointreau
- 2 dashes of Angostura bitters
- Lemon twist, for garnish

Pour all of the ingredients into a chilled Champagne Flute. Stir briefly, and add the twist.

Fish House Cocktail

Based on the Fish House Punch. Assembled by Gary Regan, circa 2003.

- 1$1/2$ ounces dark rum
- $1/2$ ounce brandy
- $1/2$ ounce peach brandy
- $1/2$ ounce simple syrup (page 35)
- $1/4$ ounce fresh lime juice
- $1/4$ ounce fresh lemon juice

Pour all of the ingredients into a shaker two-thirds full of ice cubes. Shake well. Strain into a chilled Cocktail glass.

Fish House Punch

This one was born in Philadelphia a long time ago, and it's said that George Washington himself tasted it.

MAKES ABOUT TWENTY-FOUR 6-OUNCE SERVINGS

- 1 large block of ice
- 8 ounces chilled simple syrup (page 35)
- 2 ounces ice water
- 10 ounces chilled fresh lime juice
- 10 ounces chilled fresh lemon juice
- 2 750-ml bottles chilled dark rum
- 18 ounces chilled brandy
- 12 ounces chilled peach brandy

Place the block of ice in the center of a large punch bowl. Pour in all of the remaining ingredients and stir well.

Flame of Love Martini

Created for singer and actor Dean Martin by Pepe at Chasen's, Los Angeles.

- $1/4$ ounce dry sherry
- 2 orange twists
- 3 ounces gin or vodka

Coat a chilled Cocktail glass with the sherry and discard the excess. Flame 1 of the twists over the glass. Stir the liquor over ice until very cold; strain into the glass. Flame the second twist over the drink.

Flirtini

What those girls on *Sex and the City* loved to sip on.

3 to 4 fresh raspberries
1¹/₂ ounces Stolichnaya Razberi vodka
¹/₂ ounce Cointreau
Splash of fresh lime juice
Splash of pineapple juice
Splash of cranberry juice
Brut champagne or other dry sparkling wine
Mint sprig, for garnish

Muddle the raspberries in the bottom of a chilled Champagne flute. Pour the vodka, Cointreau, and fruit juices into a shaker two-thirds full of ice cubes. Shake well. Strain into the Champagne flute. Top with the champagne; add the mint sprig.

Flying Dutchman

2 ounces gin
¹/₂ ounce triple sec

Pour both ingredients into a mixing glass two-thirds full of ice cubes. Stir well. Strain into an ice-filled Rocks glass.

Fog Cutter

Adapted from a recipe in Jones' Complete Barguide.

1¹/₂ ounces light rum
¹/₂ ounce brandy
¹/₂ ounce gin
2 ounces fresh orange juice
¹/₂ ounce fresh lemon juice
¹/₂ ounce orgeat syrup
¹/₄ ounce cream sherry

Pour the rum, brandy, gin, juices, and syrup into a shaker two-thirds full of ice cubes. Shake well. Strain into an ice-filled Collins glass. Float the sherry on top.

Footloose Cocktail

Adapted from a recipe by Wesly Moore, Pasadena, California.

2 ounces Stolichnaya Razberi vodka

1 ounce Cointreau

$1/2$ ounce fresh lime juice

Peychaud's bitters, to taste

Lime twist, for garnish

Pour all of the ingredients into a shaker two-thirds full of ice cubes. Shake well. Strain into a chilled Cocktail glass. Add the twist.

Freddy Fudpucker

This is a variation on the popular Harvey Wallbanger, but the tequila, which substitutes for the vodka, adds complexity that vodka just can't deliver.

2 ounces white tequila

3 ounces orange juice

$1/2$ ounce Galliano

Pour the tequila and orange juice into an ice-filled Highball glass; stir briefly. Carefully pour the Galliano over the back of a spoon so that it floats on top of the drink.

French Connection

You can play with the ratios of Grand Marnier to cognac to achieve sweeter or drier versions of this drink.

2 ounces cognac

1 ounce Grand Marnier

Pour both ingredients into an ice-filled Rocks glass. Stir well to chill.

French Kiss

An excellent experience.

2 ounces sweet vermouth

2 ounces dry vermouth

Lemon twist, for garnish

Pour both vermouths into an ice-filled Rocks glass; stir briefly. Add the twist.

French Rose Cocktail

1½ ounces gin
¼ ounce dry vermouth
½ ounce cherry brandy

Pour all of the ingredients into a mixing glass two-thirds full of ice cubes. Stir well. Strain into a chilled Cocktail glass.

French 75

Here's the rule to remember: The French 75 uses gin, the French 76 uses brandy.

2 ounces gin
½ ounce fresh lime juice
¼ ounce simple syrup (page 35)
4 ounces chilled champagne

Pour the gin, lime juice, and simple syrup into a shaker two-thirds full of ice cubes. Shake well. Strain the mixture into a crushed ice–filled wine goblet; top with the champagne.

French 76

2 ounces brandy
½ ounce fresh lemon juice
¼ ounce simple syrup (page 35)
4 ounces chilled champagne

Pour the brandy, lemon juice, and simple syrup into a shaker two-thirds full of ice cubes. Shake well. Strain the mixture into a crushed ice–filled wine goblet; top with the champagne.

Fresh Ginger Mojito

Adapted from a recipe by Tim Wilson, director of beverages at the Wolfgang Puck organization, Las Vegas.

6 fresh mint leaves
1½ ounces fresh lime juice
3 thin slices fresh ginger
1½ ounces Montecristo spiced rum
½ ounce ginger ale
Mint sprig and a slice of candied ginger, for garnishes

Muddle the mint leaves, lime juice, and ginger in an empty shaker. Add ice cubes and the rum; shake well. Strain into an ice-filled Collins glass; top with the ginger ale. Add the mint sprig and candied ginger.

Frontier Cocktail

$1/2$ ounce B&B liqueur

2 ounces white tequila

$1/4$ ounce DiSaronno amaretto

$1/2$ ounce pineapple juice

$1/2$ ounce fresh lime juice

Coat a chilled Cocktail glass with the B&B. Pour all of the remaining ingredients into a shaker two-thirds full of ice cubes. Shake well. Strain into the prepared glass.

Frozen Banana Daiquiri

2 ounces light, gold, or dark rum

1 ounce fresh lime juice

1 ripe banana, cut into chunks

Place all of the ingredients into a blender containing 1 cup of ice cubes. Blend well. Pour into a chilled wine goblet.

Frozen Daiquiri

$2 1/2$ ounces light rum

1 ounce fresh lime juice

$1/2$ ounce simple syrup (page 35)

Pour all of the ingredients into a blender containing 1 cup of ice cubes. Blend well. Pour into a chilled wine goblet.

Frozen Margarita

Repeat after me: "I will always use fresh lime juice in my Margaritas. Nothing else will do."

3 ounces white tequila

2 ounces triple sec

1 ounce fresh lime juice

Pour all of the ingredients into a blender containing 1 cup of ice cubes. Blend well. Pour into a chilled wine goblet.

Frozen Matador

2 ounces white tequila

1 ounce pineapple juice

1 ounce fresh lime juice

Pour all of the ingredients into a blender containing 1 cup of ice cubes. Blend well. Pour into a chilled wine goblet.

Frozen Peach Daiquiri

2 ounces light rum

1 ounce fresh lime juice

1 ripe peach, pitted and cut into 8 wedges

Place all of the ingredients into a blender containing 1 cup of ice cubes. Blend well. Pour into a chilled wine goblet.

Frozen Peach Margarita

2 ounces white tequila

1 ounce fresh lime juice

1 ripe peach, pitted and cut into 8 wedges

Place all of the ingredients into a blender containing 1 cup of ice cubes. Blend well. Pour into a chilled wine goblet.

Frozen Piña Colada

2 ounces light or dark rum

2 ounces pineapple juice

2 ounces cream of coconut

Pour all of the ingredients into a blender containing 1 cup of ice cubes. Blend well. Pour into a chilled wine goblet.

Frozen Strawberry Daiquiri

2 ounces light rum

1 ounce fresh lime juice

8 ripe strawberries, hulled and halved

Place all of the ingredients into a blender containing 1 cup of ice cubes. Blend well. Pour into a chilled wine goblet.

Frozen Strawberry Margarita

2 ounces white tequila

1 ounce fresh lime juice

8 ripe strawberries, hulled and halved

Place all of the ingredients into a blender containing 1 cup of ice cubes. Blend well. Pour into a chilled wine goblet.

Fuddy-Duddy Fruit Punch

Make this punch and let adults spike it if they please.

MAKES ABOUT THIRTY-TWO 6-OUNCE SERVINGS

2 quarts grapefruit juice

1 quart orange juice

1 quart tangerine juice

12 ounces cranberry juice

4 ounces fresh lime juice

4 ounces fresh lemon juice

6 ounces simple syrup (page 35)

2 ounces grenadine

1 ounce orgeat syrup

1 large block of ice, for serving

Pour all of the liquid ingredients into a nonreactive large pan or bowl; stir well. Cover and refrigerate until chilled, at least 4 hours.

Place the ice in the center of a large punch bowl. Add the punch.

The Fukien Mist

Adapted from a recipe by Chris Hopkins, bartender at Ana Mandara, San Francisco.

2 ounces gin

$3/4$ ounce Soho lychee liqueur

$1/4$ ounce fresh lemon juice

$1/8$ ounce simple syrup (page 35; optional)

$1/8$ ounce grenadine

Orange twist, for garnish

Pour the gin, lychee liqueur, lemon juice, and simple syrup into a shaker two-thirds full of ice cubes. Shake well. Strain into a chilled Cocktail glass. Pour the grenadine into the center of the drink, and stir gently. Add the twist.

Full Monte

*Created by "Libation Goddess," aka Audrey Saunders, New York City,
circa 2000.*

$1/4$ **ounce vodka**

$1/4$ **ounce gin**

$1/4$ **ounce light rum**

$1/4$ **ounce tequila**

$1/4$ **ounce maraschino liqueur**

$1/2$ **ounce fresh lemon juice**

$1/2$ **ounce simple syrup (page 35)**

2 dashes of Angostura bitters

Champagne or other sparkling wine

Pour the vodka, gin, rum, tequila, maraschino liqueur, lemon
juice, simple syrup, and bitters into a shaker two-thirds full of
ice cubes. Shake well. Strain into a chilled Champagne flute. Top
with the champagne.

Fuzzy Logic

2 ounces Tanqueray gin

1$1/2$ ounces fresh orange juice

$1/2$ **ounce peach schnapps**

2 dashes of Bénédictine

Pour all of the ingredients into a shaker two-thirds full of ice
cubes. Shake well. Strain into a chilled Cocktail glass.

Fuzzy Navel

My sister's favorite.

2 ounces vodka

1 ounce peach schnapps

3 to 4 ounces fresh orange juice

Pour all of the ingredients into an ice-filled Highball glass; stir
briefly.

Gibson

Named for Charles Dana Gibson, magazine illustrator and the creator of the Gibson Girl of the late 1800s.

3 ounces gin
$1/2$ ounce dry vermouth
3 pearl onions, for garnish

Pour the gin and the vermouth into a mixing glass two-thirds full of ice cubes. Stir well. Strain into a chilled Cocktail glass. Add the onions.

Gimlet

The Gin Gimlet was the first-ever Gimlet and is sometimes referred to merely as a Gimlet, the "Gin" being understood by many experienced bartenders. The drink is thought to have been created in order to entice British sailors to drink lime juice to ward off scurvy.

$2^1/2$ ounces gin
$1/2$ ounce lime juice cordial, such as Rose's
Lime wedge, for garnish

Pour both ingredients into an ice-filled Rocks glass; stir briefly. Add the lime wedge.

Gin & Bitter Lemon

2 ounces gin
$3/4$ ounce fresh lemon juice
$3/4$ ounce simple syrup (page 35)
4 ounces tonic water

Build in an ice-filled Highball glass. Stir to chill.

Gin & It

The "It" in the Gin & It refers to the sweet vermouth that often is referred to as "Italian," since Italy was the birthplace of sweet vermouth.

3 ounces gin
$1/2$ ounce sweet vermouth

Pour both ingredients into a mixing glass two-thirds full of ice cubes. Stir well. Strain into a chilled Cocktail glass.

Gin & Sin

2 ounces gin

1 ounce fresh orange juice

$1/2$ ounce fresh lemon juice

2 dashes of grenadine

Pour all of the ingredients into a shaker two-thirds full of ice cubes. Shake well. Strain into a chilled Cocktail glass.

Gin & Tonic

$2^1/2$ ounces gin

4 ounces tonic water

Lime wedge, for garnish

Pour the gin and the tonic water into an ice-filled Highball glass. Stir briefly. Squeeze the lime and drop it in.

Gin Buck

This is probably the original Buck.

1 lemon wedge

2 ounces gin

5 ounces ginger ale

Squeeze the lemon wedge into a Highball glass and drop it into the glass. Fill the glass with ice cubes. Add the gin and ginger ale. Stir briefly.

Gin Fix

This Fix is considered to be the classic.

$2^1/2$ ounces gin

1 ounce fresh lemon juice

$1/2$ ounce pineapple juice

Fresh fruit in season (your choice), for garnish

Pour all of the ingredients into a shaker two-thirds full of crushed ice. Shake well. Strain into a crushed ice–filled Highball glass. Add the fruit.

Gin Fizz

2 ounces gin

1 ounce fresh lemon juice

$1/2$ ounce simple syrup (page 35)

5 to 6 ounces club soda

Fresh fruit in season (your choice), for garnish

Pour the gin, lemon juice, and simple syrup into a shaker two-thirds full of ice cubes. Shake well; strain into a chilled wine goblet. Add the club soda; stir briefly. Add the fruit.

Gin Rickey

2^1/$_2$ ounces gin

1 ounce fresh lime juice

5 to 6 ounces club soda

Lime wedge, for garnish

Pour the gin and lime juice into an ice-filled Highball glass. Add the club soda; stir briefly. Add the lime wedge.

Gin Sais Quoi?

Adapted from a recipe by "Dr. Cocktail" (Ted Haigh).

1^1/$_2$ ounces gin

^{1}/$_2$ ounce ouzo

1 ounce fresh lemon juice

^{1}/$_4$ ounce black currant syrup or grenadine

2 dashes of orange bitters

Lemon twist, for garnish

Pour all of the ingredients into a shaker two-thirds full of ice cubes. Shake well. Strain into a chilled Cocktail glass. Garnish with the twist.

Gin Sling

Although the Singapore Sling is based on gin, this refreshing drink is completely different from it.

2^1/$_2$ ounces gin

^{1}/$_2$ ounce triple sec

^{1}/$_2$ ounce fresh lemon juice

5 to 6 ounces club soda

Lemon wedge, for garnish

Pour the gin, triple sec, and lemon juice into a shaker two-thirds full of ice cubes; shake well. Strain the drink into an ice-filled Collins glass. Add the club soda; stir briefly. Add the lemon wedge.

Ginger Beer Shandy

See also **Shandy Gaff**.

> **8 ounces ginger beer**
> **8 ounces amber ale**

Carefully pour the ginger beer and the ale into a 16-ounce beer glass.

The Ginger Blush

Created by Gary Regan and me in 2008.

> **3 ounces chilled Croft PINK Port**
> **4 ounces chilled champagne**
> **$1/2$ ounce Domaine de Canton ginger liqueur**
> **2 dashes of Angostura bitters**
> **Lemon twist, for garnish**

Pour all of the ingredients into a chilled Champagne flute. Stir briefly; add the twist.

Ginger Julep

Created at the Red Star Tavern and Road House, Portland, Oregon.

> **Leaves from 4 fresh mint sprigs**
> **1 ounce simple syrup (page 35)**
> **$1/2$ ounce fresh lime juice**
> **2 ounces chilled champagne**
> **2 ounces ginger beer**

Place the mint leaves, simple syrup, and lime juice in an empty shaker; muddle well. Add ice cubes and shake well. Strain into a chilled Champagne flute. Add the champagne and ginger beer.

Ginger Silver Coin

Adapted from a recipe by Brett Davis, beverage director at Grasshopper, Durham, North Carolina.

Sea salt and a wedge of lime for rimming the glass
2 ounces Herradura Silver tequila
1 ounce Cointreau
2 ounces fresh lime juice
1 ounce ginger simple syrup (see recipe below)
Lime wheel, for garnish

Prepare a Cocktail glass. Pour all of the ingredients into a shaker two-thirds full of ice cubes. Shake well. Strain into the prepared glass. Add the lime wheel.

GINGER SIMPLE SYRUP
²/₃ cup granulated sugar
²/₃ cup water
2 tablespoons grated fresh ginger

In a nonreactive saucepan set over moderate heat, combine the sugar and water, stirring frequently, until the sugar dissolves. Set aside to cool. Pour the syrup into a jar, add the ginger, and let infuse overnight. Strain through a double layer of dampened cheesecloth, and store in the refrigerator.

GINger Snap

Created by Gary Regan for Beefeater gin, June 2008.

1¹/₂ ounces Beefeater gin
¹/₂ ounce Domaine de Canton ginger liqueur
¹/₂ ounce Cointreau
¹/₂ ounce fresh lemon juice
Dash of Angostura bitters
Club soda
Lemon twist, for garnish

Pour the gin, liqueurs, lemon juice, and bitters into a shaker two-thirds full of ice cubes. Shake well. Strain into an ice-filled Collins glass. Top with club soda, and add the twist.

Girl Scout Cookie

1¹/₂ ounces peppermint schnapps

1¹/₂ ounces Kahlúa

3 ounces half-and-half

Pour all of the ingredients into a shaker two-thirds full of ice cubes. Shake well. Strain into a chilled Cocktail glass.

Glenkinchie Clincher

Created for a reception for singer Tony Bennett in London.

2 ounces Glenkinchie single-malt scotch

¹/₄ ounce amaretto

¹/₄ ounce triple sec

Maraschino cherry, for garnish

Pour all of the ingredients into a mixing glass two-thirds full of ice cubes. Stir well. Strain into a chilled Cocktail glass. Add the cherry.

The Glory Cocktail

Created by Pete Kendal, head bartender at Milk & Honey, London, circa 2004.

¹/₂ ounce Dubonnet

1 fresh cherry

1 fresh raspberry

4 ounces gin

2 ounces sweet vermouth

1¹/₂ ounces dry vermouth

¹/₂ ounce Cherry Heering

Orange twist, for garnish

Fill a Cocktail glass with crushed ice, and add the Dubonnet. In an empty mixing glass, lightly muddle the cherry, raspberry, and gin. Fill the mixing glass two-thirds full of ice and add both vermouths and the Cherry Heering. Stir very well. Discard the ice and Dubonnet from the cocktail glass, and strain the cocktail into the glass. Add the twist.

Godchild

Part I of the drink trilogy.

1 ounce vodka

1 ounce amaretto

1 ounce heavy cream

Build in an ice-filled Rocks glass; stir briefly.

Godfather

Part II of the trilogy.

2 ounces scotch

1 ounce amaretto

Build in an ice-filled Rocks glass; stir briefly.

Godmother

Part III of the trilogy.

2 ounces vodka

1 ounce amaretto

Build in an ice-filled Rocks glass; stir briefly.

Golden Cadillac

Almost 50 years old and still going.

2 ounces white crème de cacao

³/₄ ounce Galliano

1 ounce light cream

Pour all of the ingredients into a shaker two-thirds full of ice cubes. Shake well. Strain into a chilled Cocktail glass.

Golden Dawn Cocktail

1 ounce gin

1 ounce apricot brandy

1 ounce calvados or applejack

Pour all of the ingredients into a mixing glass two-thirds full of ice cubes. Stir well. Strain into a chilled Cocktail glass.

Golden Delicious Martini

This is a wonderful variation on the Apple Martini.

2 ounces Van Gogh Wild Appel vodka
$^1/_2$ ounce Goldschlager

Pour both ingredients into a mixing glass two-thirds full of ice cubes. Stir well. Strain into a chilled Cocktail glass.

Golden Dream

2 ounces Galliano
$^1/_2$ ounce triple sec
1 ounce orange juice
1 ounce light cream

Pour all of the ingredients into a shaker two-thirds full of ice cubes. Shake well. Strain into a chilled Cocktail glass.

Golden Eye

$1^1/_2$ ounces Appleton Estate V/X rum
$^3/_4$ ounce DiSaronno amaretto
$^1/_2$ ounce fresh lemon juice
Orange twist, for garnish

Pour all of the ingredients into a shaker two-thirds full of ice cubes. Shake well. Strain into a chilled Cocktail glass. Add the twist.

Golden Girl

Adapted from a recipe by Dale DeGroff, author of The Craft of the Cocktail.

MAKES 2 SERVINGS

2 ounces Bacardi 8-year-old rum
1 ounce simple syrup (page 35)
2 ounces pineapple juice
$1^1/_2$ ounces Offley Rich tawny port
1 small egg
Pinch of grated orange zest, for garnish

Pour all of the ingredients into a shaker two-thirds full of ice cubes. Shake very well. Strain, dividing between 2 chilled Cocktail glasses. Sprinkle the orange zest on top of each.

Golden Idol

Adapted from a recipe by Sean Bigley, bar manager at the Bellagio, Las Vegas.

> 1¹/₄ ounces Idol vodka
> ¹/₂ ounce Marie Brizard amaretto
> ¹/₄ ounce Marie Brizard crème de cassis
> 2 ounces apricot nectar
> ¹/₂ ounce fresh lemon juice
> ¹/₄ ounce simple syrup (page 35)

Pour all of the ingredients into a shaker two-thirds full of ice cubes. Shake well. Strain into a chilled Cocktail glass.

Golden Rye Flip

Adapted from a recipe from Rye, San Francisco, 2006.

> 1¹/₂ ounces straight rye whiskey
> ¹/₂ ounce advocaat liqueur
> ¹/₂ ounce half-and-half
> ¹/₂ ounce simple syrup (page 35)
> 4 dashes of orange bitters
> 2 ounces fresh clementine juice
> Orange twist, for garnish

Pour all of the ingredients into a shaker two-thirds full of ice cubes. Shake well. Strain into a chilled Cocktail glass. Add the twist.

Goldfish Martini

This was the signature drink at a Manhattan speakeasy during Prohibition.

> 2 ounces gin
> 1 ounce dry vermouth
> ¹/₄ ounce Goldwasser liqueur

Pour all of the ingredients into a mixing glass two-thirds full of ice cubes. Stir well. Strain into a chilled Cocktail glass.

Good Night Kiss

Adapted from a recipe by David Russell and friends at the Hotel Jerome, Aspen, Colorado.

> 1/2 ounce Godiva Original chocolate liqueur
>
> 1/2 ounce Baileys Irish cream liqueur
>
> 1/4 ounce Frangelico
>
> 1 ounce vodka
>
> Whipped cream and shaved chocolate, for garnishes

Pour the liqueurs and vodka into a shaker two-thirds full of ice cubes. Shake well. Strain into a chilled Cocktail glass. Add the whipped cream and shaved chocolate.

Gorilla Tits

Who knows? Who cares?

> 1/2 ounce dark rum
>
> 1/2 ounce bourbon
>
> 1/2 ounce Kahlúa

Build in an ice-filled Rocks glass. Stir with a sip-stick.

Gotham

Adapted from a recipe created by David Wondrich in 2001 for the debut issue of New York's *Gotham* magazine. Don't pass up the chance to read his wonderful book, *Imbibe From Absinthe Cocktail to Whiskey Smash; A Salute in Stories and Drinks to "Professor" Jerry Thomas*.

> 2 ounces cognac
>
> 1 ounce Noilly Prat dry vermouth
>
> 1/2 ounce crème de cassis
>
> 2 dashes of fresh lemon juice
>
> Lemon twist, for garnish

Pour all of the ingredients into a shaker two-thirds full of ice cubes. Shake well. Strain into a chilled Cocktail glass. Add the twist.

Gotham Martini

From the Four Seasons Hotel, New York City.

3 ounces Absolut vodka
$^1/_2$ ounce blackberry brandy
$^1/_2$ ounce black sambuca
3 blackberries, for garnish

Pour all of the ingredients into a mixing glass two-thirds full of ice cubes. Stir well. Strain into a chilled Cocktail glass. Add the blackberries.

The Gourmet

Created by Gary Regan for Gourmet *magazine's food-pairing challenge, 2004.*

$1^1/_2$ ounces Hennessy VSOP Privilège cognac
$1^1/_2$ ounces ruby port (any decent bottling)
$^3/_4$ ounce Monin Gingerbread syrup

Pour all of the ingredients into a snifter or a Sherry glass. Stir well to combine.

Grand Garnier

Adapted from a recipe by David Nepove, Enrico's, San Francisco.

2 fresh lime slices
2 fresh orange slices
1 ounce Grand Marnier
1 ounce green Chartreuse V.E.P.
Lime wedge, for garnish

Muddle the lime and orange slices with 4 or 5 ice cubes in a shaker. Add more ice, the Grand Marnier, and the Chartreuse. Shake well. Strain into a chilled Cocktail glass. Add the lime wedge.

Grapefruit Fizz

6 ounces fresh grapefruit juice
3 ounces lemon-lime soda
Dash of Angostura bitters

Build in an ice-filled Collins glass; stir briefly.

Grasshopper

Very popular during the 1970s, this drink is poised to make a comeback.

> 1½ ounces green crème de menthe
> 1½ ounces white crème de cacao
> ¾ ounce light cream

Pour all of the ingredients into a shaker two-thirds full of ice cubes. Shake well. Strain into a chilled Cocktail glass.

Greek Margarita

Adapted from a recipe by Heather Branch, beverage director at Dona, New York City.

> Crushed fennel seeds and salt, for rimming the glass
> 2 ounces Don Julio Blanco tequila
> ½ ounce ouzo
> ¼ ounce Cointreau
> ½ ounce fresh lime juice
> ¼ ounce simple syrup (page 35)

Prepare a Cocktail glass; chill until needed. Pour all of the ingredients into a shaker two-thirds full of ice cubes. Shake well. Strain into the chilled glass.

The Greek Vesper

Adapted from a recipe by Ektoras Binikos, Aureole restaurant, New York City.

> 1 ounce gin
> ½ ounce Grand Marnier
> ½ ounce fresh lime juice
> Dash of crème de cassis
> Lemon thyme sprig, for garnish

Pour all of the ingredients into a shaker two-thirds full of ice cubes. Shake well. Strain into a chilled Cocktail glass. Add the thyme sprig.

Green Glazier

Adapted from a recipe by Jamie Boudreau, Vessel, Seattle.

2 ounces Rémy V.S. cognac
³/₄ ounce green Chartreuse
¹/₄ ounce white crème de cacao
2 dashes of Angostura bitters

Pour all of the ingredients into a mixing glass two-thirds full of ice cubes. Stir well. Strain into a chilled Cocktail glass.

Greyhound

A cooling drink for the dog days of summer.

2¹/₂ ounces vodka
4 ounces grapefruit juice

Build in an ice-filled Highball glass; stir briefly.

Grilled Peach Old-Fashioned

Adapted from a recipe by Neyah White, head bartender at Nopa, San Francisco.

¹/₄ to ¹/₂ peach, grilled over an open flame until soft
1 orange slice
1 teaspoon brown molasses sugar*
8 heavy dashes of Angostura bitters
1¹/₂ ounces aged rum (preferably Santa Teresa Gran Reserva)

Muddle the peach, orange slice, sugar, and bitters in a Double Old-Fashioned glass. Add ice cubes and the rum; stir briefly.

Grog

2¹/₂ ounces dark rum
2¹/₂ ounces spring water
2 dashes of Angostura bitters

Pour all of the ingredients into a mixing glass two-thirds full of ice cubes. Stir well. Strain into an ice-filled Rocks glass.

* Neyah's favorite brown molasses sugar is Billington's Natural Dark Brown Molasses Sugar, which is available on Amazon.com.

Gypsy

This drink dates back to the 1930s, but the garnish is a recent addition.

> 1¹/₂ ounces gin
> 1¹/₂ ounces sweet vermouth
> Maraschino cherry, for garnish

Pour the gin and vermouth into a mixing glass two-thirds full of ice cubes. Stir well. Strain into a chilled Cocktail glass. Add the cherry.

Habana

Adapted from a recipe by Ektoras Binikos, Aureole restaurant, New York City.

> 1¹/₂ ounces añejo rum
> ¹/₂ ounce Grand Marnier
> 1 ounce fresh grapefruit juice
> ¹/₂ ounce fresh lime juice
> Dash of Angostura bitters
> 1 teaspoon confectioners' sugar
> Fresh mint sprig, for garnish

Pour all of the ingredients into a shaker two-thirds full of ice cubes. Shake well. Strain into a chilled Cocktail glass. Add the mint sprig.

The Harris Fizz

Adapted from a recipe by Adam Harris, bartender at Dylan Prime, New York City, circa 2004.

> 1 kiwi, peeled and sliced
> 1 teaspoon superfine sugar
> 1 ounce pineapple syrup (recipe follows)
> 2 ounces Stolichnaya Razberi vodka
> ¹/₄ ounce maraschino liqueur
> Club soda
> Kiwi slice, for garnish

Muddle the kiwi and sugar in an empty shaker. Add ice cubes, the pineapple syrup, vodka, and liqueur. Shake very well. Strain into an ice-filled Collins glass. Top with the club soda. Add the kiwi slice.

2 cups pineapple juice

$1/4$ cup granulated sugar

In a nonreactive saucepan, combine the pineapple juice and sugar over moderate heat. Cook, stirring constantly, until the sugar dissolves and the juice thickens slightly, about 5 minutes. Set aside to cool.

Harry Denton Martini

Named for one of San Francisco's best-loved bon vivants.

$1^1/4$ ounces Bombay Sapphire gin

$1/2$ ounce green Chartreuse

Pour both ingredients into a shaker two-thirds full of ice cubes. Shake well. Strain into a chilled Cocktail glass.

Harvard Cocktail

Go Pforzheimer, Brook, and Ryan!

$1^1/2$ ounces brandy

$1^1/2$ ounces sweet vermouth

$1/4$ ounce simple syrup (page 35)

$1/4$ ounce Angostura bitters

Pour all of the ingredients into a shaker two-thirds full of ice cubes. Shake well. Strain into a chilled Cocktail glass.

Harvey Wallbanger

Walk carefully after having one of these; look out for walls.

2 ounces vodka

6 ounces orange juice

$1/2$ ounce Galliano

Pour the vodka and the orange juice into an ice-filled Highball glass; stir briefly. Float the Galliano on top of the drink.

Havana Cocktail

2 ounces light rum

1 ounce pineapple juice

1 ounce fresh lemon juice

Pour all of the ingredients into a shaker two-thirds full of ice cubes. Shake well. Strain into a chilled Cocktail glass.

Hawaiian Cocktail

2 ounces gin

1/2 ounce triple sec

1/2 ounce pineapple juice

2 dashes of Angostura bitters

Pour all of the ingredients into a shaker two-thirds full of ice cubes. Shake well. Strain into a chilled Cocktail glass.

Hawthorne Lane's Bella Noce

Adapted from a recipe by Ray Scholz, bartender at Hawthorne Lane, San Francisco, 2006.

1 1/2 ounces kumquat- and blood orange–infused vodka (recipe follows)

1 1/2 ounces Nocino Della Cristina liqueur

1/2 teaspoon blood orange syrup (recipe follows)

1/2 slice blood orange, for garnish

Pour all of the ingredients into a shaker two-thirds full of ice cubes. Shake well. Strain into a chilled Cocktail glass. Add the blood orange slice.

KUMQUAT- AND BLOOD ORANGE–INFUSED VODKA

4 blood oranges

8 kumquats

1 liter vodka

Cut both types of fruit into halves, squeeze some juice from the fruit, and drop everything into a large sealable container. Add the vodka, seal the container, and set aside for 3 days. Strain the mixture through a double layer of dampened cheesecloth; store in the refrigerator.

1 cup granulated sugar

1 cup strained blood orange juice

Combine both ingredients in a nonreactive saucepan set over moderate heat. Stir occasionally, and cook until the sugar dissolves. Set aside to cool; refrigerate.

The Haymaker Special

Adapted from a recipe by "Dr. Cocktail" (Ted Haigh).

2 ounces calvados

$1/2$ ounce Dubonnet Rouge

$1/2$ ounce Cointreau

$1/2$ ounce fresh grapefruit juice

Lime peel spiral, for garnish

Pour all of the ingredients into a shaker two-thirds full of ice cubes. Shake well. Strain into a chilled Cocktail glass. Add the lime spiral.

The Heavenly Dram

Adapted from a recipe by Jacques Bezuindenhout, bartender at Harry Denton's Starlight Room, San Francisco, circa 2005.

$1 1/2$ ounces 25-year-old The Macallan single-malt scotch

$3/4$ ounce Pedro Ximénez sherry

$1/2$ ounce fresh lemon juice

2 teaspoons honey syrup (see recipe below)

Pour all of the ingredients into a shaker two-thirds full of ice cubes. Shake well. Strain into a chilled Cocktail glass.

HONEY SYRUP

Dissolve $1/2$ cup of honey in $1/2$ cup of hot water. Stir well; let cool to room temperature.

Helsinki Charger

2 ounces Finlandia lime vodka

Ginger beer

2 lime wedges, for garnish

Build in an ice-filled Collins glass. Add the lime wedges.

DRINKS A TO Z

Hemingway Daiquiri

Just what Papa ordered.

1$^1/_2$ ounces light rum
$^3/_4$ ounce maraschino liqueur
1 ounce fresh lime juice
1 ounce grapefruit juice

Pour all of the ingredients into a blender and add 4 to 6 ice cubes. Start slowly and increase the speed, blending until frozen. Pour into a very large Cocktail glass.

Hennessy Martini

A mixture of cognac and lemon juice was favored by the French during the late 1700s, but this drink dates back only to the 1990s, when the Hennessy cognac people promoted it heavily.

2 ounces Hennessy cognac
$^1/_4$ ounce fresh lemon juice

Pour both ingredients into a mixing glass two-thirds full of ice cubes. Stir well. Strain into a chilled Cocktail glass.

Highland Cream

Adapted from a recipe by Colin Peter Field, head bartender, The Ritz Hotel, Paris.

1$^1/_2$ ounces scotch
$^3/_4$ ounce Kahlúa
$^3/_4$ ounce dark crème de cacao
2 ounces heavy cream

Pour all of the ingredients into a shaker two-thirds full of ice cubes. Shake well. Strain into a chilled Cocktail or an ice-filled Double Old-Fashioned glass.

Highland Fling

2$^1/_2$ ounces scotch
$^3/_4$ ounce sweet vermouth
2 dashes of orange bitters

Pour all of the ingredients into a mixing glass two-thirds full of ice cubes. Stir well. Strain into a chilled Cocktail glass.

Highlander Revisited

1¹/₂ ounces Glenmorangie 10-year-old single-malt scotch

³/₄ ounce Dubonnet Blanc

¹/₂ ounce Galliano

Lemon twist, for garnish

Pour all of the ingredients into a mixing glass two-thirds full of ice cubes. Stir well. Strain into a chilled Cocktail glass. Add the twist.

Hogmanay Cocktail

Hogmanay is the Scottish word for "New Year's Eve celebrations," the origins of said celebrations dating back to the pagan practice of sun and fire worship in the deep midwinter. If you want to celebrate New Year's in grand fashion, Scotland is the place to be.

2¹/₂ ounces scotch

¹/₄ ounce absinthe

Pour both ingredients into a mixing glass two-thirds full of ice cubes. Stir well. Strain into a chilled Cocktail glass.

Hogmanay Eggnog

Serve this on New Year's Day.

MAKES EIGHT 6-OUNCE SERVINGS

4 eggs

6 ounces scotch

2 ounces Drambuie

1 teaspoon vanilla extract

¹/₂ teaspoon ground cinnamon

¹/₂ teaspoon ground allspice

1 quart whole milk

Freshly grated nutmeg, for garnish

Break the eggs into a large bowl and whisk until frothy. Add the scotch, Drambuie, vanilla, cinnamon, and allspice; whisk to combine. Slowly add the milk, whisking until thoroughly mixed. Ladle into Irish Coffee glasses; sprinkle on the nutmeg.

Hole-in-One

2 ounces scotch

1 ounce dry vermouth

1/4 ounce fresh lemon juice

Dash of orange bitters

Pour all of the ingredients into a shaker two-thirds full of ice cubes. Shake well. Strain into a chilled Cocktail glass.

Holy Vesper

1 1/2 ounces Türi Vodka

3/4 ounce Tanqueray No. Ten Gin

3 dashes of B&B

Lemon twist, for garnish

Pour all of the ingredients into a mixing glass two-thirds full of ice cubes. Stir well. Strain into a chilled Cocktail glass. Add the twist.

Hop-Scotch

Yellow Chartreuse, for rinsing the glass

1 1/2 ounces Balvenie Doublewood single-malt scotch

1 barspoon simple syrup (page 35)

2 dashes of Peychaud's bitters

Lemon twist, for garnish

Prepare a Rocks glass with the Chartreuse. Pour all of the ingredients into a mixing glass two-thirds full of ice cubes. Stir well. Strain into the prepared glass. Add the twist.

Hop Toad

Believe it or not, this drink has graced cocktail menus since the early 1900s, but the bitters are a recent addition.

1 1/2 ounces dark rum

1 ounce apricot brandy

1/2 ounce fresh lime juice

2 dashes of Angostura bitters

Pour all of the ingredients into a shaker two-thirds full of ice cubes. Shake well. Strain into a chilled Cocktail glass.

Horse's Neck

This was originally a nonalcoholic drink, but the whiskey made its way into it sometime around, or just after, Prohibition.

> **Lemon peel spiral (page 41)**
> **2¹/₂ ounces bourbon**
> **4 to 5 ounces ginger ale**

Place the lemon peel spiral into a Collins glass; fill the glass with ice cubes. Pour the bourbon and ginger ale into the glass; stir briefly.

The Horseshoe Sling

Created by Gary Regan, circa 2004.

> **2 ounces Herradura Silver 100% blue agave tequila**
> **³/₄ ounce fresh lime juice**
> **¹/₄ ounce Bénédictine**
> **¹/₄ ounce Cherry Heering**
> **¹/₂ ounce Cointreau**
> **¹/₄ ounce pineapple juice**
> **2 dashes of Angostura bitters**
> **Club soda or chilled sparkling wine**
> **Lime wedge and an orange wheel, for garnishes**

Pour the tequila, lime juice, Bénédictine, Cherry Heering, Cointreau, pineapple juice, and bitters into a shaker two-thirds full of ice cubes. Shake well. Strain into an ice-filled Collins glass. Top with the club soda. Add the lime wedge and orange wheel.

The Hoskins Cocktail

Adapted from a recipe by Chuck Taggart, circa 2004.

> **2 ounces Plymouth gin**
> **³/₄ ounce Torani Amer liqueur**
> **¹/₂ ounce maraschino liqueur**
> **¹/₄ ounce Cointreau**
> **Dash of orange bitters**
> **Orange twist, for garnish**

Pour all of the ingredients into a mixing glass two-thirds full of ice cubes. Stir well. Strain into a chilled Cocktail glass. Carefully flame the twist, and add it to the drink.

Hot Buttered Rum

Americans have been enjoying this delectable potion for more than 150 years.

2 ounces dark rum

$1/2$ ounce simple syrup (page 35)

3 whole cloves

1 cinnamon stick (about 3 inches long)

4 to 5 ounces boiling water

2 teaspoons unsalted butter

Freshly grated nutmeg, for garnish

Pour the rum and simple syrup into an Irish Coffee glass. Add the cloves and cinnamon stick. Add boiling water to almost fill the glass. Add the butter; stir briefly. Sprinkle with the nutmeg.

Hot Honeyed Mulled Wine

Prepare this drink just prior to party time so that the aroma will greet guests as they walk in the door.

MAKES SIX 6-OUNCE SERVINGS

8 whole cloves

1 teaspoon freshly grated nutmeg

1 teaspoon ground allspice

1 cinnamon stick (about 3 inches long)

2 ounces honey

12 ounces hot water

1 750-ml bottle dry red wine

6 lemon twists, for garnish

Place the cloves, nutmeg, allspice, and cinnamon stick into a large saucepan; add the honey and hot water. Bring the mixture to a boil over high heat. Reduce the heat to low and simmer for 10 minutes. Strain the mixture through a sieve lined with a double layer of dampened cheesecloth and return it to the pan. Pour in the wine and warm over moderate heat until hot. Divide among 6 Irish Coffee glasses; add a lemon twist to each serving.

Hot Spiced Halloween Cider Punch

MAKES EIGHT 6-OUNCE SERVINGS

8 whole cloves

1 teaspoon freshly grated nutmeg

1 teaspoon ground allspice

$1/2$ teaspoon ground mace

2 cinnamon sticks (each about 3 inches long)

12 ounces hot water

36 ounces hard cider

4 ounces applejack

8 apple slices, for garnish

Place the cloves, nutmeg, allspice, mace, and cinnamon sticks into a large saucepan; add the hot water. Bring the mixture to a boil over high heat. Reduce the heat to low and simmer for 10 minutes. Strain the mixture through a sieve lined with a double layer of dampened cheesecloth and return it to the pot. Pour in the hard cider and warm over moderate heat until hot. Divide among 8 Irish Coffee glasses; add $1/2$ ounce of the applejack and an apple slice to each serving.

Hot Spiked Chocolate

Brandy and hot chocolate create a marriage made in heaven, and if you use Mexican chocolate, which is flavored with almonds and cinnamon, you'll think you're attending the wedding reception. Phone your neighbors.

MAKES 6 SERVINGS

48 ounces prepared hot chocolate

6 ounces brandy

3 ounces dark crème de cacao

Whipped cream and freshly grated nutmeg, for garnishes

Pour the prepared hot chocolate into a large bowl. Add the brandy and crème de cacao; stir to blend. Ladle into 6 mugs. Top each serving with whipped cream and a sprinkling of nutmeg.

Hot Toddy

Toddies have been popular among Americans since the 1700s, and at that time, the drink wasn't always heated.

> 1¹/₂ ounces bourbon, rum, or brandy
>
> 2 whole cloves
>
> Pinch of ground mace
>
> Pinch of ground cinnamon
>
> 4 to 5 ounces boiling water
>
> Lemon twist and cinnamon sugar, for garnishes

Pour the spirit into an Irish Coffee glass; stir in the cloves, mace, and cinnamon. Add boiling water to almost fill the glass. Add the twist and a sprinkle of cinnamon sugar.

The Hpnotiq Breeze

Created by Jaime Wong, bar manager at Cliff House on Point Lobos, San Francisco, circa 2004.

> 1¹/₂ ounces Hpnotiq liqueur
>
> ³/₄ ounce vodka
>
> 2 ounces pineapple juice
>
> 2 ounces white cranberry juice
>
> Lemon twist, for garnish

Pour all of the ingredients into a shaker two-thirds full of ice cubes. Shake well. Strain into a chilled Cocktail glass. Add the twist.

The Hpnotiq Margarita

Created for Phil Ward by Gary Regan.

> 1¹/₂ ounces Herradura Silver 100% blue agave tequila
>
> ¹/₂ ounce Cointreau
>
> ¹/₂ ounce Hpnotiq liqueur
>
> ¹/₂ ounce fresh lime juice

Pour all of the ingredients into a shaker two-thirds full of ice cubes. Shake well. Strain into a chilled Cocktail glass.

The Bartender's Best Friend

Hurricane

Batten down the hatches—this drink was created at Pat O'Brien's restaurant in New Orleans, circa 1945.

1 ounce light rum

1 ounce dark rum

$^1/_2$ ounce passion fruit juice

$^1/_2$ ounce fresh lime juice

$^1/_4$ ounce simple syrup (page 35)

Pour all of the ingredients into a shaker two-thirds full of ice cubes. Shake well. Strain into a chilled Cocktail glass.

Ice 'T' Knee

Adapted from a recipe by Mirko Cattini, The Blue Bar, London.

2 ounces Belvedere vodka

$^3/_4$ ounce Inniskillin Icewine

$^1/_2$ ounce cold jasmine tea

Lemon twist, for garnish

Pour all of the ingredients into a mixing glass two-thirds full of ice cubes. Stir well. Strain into a chilled Cocktail glass. Add the twist.

Ideal Cocktail

2 ounces gin

1 ounce dry vermouth

$^1/_2$ ounce grapefruit juice

Pour all of the ingredients into a shaker two-thirds full of ice cubes. Shake well. Strain into a chilled Cocktail glass.

Immermost Secret

Created by Gary Regan for Andrea Immer, 2004.

1 ounce bourbon

1 ounce Hpnotiq liqueur

$^1/_2$ ounce triple sec

2 dashes of Peychaud's bitters

Maraschino cherry, for garnish

Pour all of the ingredients into a shaker two-thirds full of ice cubes. Shake well. Strain into a chilled Cocktail glass. Add the cherry.

Imperial Cocktail

1 1/2 ounces gin

3/4 ounce dry vermouth

Dash of maraschino liqueur

Maraschino cherry, for garnish

Pour all of the ingredients into a mixing glass two-thirds full of ice cubes. Stir well. Strain into a chilled Cocktail glass. Add the cherry.

In & Out Martini

The name of this Martini comes from the method used to make it.

2 1/2 ounces gin

Splash of dry vermouth

Pour the gin into a mixing glass two-thirds full of ice cubes. Stir well. Pour the vermouth into a chilled Cocktail glass; swirl to coat the entire interior of the glass. Pour out any excess. Strain the gin into the glass.

In the Red

Adapted from a recipe by Daniel Hartenstein and Mike Kozek, Tavern on the Green, New York City, 2003.

1 ounce armagnac

1 ounce vodka

1/4 ounce Campari

3/4 ounce simple syrup (page 35)

1/2 ounce fresh orange juice

1/2 ounce fresh lime juice

Orange twist, for garnish

Pour all of the ingredients into a shaker two-thirds full of ice cubes. Shake well. Strain into a chilled Cocktail glass. Add the twist.

Income Tax Cocktail

This is an ideal cocktail to serve on April 15, August 15, or whatever day you finally file your taxes.

1¹/₂ ounces gin
³/₄ ounce dry vermouth
³/₄ ounce sweet vermouth
1 ounce orange juice
2 dashes of Angostura bitters

Pour all of the ingredients into a shaker two-thirds full of ice cubes. Shake well. Strain into a chilled Cocktail glass.

The Interesting Cocktail

Created by Gary Regan, 2007.

2 ounces Don Julio, El Tesoro, Milagro, or Partida Blanco tequila
³/₄ ounce Aperol
¹/₄ ounce dark crème de cacao
¹/₄ ounce fresh lemon juice
4 grapefruit twists

Pour the tequila, Aperol, crème de cacao, and lemon juice into a shaker. Release the oils from 3 of the grapefruit twists over the ingredients by gently twisting them. Then add them, along with lots of ice, to the shaker. Shake well. Strain into a chilled Champagne flute. Add the remaining grapefruit twist as garnish.

International Cocktail

Created by "King Cocktail," Dale DeGroff, New York City.

2 ounces Gentleman Jack Rare Tennessee whiskey
1 ounce Dry Sack sherry
2 dashes of Angostura bitters
Orange twist, for garnish

Pour all of the ingredients into a shaker two-thirds full of ice cubes. Shake well. Strain into a chilled Cocktail glass. Flame the orange twist over the glass.

Irish Coffee

When in San Francisco, have one of these at the Buena Vista.

> **1¹/₂ ounces Irish whiskey**
> **¹/₂ ounce simple syrup (page 35)**
> **4 ounces hot coffee**
> **Dollop of whipped cream**
> **Dash of green crème de menthe**

Pour the whiskey, simple syrup, and coffee into an Irish Coffee glass; stir briefly. Spoon the whipped cream onto the coffee so that it floats on top. Drizzle the crème de menthe over the cream.

Irresistible Manhattan

I'm not sure who created this drink, but the amaretto works just perfectly with both the whisky and the vermouth in this recipe.

> **1¹/₂ ounces blended Canadian whisky**
> **1 ounce sweet vermouth**
> **1 ounce amaretto**
> **¹/₄ ounce maraschino cherry juice (straight from the jar)**
> **Dash of Angostura bitters**

Pour all of the ingredients into a mixing glass two-thirds full of ice cubes. Stir well. Strain into a chilled Cocktail glass.

Is Paris Burning?

Named for the 1966 film starring Jean-Paul Belmondo, Gert Fröbe, Orson Welles, and Leslie Caron, the combination of these two ingredients is a classic.

> **2 ounces cognac**
> **1 ounce Chambord raspberry liqueur**

Pour both ingredients into a mixing glass two-thirds full of ice cubes. Stir well. Strain into a chilled Cocktail glass.

Island Breeze

MAKES TWO 8-OUNCE SERVINGS

2 ripe bananas, peeled and roughly chopped

3 ounces dark rum

3 ounces canned coconut cream

2 dashes of Angostura bitters

Place all of the ingredients into a blender containing 1 cup of ice cubes. Blend well. Pour into 2 chilled wine goblets.

Islander

2 ounces Martini & Rossi sweet vermouth

$1/2$ ounce Ardbeg 10-year-old single-malt scotch

2 dashes of Pernod

Lemon twist, for garnish

Pour all of the ingredients into a mixing glass two-thirds full of ice cubes. Stir well. Strain into a chilled Cocktail glass. Add the twist.

Italian Champagne Cocktail

Even if you are not a fan of the bitter herbal flavors of Campari, you might enjoy this variation on the Champagne Cocktail, since the sugar will counteract the bitterness somewhat.

1 sugar cube

1 ounce Campari

5 ounces Prosecco, champagne, or other sparkling wine

Orange twist, for garnish

Drop the sugar cube into the bottom of a Champagne flute; add the Campari. Carefully pour in the Prosecco. Add the twist.

Italian Coffee

Amaretto is an equally Italian substitute for the Frangelico in this recipe.

$1^1/2$ ounces Frangelico

4 ounces hot coffee

Dollop of whipped cream

Pour the Frangelico and coffee into an Irish Coffee glass; stir briefly. Float the whipped cream on top.

Italian Mojito

Adapted from a recipe by Xavier Herit, Francesco at Mix, Manhattan.

10 mint leaves

1 tablespoon brown sugar

1 teaspoon simple syrup (page 35)

$1/2$ lime, cut into wedges

2 ounces light rum

2 ounces Prosecco

Fresh mint and a lime wheel, for garnishes

Muddle the mint leaves, sugar, simple syrup, and lime wedges in an empty mixing glass. Add ice cubes and the rum. Shake well. Strain into an ice-filled Highball glass. Top with the Prosecco; stir briefly. Add the mint and lime wheel.

Italian Pirate

Adapted from a recipe by Robert Hess, 2000.

2 ounces dark rum

1 ounce Campari

$1/2$ ounce Falernum liqueur

Lime twist, for garnish

Pour all of the ingredients into a mixing glass two-thirds full of ice cubes. Stir well. Strain into a chilled Cocktail glass. Add the twist.

Italian Stallion Martini

From Villa Christina, Atlanta, Georgia.

3 ounces Tanqueray Sterling vodka

Splash of Galliano

Splash of Frangelico

Pour all of the ingredients into a mixing glass two-thirds full of ice cubes. Stir well. Strain into a chilled Cocktail glass.

Jack & Coke

2 ounces Jack Daniel's Tennessee whiskey

4 ounces Coca-Cola

Build in an ice-filled Highball glass. Stir briefly.

Jack Rose

Created prior to 1920 and reportedly named for its color, which was compared to a Jacqueminot rose.

2¹/₂ ounces applejack
¹/₂ ounce fresh lemon juice
¹/₄ ounce grenadine

Pour all of the ingredients into a shaker two-thirds full of ice cubes. Shake well. Strain into a chilled Cocktail glass.

Jack Rose Royale

3 ounces applejack
¹/₂ ounce Chambord raspberry liqueur
¹/₂ ounce fresh lemon juice

Pour all of the ingredients into a shaker two-thirds full of ice cubes. Shake well. Strain into a chilled Cocktail glass.

Jade

2 ounces light rum
¹/₂ ounce white curaçao
¹/₂ ounce green crème de menthe
¹/₂ ounce fresh lime juice

Pour all of the ingredients into a shaker two-thirds full of ice cubes. Shake well. Strain into a chilled Cocktail glass.

Jamaican Coffee

1¹/₂ ounces Tia Maria
4 ounces hot coffee
Dollop of whipped cream

Pour the Tia Maria and coffee into an Irish Coffee glass; stir briefly. Float the whipped cream on top.

Jamaican Farewell

Adapted from a recipe by Daniel Reichert, Vintage Cocktails, Los Angeles, circa 2005.

> 2 ounces Appleton Estate V/X rum
> 3/4 ounce Apry apricot liqueur
> 3/4 ounce fresh lime juice
> 2 dashes of Angostura bitters
> Lime wedge, for garnish

Pour all of the ingredients into a shaker two-thirds full of ice cubes. Shake well. Strain into a chilled Cocktail glass. Add the lime wedge.

Jamaican Ten Speed

Created by Roger Gobbler, Café Terra Cotta, Tucson, Arizona.

> 1 ounce vodka
> 3/4 ounce melon liqueur
> 1/4 ounce crème de banane
> 1/4 ounce Malibu rum
> 1/2 ounce half-and-half

Pour all of the ingredients into a shaker two-thirds full of ice cubes. Shake well. Strain into a chilled Cocktail glass.

James Joyce

A variation on the Oriental Cocktail, this was named for the Irish writer because of its Irish whiskey base. As James Joyce noted, "Christopher Columbus, as everyone knows, is honoured by posterity because he was the last to discover America."

> 1 1/2 ounces Irish whiskey
> 3/4 ounce sweet vermouth
> 3/4 ounce triple sec
> 1/2 ounce fresh lime juice

Pour all of the ingredients into a shaker two-thirds full of ice cubes. Shake well. Strain into a chilled Cocktail glass.

Japanese Cocktail

1¹/₂ ounces brandy
¹/₂ ounce orgeat syrup
Dash of Angostura bitters

Pour all of the ingredients into a shaker two-thirds full of ice cubes. Shake well. Strain into a chilled Cocktail glass.

JDSB Strawberry Mint Martini

Adapted from a recipe by Cindy Crockett, Bourbon Street Café, Louisville, Kentucky.

6 fresh mint leaves
2 ounces Jack Daniel's Single Barrel Tennessee whiskey
1 ounce strawberry liqueur
Thin strawberry slice and a mint sprig, for garnishes

Press the mint leaves into the bottom and sides of a chilled Cocktail glass to release the oils. Discard the leaves. Pour the whiskey and liqueur into a mixing glass two-thirds full of ice cubes. Stir well. Strain into the glass. Add the strawberry slice and mint sprig.

Jell-O Shots

1 package Jell-O, flavor of choice
8 ounces boiling water
8 ounces vodka

Dissolve the Jell-O in the boiling water; stir very well. Add the vodka and stir well. Pour the mixture into a shallow pan, ice-cube trays, tiny disposable cups, or whatever you choose. Chill until set.

Jerez Manhattan

Adapted from a recipe by Tim Wilson, beverage director for Wolfgang Puck Fine Dining Group, Las Vegas, Nevada.

2 ounces Maker's Mark bourbon
1 ounce Lustau Pedro Ximénez sherry
Thin fig slice, for garnish

Pour both ingredients into a shaker two-thirds full of ice cubes. Shake well. Strain into a chilled Cocktail glass. Add the fig slice.

Jockey Club Cocktail

Adapted from a formula set down in the 1920s by Harry McElhone of Harry's New York Bar, Paris.

> **1¹/₂ ounces gin**
> **¹/₄ ounce crème de noyaux**
> **¹/₄ ounce fresh lemon juice**
> **Dash of Angostura bitters**
> **Dash of orange bitters**
> **Lemon twist, for garnish**

Pour all of the ingredients into a shaker two-thirds full of ice cubes. Shake well. Strain into a chilled Cocktail glass. Add the twist.

John Collins

I always thought this classic was made with bourbon. But, noooo, Dave Wondrich's fabulous sleuthing proved me wrong, wrong, wrong. Cheers, David!

> **2 ounces genever gin**
> **¹/₂ ounce fresh lemon juice**
> **¹/₂ ounce simple syrup (page 35)**
> **5 to 6 ounces club soda**
> **Fresh fruit in season (your choice), for garnish**

Pour the gin, lemon juice, and simple syrup into a shaker two-thirds full of ice cubes. Shake well. Strain into an ice-filled Collins glass. Add the club soda; stir briefly. Add the fruit.

Jolly Roger

Adapted from a recipe by Robert Hess, who created it during his "pirate phase" in 2000.

> **2 ounces dark rum**
> **1 ounce fresh orange juice**
> **¹/₄ ounce Falernum liqueur**
> **Dash of Angostura bitters**
> **Orange twist, for garnish**

Pour all of the ingredients into a shaker two-thirds full of ice cubes. Shake well. Strain into a chilled Cocktail glass. Add the twist.

Journalist Cocktail

This drink appears in a Prohibition-era British cocktail book, so it might have been named for the hard-drinking newspapermen of Fleet Street.

> **2 ounces gin**
> **1/4 ounce dry vermouth**
> **1/4 ounce sweet vermouth**
> **1/4 ounce triple sec**
> **1/4 ounce fresh lemon juice**
> **2 dashes of orange bitters**

Pour all of the ingredients into a shaker two-thirds full of ice cubes. Shake well. Strain into a chilled Cocktail glass.

Joy Division

Adapted from a recipe by Phil Ward, Death & Co., New York City, 2008.

> **2 ounces Beefeater gin**
> **1 ounce Noilly Pratt dry vermouth**
> **1/2 ounce Cointreau**
> **4 dashes of absinthe**

Stir over ice and strain into a chilled glass slipper. No garnish.

Julia's Cup

Adapted from a recipe created at Hemingway's Restaurant, Killington, Vermont, and dedicated to Julia Child on the occasion of her death in 2004.

> **1 ounce cognac**
> **1/4 ounce green Chartreuse**
> **1 teaspoon simple syrup (page 35)**
> **1 teaspoon fresh lemon juice**
> **Champagne**

Pour the cognac, Chartreuse, simple syrup, and lemon juice into a shaker two-thirds full of ice cubes. Shake well. Strain into a chilled Cocktail glass. Top with the champagne.

Junior Mint

Just the drink for watching DVDs.

> 1¹/₂ ounces white crème de cacao
> 1¹/₂ ounces white crème de menthe
> ¹/₂ ounce Malibu rum
> 1 Junior Mint candy, for garnish

Pour all of the ingredients into an ice-filled Rocks glass; stir briefly. Pierce the Junior Mint with a sip-stick and add it to the drink.

Kahlúa & Cream

> 2 ounces Kahlúa
> 1 ounce heavy cream

Pour both ingredients into an ice-filled Rocks glass. Stir, if desired.

Kamikaze

This drink started out as a shooter but has turned more respectable; it's now a sipping cocktail.

> 2 ounces vodka
> ¹/₂ ounce triple sec
> ¹/₄ ounce fresh lime juice

Pour all of the ingredients into a shaker two-thirds full of ice cubes. Shake well. Strain into a chilled Cocktail glass.

Kentucky Black Hawk

> 2¹/₂ ounces bourbon
> ¹/₄ ounce sloe gin
> ¹/₂ ounce fresh lemon juice
> ¹/₂ ounce simple syrup (page 35)

Pour all of the ingredients into a shaker two-thirds full of ice cubes. Shake well. Strain into a chilled Cocktail glass.

Kentucky Champagne Cocktail

1 sugar cube

2 to 3 dashes of Peychaud's bitters

1 ounce bourbon

5 ounces champagne or other sparkling wine

Lemon twist, for garnish

Drop the sugar cube into the bottom of a Champagne flute; add the bitters and bourbon. Carefully pour in the champagne. Add the twist.

Kentucky Colonel

Notable Kentucky colonels include Lyndon B. Johnson; Winston Churchill; America's first man to orbit the earth, John Glenn; and Mardee Haidin Regan (honest), who's still orbiting in her own way.

2¹/₂ ounces bourbon

¹/₂ ounce Bénédictine

Lemon twist, for garnish

Pour both ingredients into a mixing glass two-thirds full of ice cubes. Stir well. Strain into a chilled Cocktail glass. Add the twist.

Kentucky Distillery Punch

This punch packs a wallop—feel free to dilute it with more club soda or some ginger ale.

MAKES ABOUT TWENTY-FOUR 6-OUNCE SERVINGS

1 750-ml bottle bourbon

1 750-ml bottle dark rum

1 750-ml bottle brandy

6 ounces simple syrup (page 35)

1 cup fresh lemon juice

2 ounces grenadine

1 large block of ice

16 ounces ginger ale

Pour the bourbon, rum, brandy, simple syrup, lemon juice, and grenadine into a nonreactive large pan or bowl; stir well. Cover and refrigerate until chilled, at least 4 hours.

Place the ice in the center of a large punch bowl; add the punch. Pour in the ginger ale.

DRINKS A TO Z

Kentucky Longshot

Created by the late Bartender Emeritus Max Allen, Jr., of Louisville's Seelbach Hotel as the signature drink for the 1998 Breeder's Cup race.

> 1^1/$_2$ ounces bourbon
>
> ^{1}/$_2$ ounce Domaine de Canton ginger liqueur
>
> ^{1}/$_2$ ounce peach brandy
>
> 1 dash each of Peychaud's bitters and Angostura bitters
>
> 3 strips candied ginger, for garnish

Pour all of the ingredients into a mixing glass two-thirds full of ice cubes. Stir well. Strain into a chilled Cocktail glass. Add the candied ginger.

The Kentucky Mojito

Adapted from a recipe by Mark Czechowski, mixologist at Manhattan's Noche restaurant.

> 2 ounces Maker's Mark bourbon
>
> ^{1}/$_2$ ounce Rainwater Madeira
>
> 4 to 6 fresh mint leaves
>
> 3^1/$_2$ ounces lemon-lime soda
>
> ^{1}/$_2$ ounce club soda
>
> 2 to 3 mint sprigs, for garnish

Muddle the bourbon, Madeira, and mint leaves in an empty mixing glass until the mint leaves break into flecks. Pour into an ice-filled Collins glass. Add the lemon-lime soda and the club soda. Stir briefly. Add the mint sprigs.

Kentucky's Best Manhattan

Loosely adapted from a recipe from the Bull's Head Inn, Campbell Hall, New York, by Jeff Traphagen, Charles Bennedetti, and Fred Whittle. Winner of Knob Creek's Manhattan competition, New York City, 1998.

> 2 ounces Knob Creek bourbon
>
> ^{1}/$_4$ ounce maraschino cherry juice
>
> 3 dashes of ruby port

3 dashes of Martini & Rossi sweet vermouth

2 dashes of crème de cassis

Dash of Angostura bitters

Maraschino cherry, for garnish

Pour all of the ingredients into a mixing glass two-thirds full of ice cubes. Stir well. Strain into a chilled Cocktail glass. Add the cherry.

Keoki Coffee

1 ounce brandy

1 ounce Kahlúa

4 ounces hot coffee

Dollop of whipped cream

Pour the brandy, Kahlúa, and coffee into an Irish Coffee glass; stir briefly. Float the whipped cream on top.

The Kew Club

Adapted from a recipe by Pete Kendall, head bartender at London's Milk & Honey club.

2 orange twists

2 ounces Compass Box Orangerie scotch

Splash of Grand Marnier

Splash of Bénédictine

3 dashes of Angostura bitters

Lemon twist, for garnish

Twist 1 of the orange twists into an empty Old-Fashioned glass; discard the twist. Add ice cubes, the scotch, Grand Marnier, Bénédictine, and bitters, and stir briefly. Carefully flame the remaining orange twist on top. Repeat with the lemon twist.

Key Lime Pie

Adapted from a recipe from Dylan Prime, New York City.

1 tablespoon whipped cream
1 tablespoon graham cracker crumbs
1/2 ounce Quarenta y Tres Licor 43
1 ounce heavy cream
2 ounces Malibu rum
1 ounce triple sec
1 ounce fresh lime juice

Rim a chilled Cocktail glass with the whipped cream and the cracker crumbs. Pour the Licor 43 and the heavy cream into a shaker two-thirds full of ice cubes. Shake well; reserve. In another ice-filled shaker, combine the rum, triple sec, and lime juice. Strain this mixture into the prepared glass, leaving about 1/2 inch of space at the top of the glass. Carefully float the reserved liqueur–heavy cream mixture on top.

KGB

A top-secret recipe.

1 1/2 ounces gin
1/2 ounce Kirschwasser
1/4 ounce apricot brandy
1/2 ounce fresh lemon juice
1/2 ounce simple syrup (page 35)
Lemon twist, for garnish

Pour all of the ingredients into a shaker two-thirds full of ice cubes. Shake well. Strain into a chilled Cocktail glass. Add the twist.

The Kildalton Cross

Created by Gary Regan, circa 2000.

2 ounces Martini & Rossi sweet vermouth
1/2 ounce Ardbeg 10-year-old single-malt scotch
Pernod, to taste (2 or 3 drops should do it)
Lemon twist, for garnish

Pour all of the ingredients into a mixing glass two-thirds full of ice cubes. Stir well. Strain into a chilled Cocktail glass. Add the twist.

King Alphonse

Possibly named for the thirteenth-century Spanish king who conquered the city of Jerez in 1264 and owned vineyards in that area.

2 ounces Kahlúa
Large dollop of whipped cream

Pour the Kahlúa into an ice-filled Rocks glass. Spoon the whipped cream onto the drink so that it floats on top.

Kir

Named for Canon Felix Kir, Mayor of Dijon, in the Burgundy region of France, from 1945 to 1965. Burgundy produces wonderful black currants, and this is where crème de cassis originated.

5 ounces chilled dry white wine
$1/4$ ounce crème de cassis
Lemon twist, for garnish

Pour both ingredients into a wine glass; stir briefly. Add the twist.

Kir Martini

$2^1/2$ ounces gin
$1/2$ ounce dry vermouth
$1/4$ ounce crème de cassis

Pour all of the ingredients into a mixing glass two-thirds full of ice cubes. Stir well. Strain into a chilled Cocktail glass.

Kir Royale

5 ounces chilled champagne or other sparkling wine
$1/4$ ounce crème de cassis
Lemon twist, for garnish

Pour both ingredients into a Champagne flute; stir briefly. Add the twist.

The Knack

The Knack, created by Thomas Waugh, won first prize at the U.S. Bartenders' Guild 2006 competition in San Francisco, at which time Waugh was working at Harry Denton's Starlight Room.

> **1³/₄ ounces cognac**
> **¹/₂ ounce Bénédictine**
> **¹/₄ ounce Mandarine Napoléon liqueur**
> **¹/₄ ounce fresh lemon juice**
> **Dash of Regans' Orange Bitters No. 6**

Pour all of the ingredients into a shaker two-thirds full of ice cubes. Shake well. Strain into a chilled Cocktail glass.

Knickerbocker Cocktail

A great Martini variation from the 1930s.

> **2 ounces gin**
> **¹/₂ ounce dry vermouth**
> **¹/₄ ounce sweet vermouth**
> **Lemon twist, for garnish**

Pour all of the ingredients into a mixing glass two-thirds full of ice cubes. Stir well. Strain into a chilled Cocktail glass. Add the twist.

Knockout Cocktail

The dash of crème de menthe is the "knockout" drop in this cocktail. Use just a drop if you find that it dominates the drink too much.

> **1 ounce gin**
> **1 ounce dry vermouth**
> **¹/₄ ounce absinthe**
> **Dash of white crème de menthe**

Pour all of the ingredients into a mixing glass two-thirds full of ice cubes. Stir well. Strain into a chilled Cocktail glass.

Kretchma

2 ounces vodka

1 ounce white crème de cacao

³/₄ ounce fresh lemon juice

¹/₄ ounce grenadine

Pour all of the ingredients into a shaker two-thirds full of ice cubes. Shake well. Strain into a chilled Cocktail glass.

Kumquat Caipiroshka

Created by David Nepove, Enrico's, San Francisco, circa 2004.

5 kumquats, roughly chopped

2 teaspoons granulated sugar

2 ounces Skyy Citrus vodka

Muddle the kumquats, sugar, and 4 or 5 small ice cubes in an empty shaker, continuing until the fruit is entirely pulverized. Fill the shaker two-thirds full of ice cubes; add the vodka. Shake well. Pour (do not strain) into a Double Old-Fashioned glass.

La Cola Nostra

Created by Don Lee, PDT, New York City, 2008. Joint winner of the Northeast Averna Cocktail Competition.

1¹/₂ ounces Ron Zacapa 23-year-old rum

1 ounce Averna amaro

³/₄ ounce fresh lime juice

¹/₂ ounce simple syrup (page 35)

¹/₄ ounce St. Elizabeth Allspice Dram

2 ounces Moët & Chandon White Star champagne

Pour the rum, Averna, lime juice, simple syrup, and allspice into a shaker two-thirds full of ice cubes. Shake well. Strain into an ice-filled Collins glass. Top with the champagne.

La Grand Feu

Adapted from a recipe by Tony Venci, La Femme Bar, MGM Grand Hotel, Las Vegas.

1¹/₂ ounces Hennessey cognac
1¹/₂ ounces Navan liqueur
³/₄ ounce Baileys Irish cream liqueur
³/₄ ounce chai tea
Fresh mint sprig, for garnish

Pour all of the ingredients into a shaker two-thirds full of ice cubes. Shake well. Strain into a chilled Cocktail glass. Add the mint sprig.

La Perla

Created by Jacques Bezuidenhout, bar manager at Tres Agaves, San Francisco.

1¹/₄ ounces manzanilla sherry
1¹/₂ ounces Centenario reposado tequila
1 ounce Mathilde Liqueur de Poires

Pour all of the ingredients into a mixing glass two-thirds full of ice cubes. Stir well. Strain into a chilled Cocktail glass.

Lager & Lime

1 to 2 ounces lime juice cordial, such as Rose's
12 ounces chilled lager

Pour both ingredients into a 16-ounce beer glass.

Lark Creek Inn Tequila Infusion

Absolutely fabulous—and totally addictive—this *must be* tried. Created by Bradley Ogden, Lark Creek Inn, Larkspur, California, 1995.

1 serrano chile
1 pineapple, peeled and cut into 1-inch chunks
1 tarragon sprig
1 750-ml bottle reposado tequila

Cut the top and tail from the chile and discard them. Slice the chile lengthwise down the center; discard the seeds. Place the

chile in a large glass container; add the pineapple chunks and the tarragon. Pour in the tequila, cover, and set aside in a cool, dark place to rest for 48 to 60 hours.

Strain the mixture through a sieve lined with a double layer of dampened cheesecloth; discard the solids. Return the tequila to the bottle and chill it in the refrigerator or freezer for at least 12 hours. Serve neat, in a Margarita, or however you want.

The Last Word

3/4 ounce dry gin

3/4 ounce maraschino liqueur

3/4 ounce green Chartreuse

3/4 ounce fresh lime juice

Pour all of the ingredients into a shaker two-thirds full of ice cubes. Shake well. Strain into a chilled Cocktail glass.

Latin Love

Adapted from a recipe from the Naked Fish restaurant, Boston.

Grenadine and coconut shavings, for rimming the glass

1 1/2 ounces Cruzan Coconut rum

1 1/2 ounces Cruzan Banana rum

3 ounces pineapple juice

1 1/2 ounces cream of coconut

1 1/2 ounces raspberry purée

Prepare a Hurricane glass. Pour the rums, juice, cream of coconut, and purée into a blender and add 1 cup of ice cubes. Blend until smooth. Pour into the prepared glass.

Le Grande Cocktail

1/2 ounce B&B

2 ounces Bacardi 8 rum

3/4 ounce Cointreau

1 ounce fresh orange juice

2 dashes of Angostura bitters

Rinse a chilled Cocktail glass with the B&B. Combine the remaining ingredients in a cocktail shaker two-thirds full of ice cubes. Shake well. Strain into the prepared glass.

Leap Year

Created on February 29, 1928, at London's Savoy Hotel.

2 ounces gin

1/2 ounce sweet vermouth

1/2 ounce Grand Marnier

1/4 ounce fresh lemon juice

Lemon twist, for garnish

Pour all of the ingredients into a shaker two-thirds full of ice cubes. Shake well. Strain into a chilled Cocktail glass. Add the twist.

Leatherneck Cocktail

Adapted from a recipe in Vintage Spirits and Forgotten Cocktails *by Ted Haigh.*

2 ounces blended whiskey

3/4 ounce blue curaçao

1/2 ounce fresh lime juice

Lime wheel, for garnish

Pour all of the ingredients into a shaker two-thirds full of ice cubes. Shake well. Strain into a chilled Cocktail glass. Add the lime wheel.

Leg Spreader

1 1/2 ounces Midori melon liqueur

1 1/2 ounces coconut rum

6 to 8 ounces pineapple juice

2 splashes of lemon-lime soda

Pour the Midori, rum, and pineapple juice into a shaker two-thirds full of ice cubes. Shake well. Strain into an ice-filled Hurricane glass. Top with the soda.

Lemon Drop

As guests of a Christmas Day celebration at my house will tell you, this is a great drink served straight up or on the rocks. Don't drink it as a shooter unless you want to fall asleep before Christmas dinner is served.

Superfine sugar and a lemon wedge, for rimming the glass

2 ounces citrus vodka

$1/2$ ounce triple sec

$1/2$ ounce fresh lemon juice

Prepare a chilled Cocktail glass. Pour all of the remaining ingredients into a shaker two-thirds full of ice cubes. Shake well. Strain into the prepared glass.

Lemon Kiss Cocktail

$1^1/2$ ounces limoncello

$1^1/2$ ounces vodka

Lemon twist, for garnish

Pour both ingredients into a mixing glass two-thirds full of ice cubes. Stir well. Strain into a chilled Cocktail glass. Add the twist.

Lemon-Top

12 ounces amber ale

2 ounces lemon-lime soda

Pour the ale into a beer glass and top with the soda.

Lemon Wedge Highball

$1^1/2$ ounces gin

1 ounce limoncello

4 ounces tonic water

Build in an ice-filled Highball glass. Stir with a sip-stick.

Lemon Wedge Martini

$1^1/2$ ounces limoncello

$1^1/2$ ounces gin

Lemon twist, as garnish

Pour both ingredients into a mixing glass two-thirds full of ice cubes. Stir well. Strain into a chilled Cocktail glass. Add the twist.

The Lewis & Martin Cocktail

Adapted from a recipe by Ted Haigh, "Dr. Cocktail," Los Angeles.

2 ounces bourbon
1 ounce Lillet Blanc
3/4 ounce crème de banane
2 dashes of Peychaud's bitters
Lemon twist, for garnish

Pour all of the ingredients into a shaker two-thirds full of ice cubes. Shake well. Strain into a chilled Cocktail glass. Add the twist.

The Libation Goddess

Created by Gary Regan and me in 2002.

2 ounces gin
3/4 ounce white crème de cacao
1/2 ounce cranberry juice
Lime wedge, for garnish

Pour all of the ingredients into a mixing glass two-thirds full of ice cubes. Stir well. Strain into a chilled Cocktail glass. Add the lime wedge.

The Librarian

Adapted from a recipe by Ethan Kelley, spirit sommelier at Brandy Library, New York City.

2 1/2 ounces cognac
1 ounce late-bottled vintage ruby port
1/2 ounce Chambord raspberry liqueur
Orange twist and a raspberry, for garnishes

Pour all of the ingredients into a shaker two-thirds full of ice cubes. Shake well. Strain into a chilled Cocktail glass. Add the twist and raspberry.

Licorice Martini

2 ounces Kahlúa

¹/₂ ounce sambuca

Pour both ingredients into a mixing glass two-thirds full of ice cubes. Stir well. Strain into a chilled Cocktail glass.

Liquid Cocaine #1

Liquid Cocaine is fun to order just because of the reaction you get from some bartenders and waitpeople.

1 ounce Southern Comfort

1 ounce dark rum

1 ounce amaretto

1 ounce pineapple juice

Dash of grenadine

Pour all of the ingredients into a shaker two-thirds full of ice cubes. Shake well. Strain into a chilled Cocktail glass.

Liquid Heroin

Another "drug drink."

2 ounces Jägermeister

¹/₂ ounce peppermint schnapps

Pour both ingredients into a mixing glass two-thirds full of ice cubes. Stir well. Strain into a chilled Cocktail glass.

Liquid Joy

Created by Ryan Damm at Harvard University, circa 2000.

This does not taste like dishwashing detergent, I promise.

2 ounces light rum

3 ounces pineapple juice

3 ounces ginger ale

Build in an ice-filled Highball glass. Stir with a sip-stick.

Lola Martini

Adapted from a recipe by Alex Freuman and Kurt Eckert, Jean Georges restaurant, New York City.

2 ounces OP vodka
1/2 ounce Cointreau
1/2 ounce fresh lime juice
1/2 ounce elderflower syrup
Splash of cranberry juice
Thin strawberry slice, for garnish

Pour all of the ingredients into a shaker two-thirds full of ice cubes. Shake well. Strain into a chilled Cocktail glass. Add the strawberry slice.

Londoner #1

Adapted from a recipe by Philip Ward, Pegu Club, New York City.

2 ounces Plymouth gin
1/2 ounce sweet vermouth
1/2 ounce Grand Marnier
2 to 3 dashes of orange bitters
Orange twist, as garnish

Pour all of the ingredients into a mixing glass two-thirds full of ice cubes. Stir well. Strain into a chilled Cocktail glass. Carefully flame the twist over the glass.

Londoner #2

Adapted from a recipe by Joe Wood, CocktailStars, England.

2 lime wedges
2 ounces Broker's gin
1/2 ounce crème de mûre
1 ounce pink grapefruit juice
1/4 ounce fresh lime juice

Pour all of the ingredients into a shaker two-thirds full of ice cubes. Shake well. Strain into a chilled Cocktail glass.

Long Beach Iced Tea

$1/2$ ounce vodka

$1/2$ ounce gin

$1/2$ ounce light rum

$1/2$ ounce tequila

$1/2$ ounce triple sec

$1/2$ ounce fresh lemon juice

$1^1/2$ ounces cranberry juice

Lemon wedge, for garnish

Pour all of the ingredients into a shaker two-thirds full of ice cubes. Shake well. Strain into an ice-filled Highball glass. Add the lemon wedge.

Long Island Iced Tea

$1/2$ ounce vodka

$1/2$ ounce gin

$1/2$ ounce light rum

$1/2$ ounce tequila

$1/2$ ounce triple sec

$1/2$ ounce fresh lemon juice

Cola

Lemon wedge, for garnish

Pour the vodka, gin, rum, tequila, triple sec, and lemon juice into a shaker two-thirds full of ice cubes. Shake well. Strain into an ice-filled Collins glass. Top with the cola. Add the lemon wedge.

Louisville Cocktail

This is a variation on the Manhattan, with a touch of Bénédictine —feel free to increase or decrease the liqueur to suit your taste. It's just the drink for Derby Day when you've tired of Mint Juleps.

2 ounces bourbon

$1/2$ ounce sweet vermouth

$1/2$ ounce Bénédictine

Pour all of the ingredients into a mixing glass two-thirds full of ice cubes. Stir well. Strain into a chilled Cocktail glass.

DRINKS A TO Z

Love Jones

Adapted from a recipe by Ted Kilgore, bar manager at Monarch, Maplewood, Missouri.

2 ounces Captain Morgan spiced rum

$1/2$ ounce Damiana liqueur

1 ounce passion fruit juice

$1/4$ ounce grenadine

Strawberry and a kiwi slice, for garnishes

Pour all of the ingredients into a shaker two-thirds full of ice cubes. Shake well. Strain into a chilled Cocktail glass. Add the strawberry and kiwi.

Love Potion

1 ounce orange vodka

$1/2$ ounce Chambord raspberry liqueur

$1/2$ ounce cranberry juice

Pour all of the ingredients into a mixing glass two-thirds full of ice cubes. Stir well. Strain into a chilled Pony glass.

Lutteur Horse's Neck

Adapted from a recipe created by Colin Peter Field, head barman at The Ritz, Paris.

2 ounces Hennessy cognac

4 ounces ginger ale

2 to 4 dashes of Angostura bitters

Orange peel spiral, for garnish

Pour all of the ingredients into an ice-filled Collins glass. Stir briefly; add the orange peel spiral.

Lychee & Lemongrass Fizz

Adapted from a recipe by Julie Reiner, co-owner of the Flatiron Lounge, New York City.

2 lychees

2 ounces Tanqueray gin

1 ounce lychee juice

$^3/_4$ ounce Belvoir Lime and Lemongrass cordial

$^1/_2$ ounce fresh lime juice

Club soda

Lime wheel and a lemongrass stalk, for garnishes

Muddle the lychees in the bottom of an empty shaker. Add ice cubes, the gin, lychee juice, cordial, and lime juice. Shake well. Strain into an ice-filled Collins glass. Top with club soda. Add the lime wheel and lemongrass stalk.

Lynchburg Lemonade

Lynchburg, Tennessee, where Jack Daniel's is made, is a dry town. Whiskey, whiskey everywhere—but not a drop to drink.

$1^1/_2$ ounces Jack Daniel's Tennessee whiskey

$1^1/_2$ ounces triple sec

1 ounce fresh lemon juice

$^1/_2$ ounce simple syrup (page 35)

4 ounces lemon-lime soda

Pour all of the ingredients into an ice-filled 16-ounce Mason jar. Stir to blend.

Mad Dog Cocktail

Created by Gary Regan, circa 2005.

2 ounces Laphroaig single-malt scotch

1 ounce Galliano

2 dashes of Ricard

$^1/_2$ ounce fresh lemon juice

Lemon twist, for garnish

Pour all of the ingredients into a shaker two-thirds full of ice cubes. Shake well. Strain into a chilled Cocktail glass. Add the twist.

Madam Geneva

Adapted from a recipe by Bob Brunner, Paragon restaurant and bar, Portland, Oregon.

> **1 ounce Pimm's No. 1 Cup**
>
> **1 ounce gin**
>
> **6 ounces San Pellegrino Aranciata soda**
>
> **3 cucumber slices, for garnish**

Pour all of the ingredients into a 16-ounce ice-filled glass; stir briefly. Float the cucumber slices on top.

Madame Wu

Adapted from a recipe by "Curly" Haslam-Coates, bar manager, Trio, Leeds, England.

> **1¹/₂ ounces Don Eduardo reposado tequila**
>
> **¹/₂ ounce Martini & Rossi sweet vermouth**
>
> **Dash of dark crème de cacao**
>
> **2 dashes of Peychaud's bitters**

Pour all of the ingredients into a mixing glass two-thirds full of ice cubes. Stir well. Strain into a chilled Cocktail glass.

Madras

> **2 ounces vodka**
>
> **2 ounces orange juice**
>
> **1¹/₂ ounces cranberry juice**

Build in an ice-filled Highball glass; stir briefly.

Madroño (Strawberry Bush) Cobbler

Created by Giuseppe Gonzalez, Flatiron Lounge, New York City; winner of the 2007 Vinos de Jerez Cocktail Competition.

> **1 strawberry**
>
> **¹/₂ ounce Torani Amer liqueur**
>
> **3 ounces Williams & Humbert Dry Sack Medium amontillado sherry**
>
> **2 barspoons of rich Demerara sugar syrup**
>
> **1 cinnamon stick (3 inches long), broken in half**
>
> **Fan-cut strawberry and a cinnamon stick, for garnishes**

Lightly muddle the strawberry and the Torani Amer in an empty shaker. Add the sherry, sugar syrup, cinnamon stick, and a little crushed ice. Shake lightly. Strain into a wine goblet. Top with more crushed ice. Add the cut strawberry and cinnamon stick.

Mae West Royal Diamond Fizz

Adapted from a recipe by LeNell Smothers, circa 2007.

Hot sugar (recipe follows) and a grapefruit segment, for rimming the glass

2 ounces goji-infused bourbon (recipe follows)

$1/2$ ounce PAMA pomegranate liqueur

1 ounce fresh grapefruit juice

1 egg

Brut champagne

2 macerated goji berries, for garnish

Prepare a Champagne Saucer glass, rimming it only halfway around. Pour the bourbon, liqueur, grapefruit juice, and egg into an empty shaker. Shake well to emulsify the egg. Add ice cubes and shake very well again. Strain into the prepared glasses. Top with the champagne to make a foamy head right to the rim of the glass. Garnish with 2 reserved goji berries, spearing them on a toothpick at the side of the glass.

HOT SUGAR

Combine 4 tablespoons granulated sugar, $1/4$ teaspoon cayenne pepper, and a pinch of unsweetened cocoa powder.

GOJI-INFUSED BOURBON

Macerate 4 ounces of dried goji berries in 1 750-ml bottle of Four Roses Single Barrel 100-proof bourbon. Let sit overnight, at least. Strain through a gold coffee filter or a double layer of dampened cheesecloth. Reserve some of the macerated goji berries for drink garnishes.

Magic Carp

Created by Gary Regan, 2005.

2¹/₂ ounces Johnnie Walker Green Label blended scotch
³/₄ ounce Compass Box Orangerie scotch
¹/₂ ounce fresh lemon juice
Maraschino cherry, for garnish

Pour all of the ingredients into a shaker two-thirds full of ice cubes. Shake well. Strain into an ice-filled wine goblet. Add the cherry.

Mahogany

Adapted from a recipe by Robert Hess, 2003.

Instead of the cinnamon schnapps, Robert uses a cinnamon tincture that he makes by soaking 4 cinnamon sticks in 1 cup of vodka for about a week.

¹/₂ ounce cinnamon schnapps (optional)
1¹/₂ ounces dry vermouth
³/₄ ounce Jägermeister
³/₄ ounce Bénédictine

If desired, coat the interior of a chilled Cocktail glass with the cinnamon schnapps; discard any excess. Pour the remaining ingredients into a mixing glass two-thirds full of ice cubes. Stir well. Strain into the prepared glass.

Maiden's Blush Cocktail

Adapted from Harry Craddock's 1930 recipe in the *Savoy Cocktail Book*, this gin-based New Orleans Sour calls for grenadine for color and to soften the spirit a bit—a good lesson when creating gin-based cocktails.

2 ounces gin
³/₄ ounce Cointreau
¹/₂ ounce fresh lemon juice
Grenadine, to taste

Pour all of the ingredients into a shaker two-thirds full of ice cubes. Shake well. Strain into a chilled Cocktail glass.

Maiden's Prayer

1 ounce gin

1 ounce triple sec

$^1/_2$ ounce fresh lemon juice

$^1/_2$ ounce orange juice

Pour all of the ingredients into a shaker two-thirds full of ice cubes. Shake well. Strain into a chilled Cocktail glass.

Mai Tai

Vic Bergeron, better known to most people as Trader Vic, created the Mai Tai in the 1940s. Bergeron wrote that after he first made the drink, he "gave two of them to Ham and Carrie Guild, friends from Tahiti, who were there that night. Carrie took one sip and said, '*Mai Tai—Roa Ae.*' In Tahitian this means 'Out of This World— The Best.' Well, that was that. I named the drink 'Mai Tai.'"

$1^1/_2$ ounces dark rum

1 ounce light rum

1 ounce triple sec

$^1/_2$ ounce apricot brandy

1 ounce fresh lime juice

1 ounce simple syrup (page 35)

Dash of orgeat syrup

Pour all of the ingredients into a shaker two-thirds full of ice cubes. Shake well. Strain into a large, ice-filled wine goblet.

Mai Tai Royal

Adapted from a recipe by Dale DeGroff, director of cocktail arts at the Halekulani Hotel, Honolulu, Hawaii.

$^3/_4$ ounce añejo rum

$^1/_2$ ounce white curaçao

$^1/_2$ ounce orgeat syrup

$^1/_4$ ounce fresh lime juice

3 ounces chilled champagne

Lime wedge, for garnish

Pour all of the ingredients into an ice-filled mixing glass and stir gently to avoid losing bubbles from the champagne. Strain into a chilled Champagne flute. Add the lime wedge.

Malibu Bay Breeze

2 ounces Malibu rum

2 ounces cranberry juice

2 ounces pineapple juice

Pour all of the ingredients into an ice-filled Highball glass; stir briefly.

Mamere

Adapted from a recipe by Kieran Walsh, bar manager at Solstice Lounge, San Francisco, 2006.

3 kumquats, halved

1/3 ounce simple syrup (page 35)

2 dashes of Peychaud's bitters

2 dashes of orange bitters

1 3/4 ounces Bulleit bourbon

1/3 ounce Qi White liqueur

Kumquat, for garnish

Muddle the halved kumquats, simple syrup, and both bitters in an empty mixing glass. Add ice cubes, the bourbon, and the liqueur; stir very well. Strain into an ice-filled Old-Fashioned glass. Add the kumquat.

Mamie Taylor

What you'd get if Mamie Eisenhower married Zachary Taylor. In fact, Margaret Taylor, Zachary's wife, was nicknamed "Mamie."

2 ounces scotch

5 ounces ginger ale

1 ounce fresh lemon juice

Build in a Highball glass three-quarters full of crushed ice. Stir briefly.

Mandarine Colada

Adapted from a recipe developed at Veranda Bar and Lounge at Elbow Beach, Bermuda.

³/₄ ounce dark rum

1 ounce Amarula Cream liqueur

1 ounce pineapple juice

1 ounce cream of coconut

2 ounces mango nectar

Maraschino cherry, for garnish

Reserve ¹/₄ ounce of the dark rum. Pour the remaining rum, the liqueur, juice, cream of coconut, and nectar into a blender along with 1 to 2 cups of ice. Blend until smooth. Pour into a Hurricane glass. Float the reserved rum on top; add the cherry.

Mandrintini #1

Created by Peter George, Trotters, Port of Spain, Trinidad.

2¹/₂ ounces Absolut Mandrin vodka

³/₄ ounce orange juice

³/₄ ounce cranberry juice

Pour all of the ingredients into a shaker two-thirds full of ice cubes. Shake well. Strain into a chilled Cocktail glass.

Mandrintini #2

2¹/₂ ounces Absolut Mandrin vodka

³/₄ ounce orange juice

³/₄ ounce Cointreau

Pour all of the ingredients into a shaker two-thirds full of ice cubes. Shake well. Strain into a chilled Cocktail glass.

Manhattan

Created in the late 1800s, the Manhattan was one of the first popular drinks to use vermouth. It has spawned many children, the Rob Roy, to me, the most memorable among them.

2^1/$_2$ ounces straight rye, bourbon, or blended whiskey
^{3}/$_4$ ounce sweet vermouth
2 dashes of Angostura bitters
Maraschino cherry, for garnish

Pour all of the ingredients into a mixing glass two-thirds full of ice cubes. Stir well. Strain into a chilled Cocktail glass. Add the cherry.

Manhattan, Dry

2^1/$_2$ ounces straight rye, bourbon, or blended whiskey
^{3}/$_4$ ounce dry vermouth
2 dashes of Angostura bitters
Lemon twist, for garnish

Pour all of the ingredients into a mixing glass two-thirds full of ice cubes. Stir well. Strain into a chilled Cocktail glass. Add the twist.

Manhattan, Perfect

2^1/$_2$ ounces straight rye, bourbon, or blended whiskey
^{1}/$_2$ ounce sweet vermouth
^{1}/$_2$ ounce dry vermouth
2 dashes of Angostura bitters
Maraschino cherry and a lemon twist, for garnish

Pour all of the ingredients into a mixing glass two-thirds full of ice cubes. Stir well. Strain into a chilled Cocktail glass. Add the cherry and the twist.

Manhattan Perfecto

Adapted from a recipe by bartender and manager Ted Kilgore, Agrario, Springfield, Missouri.

¹/₂ ounce Luxardo maraschino liqueur

2 ounces straight rye whiskey

³/₄ ounce Noilly Prat dry vermouth

³/₄ ounce Noilly Prat sweet vermouth

4 dashes of Angostura bitters

Lemon twist and a maraschino cherry, for garnishes

Rinse a chilled Cocktail glass with the maraschino liqueur; discard the excess. Pour the whiskey, both vermouths, and the bitters into a mixing glass two-thirds full of ice cubes. Stir well. Strain into the glass. Add the twist and the cherry.

Mansion Martini

From the Mansion on Turtle Creek, Dallas, Texas.

Splash of tequila

3 ounces Bombay Sapphire gin or Stolichnaya Cristall vodka

2 jalapeño-stuffed olives, for garnish

Rinse a chilled Cocktail glass with the tequila; pour out any excess. Pour the gin or vodka into a mixing glass two-thirds full of ice cubes. Stir well. Strain into the glass. Add the olives.

The Maravel Sling

Created by Gary Regan in 2001 for Trotters, Port of Spain, Trinidad.

2 ounces gin

¹/₄ ounce Bénédictine

¹/₄ ounce mango nectar

¹/₂ ounce fresh lemon juice

Tamarind juice, to taste

Angostura bitters, to taste

Club soda

Pineapple cube and a maraschino cherry, for garnishes

Pour the gin, Bénédictine, lemon juice, mango nectar, tamarind juice, and bitters into a shaker two-thirds full of ice cubes. Shake well. Strain into an ice-filled Collins glass. Top with the club soda. Add the pineapple and cherry.

Mardeeni

A delicious drink, if I do say so myself.

> **Granulated sugar and 1 teaspoon finely grated orange zest, for rimming the glass**
>
> **3 ounces orange vodka**
>
> **Splash of Lillet Blanc**
>
> **Orange twist, for garnish**

Stir the sugar and the orange zest together and use it to rim a chilled Cocktail glass. Pour the vodka and Lillet into a mixing glass two-thirds full of ice. Stir well. Strain into the glass. Add the twist.

Margarita

Margarita Sames, a socialite from San Antonio, Texas, claims to have created this drink in the 1940s, when she threw extravagant parties at her ranch. It's said that she first made the drink for Nicky Hilton of the hotel Hiltons, and her husband not only named the drink for her, but also had a set of glasses made that were etched with her name.

> **Kosher salt and a lime wedge, for rimming the glass**
>
> **3 ounces white tequila**
>
> **2 ounces Cointreau or triple sec**
>
> **1 ounce fresh lime juice**

Prepare a Cocktail glass. Pour the remaining ingredients into a shaker two-thirds full of ice cubes. Shake well. Strain into the salt-rimmed glass.

Maria Sta Note

Adapted from a recipe from Joseph Bastianich, co-owner of Esca, New York City.

> **1 sugar cube**
>
> **Dash of grappa**
>
> **Dash of limoncello**
>
> **Chilled Prosecco**

Place the sugar cube into a Champagne flute and soak it with the grappa. Add the limoncello. Top with the Prosecco.

Marin-i-tini

Adapted from a recipe by Manne Hinojosa, Walnut Creek Yacht Club, Walnut Creek, California.

1¹/₂ ounces Pearl vodka
¹/₂ ounce Cointreau
¹/₂ ounce peach schnapps
¹/₂ ounce fresh lime juice
¹/₄ ounce blue curaçao
Lime twist, for garnish

Pour the vodka, Cointreau, schnapps, and lime juice into a shaker two-thirds full of ice cubes. Shake well. Strain into a chilled Cocktail glass. Gently pour the blue curaçao down the side of the glass so that it rests on the bottom. Add the twist.

The Marketa Cocktail

Created at the Prague Hilton by Gary Regan, 2007.

2 ounces dry vermouth
1 ounce grappa
1 ounce Becherovka liqueur
2 dashes of grenadine
Lemon twist, for garnish

Pour all of the ingredients into a mixing glass two-thirds full of ice cubes. Stir well. Strain into a chilled Cocktail glass. Add the twist.

Marmalade Martini

This is jammin'.

2 ounces gin
¹/₄ ounce dry vermouth
1 teaspoon orange marmalade

Pour all of the ingredients into a shaker two-thirds full of ice cubes. Shake well. Strain into a chilled Cocktail glass.

Martinez

Arguably the predecessor of the Martini, this drink dates back to the 1880s, and it's been suggested that it came about as a gin-based variation of the Manhattan.

> **2 ounces gin**
> **$1/2$ ounce sweet vermouth**
> **$1/4$ ounce maraschino liqueur**
> **$1/2$ ounce simple syrup (page 35)**

Pour all of the ingredients into a mixing glass two-thirds full of ice cubes. Stir well. Strain into a chilled Cocktail glass.

Martini

The Martini has been around for more than 100 years. It slowly evolved from a drink made with equal parts of gin and dry vermouth, with orange bitters as an additional ingredient that didn't disappear until the 1940s, to a drink that sometimes barely sees the vermouth bottle. This is a cocktail that everyone wants to be made "their" way, so be prepared to go through some strange rituals when making this one. One writer in the 1960s suggested that, by placing a lightbulb close to a bottle of dry vermouth and putting a bottle of gin on the other side, enough vermouth would be "radiated" into the gin to make the perfect dry Martini.

Make your Martini the way you like it by experimenting with gin to vermouth ratios, and when making Martinis for others, ask how they like theirs to be made. You can also try using sweet vermouth instead of dry, since that was the way the drink was first made in the late 1800s. The recipe below works if a simple "Dry Martini" is called for. Use less vermouth for an Extra-Dry Martini, and more for a Medium Martini.

> **3 ounces gin**
> **$1/2$ ounce dry vermouth**
> **Lemon twist or cocktail olive, for garnish**

Pour both ingredients into a mixing glass two-thirds full of ice cubes. Stir well. Strain into a chilled Cocktail glass. Add the garnish.

Martini Jo

Created by Chef Jean Joho, Brasserie Jo, Chicago, Illinois.

3¹/₂ ounces Skyy vodka
¹/₂ ounce Lillet Rouge
Orange twist, for garnish

Pour both ingredients into a mixing glass two-thirds full of
ice cubes. Stir well. Strain into a chilled Cocktail glass. Add
the twist.

Mary Pickford

Named for the popular silent-screen movie actress, who played in
238 films between 1908 and 1942.

2 ounces light rum
1 ounce pineapple juice
Dash of maraschino liqueur
Dash of grenadine

Pour all of the ingredients into a shaker two-thirds full of ice
cubes. Shake well. Strain into a chilled Cocktail glass.

Massa Margarita

1¹/₂ ounces Herradura Silver tequila
1¹/₂ ounces Villa Massa limoncello
¹/₂ ounce fresh lemon juice

Pour all of the ingredients into a shaker two-thirds full of ice
cubes. Shake well. Strain into a chilled Cocktail glass.

Massa Mojito

Adapted from Pizzicato Restaurant, Philadelphia.

1 ounce fresh lemon juice
$3/4$ ounce simple syrup (page 35)
15 fresh mint leaves
$2^1/2$ ounces Villa Massa limoncello
Club soda
Mint sprig, for garnish

Muddle the lemon juice, simple syrup, and mint leaves in an empty mixing glass. Add ice cubes and the limoncello. Stir well. Strain into an ice-filled Collins glass. Top with the soda. Add the mint sprig.

Maurice

Chevalier, anyone? This is a variation on the pre-Prohibition drink the Bronx Cocktail, which appeared in Europe during the 1920s.

2 ounces gin
$1/4$ ounce dry vermouth
$1/4$ ounce sweet vermouth
$1/4$ ounce absinthe
1 ounce fresh orange juice

Pour all of the ingredients into a shaker two-thirds full of ice cubes. Shake well. Strain into a chilled Cocktail glass.

Mayahuel

Adapted from a recipe by Junior Merino, cocktail consultant, The Liquid Chef, Inc., New York.

$1^1/2$ ounces Partida reposado tequila
$1/2$ ounce butterscotch schnapps
$1/4$ ounce d'Aristi Xtabentun (honey) liqueur
4 ounces hot apple cider
Cinnamon stick and a star anise pod, for garnishes

Combine all the ingredients in an Irish Coffee glass. Stir briefly. Add the cinnamon stick and star anise.

The McEwan

Adapted from a recipe by Jacques Bezuidenhuit, The Irish Bank, San Francisco.

2 ounces Bruichladdich 10-year-old single-malt scotch

$1/4$ ounce Poire William eau-de-vie

$1/2$ ounce fresh lemon juice

$1/2$ ounce clove and cinnamon simple syrup (see recipe below)

1 teaspoon raw egg white (optional)

Freshly grated nutmeg, for garnish

Pour all of the ingredients into a shaker two-thirds full of ice cubes. Shake very well. Strain into an ice-filled Old-Fashioned glass. Add the nutmeg.

CLOVE AND CINNAMON SIMPLE SYRUP

$2^{1}/2$ cups hot water

$2^{1}/2$ cups granulated sugar

2 cinnamon sticks, broken into 2-inch pieces

30 whole cloves

Combine the water and sugar in a saucepan and cook, stirring frequently, over moderate heat, until the sugar dissolves. Reduce the heat and add the cinnamon sticks and cloves. Simmer for 10 minutes. Let cool to room temperature. Bottle and refrigerate.

Melon Ball

$1^{1}/2$ ounces Midori melon liqueur

1 ounce vodka

2 ounces pineapple juice

Pour all of the ingredients into a shaker two-thirds full of ice cubes. Shake well. Strain into an ice-filled Rocks glass.

Ménage au Poire

Adapted from a recipe by Victoria Damato-Moran, bar manager, Tony Nik's, San Francisco.

1¹/₄ ounces Pitú cachaça

1 ounce Belle de Brillet liqueur

¹/₂ ounce Chinaco reposado tequila

2¹/₂ ounces Santa Cruz pear nectar

¹/₂ ounce fresh lime juice

Pinch of sea salt

Pear slice and a lime twist, for garnishes

Pour all of the ingredients into a shaker two-thirds full of ice cubes. Shake well. Strain into a chilled Cocktail glass. Add the pear slice and the twist.

Mercy, Mercy

Campari, for rinsing the glass

2 ounces Sazerac straight rye whiskey

2 dashes of Peychaud's bitters

¹/₂ ounce Martini & Rossi sweet vermouth

¹/₄ ounce Luxardo maraschino liqueur

Lemon twist, for garnish

Rinse a Champagne flute with Campari; discard any excess. Pour the remaining ingredients into a mixing glass two-thirds full of ice cubes. Stir well. Strain into the glass. Add the twist.

Merry Widow

Created at the Waldorf-Astoria to celebrate the 1907 Broadway opening of Franz Lehar's operetta of the same name. The show was so popular that unauthorized products, including a line of corsets, were named "Merry Widow" to cash in on the craze.

1¹/₂ ounces Dubonnet Rouge

1¹/₂ ounces dry vermouth

Pour both ingredients into a mixing glass two-thirds full of ice cubes. Stir well. Strain into a chilled Cocktail glass.

Metaxa Blaster

MAKES 2 SHOOTERS

2 ounces Metaxa 5-star brandy liqueur

$^1/_2$ ounce B&B

$^1/_4$ ounce fresh lemon juice

2 dashes of Angostura bitters

Pour all of the ingredients into a shaker two-thirds full of ice cubes. Shake very well. Divide between two Pony glasses.

Metropolitan

A variation on the Cosmopolitan that is oh-so-fine.

Created by Chuck Coggins at Marion's Continental Restaurant and Lounge in Manhattan's East Village.

2$^1/_2$ ounces Absolut Kurant vodka

$^1/_2$ ounce lime juice cordial, such as Rose's

$^1/_2$ ounce fresh lime juice

$^1/_2$ ounce cranberry juice

Lime wedge, for garnish

Pour all of the ingredients into a shaker two-thirds full of ice cubes. Shake well. Strain into a chilled Cocktail glass. Add the lime wedge.

Mexican Aperitivo

Adapted from a recipe by Jonny Raglin and Raul Tamayo, Absinthe, San Francisco.

MAKES 2 SHOOTERS

1 ounce green Chartreuse

$^1/_2$ ounce yellow Chartreuse

$^2/_3$ ounce fresh lemon juice

$^1/_3$ ounce fresh lime juice

Chilled champagne

$^1/_4$ ounce Campari, as a "sink"

Pour both chartreuses and both juices into a shaker two-thirds full of ice cubes. Shake very well. Strain, dividing between two tall shot glasses, leaving about $^1/_4$ inch of room at the top of each. Fill each shot to the top with the champagne. Sink a little Campari into the bottom for color. Look your friend in the eye, clink glasses, say cheers, and knock 'em back.

Mexican Coffee

1¹/₂ ounces Kahlúa

4 ounces hot coffee

Dollop of whipped cream

Pour the Kahlúa and coffee into an Irish Coffee glass; stir briefly. Spoon the whipped cream onto the coffee so that it floats on top.

The Mexican Mojito

Adapted from a recipe by Dave Singh, "Ambassador" for Gran Centenario tequila.

1¹/₂ ounces Gran Centenario Plata tequila

2 teaspoons granulated sugar

6 to 8 fresh mint leaves

Club soda

1 to 2 dashes of Angostura bitters

2 or 3 mint sprigs, for garnish

Muddle the tequila, sugar, and mint leaves in an empty mixing glass until the mint leaves break into flecks. Pour into an ice-filled Collins glass. Add the club soda and bitters; stir briefly. Add the mint sprigs.

Mexican Sidecar

Adapted from a recipe by Jeffrey Morgenthaler, head bartender at El Vaquero, Eugene, Oregon.

Granulated sugar, for rimming the glass

1 ounce Presidente Mexican brandy

1 ounce Patrón Citrónge orange liqueur

1 ounce fresh lemon juice

Lemon twist, for garnish

Prepare a Cocktail glass. Pour all of the ingredients into a shaker two-thirds full of ice cubes. Shake well. Strain into the prepared glass. Add the twist.

Miami Martini

Adapted from a recipe by Alexandra Fiot, Lonsdale, United Kingdom.

2 ounces Belvedere vodka

1/4 ounce Campari

1 ounce watermelon juice (fresh watermelon blended then strained)

3/4 ounce Teisseire Sirop de Gomme (sugarcane syrup)

1/2 ounce fresh lemon juice

2 dashes of orange bitters

Edible flower, for garnish

Pour all of the ingredients into a shaker two-thirds full of ice cubes. Shake well. Strain into a chilled Cocktail glass. Add the flower.

Midnight Smash

Adapted from a recipe by Duggan McDonnell, Cantina, San Francisco, circa 2008.

3 ripe blackberries

1 ounce fresh Meyer lemon juice

1 ounce Averna amaro

1 ounce Cointreau

2 ounces ginger beer

Orange wheel, for garnish

Muddle the blackberries in the bottom of an empty shaker. Add ice cubes, the lemon juice, the Averna, and the Cointreau. Shake well. Strain into an ice-filled Highball glass. Add the ginger beer; stir briefly. Add the orange wheel.

Midnight Train

Created by Gary Regan to honor Gladys Knight, circa 2000.

2 1/2 ounces bourbon

1/2 ounce peach schnapps

3 dashes of Angostura bitters

Lemon twist, for garnish

Pour all of the ingredients into a mixing glass two-thirds full of ice cubes. Stir well. Strain into a chilled Cocktail glass. Add the twist.

Millennium Manhattan

2 ounces bourbon

1 ounce sweet vermouth

$1/2$ ounce peach schnapps

3 dashes of Angostura bitters

Maraschino cherry, for garnish

Pour all of the ingredients into a mixing glass two-thirds full of ice cubes. Stir well. Strain into a chilled Cocktail glass. Add the cherry.

Millionaire Cocktail #1

In the early twentieth century there was a Millionaire Cocktail made with gin, dry vermouth, and grenadine. The ingredients in this version were detailed in a 1930s cocktail book.

$1^1/2$ ounces dark rum

$1/2$ ounce sloe gin

$1/2$ ounce apricot brandy

$1/2$ ounce fresh lime juice

Pour all of the ingredients into a shaker two-thirds full of ice cubes. Shake well. Strain into a chilled Cocktail glass.

Millionaire Cocktail #4

Millionaire Cocktails #2 and #3 have been omitted intentionally.

Adapted from a recipe by "Dr. Cocktail" (Ted Haigh).

2 ounces Myers's rum

1 ounce sloe gin

1 ounce apricot brandy

1 ounce fresh lime juice

Pour all of the ingredients into a shaker two-thirds full of ice cubes. Shake well. Strain into a chilled Cocktail glass.

Millionaire's Margarita

Adapted from a recipe by well-known beverage consultant Steve Olsen, New York City.

2 ounces El Tesoro de Don Felipe Paradiso añejo tequila
$1/_2$ ounce Grand Marnier Cuvée du Centenaire
$1^1/_2$ ounces fresh lime juice
Lime wheel or orange wedge, for garnish

Pour all of the ingredients into a shaker two-thirds full of ice cubes. Shake well. Strain into a chilled Cocktail glass or ice-filled Rocks glass. Add the garnish.

Mimosa

Many people forget to put the triple sec in this drink—don't be one of them.

$1/_2$ ounce triple sec
1 ounce fresh orange juice
4 ounces champagne or other sparkling wine
Orange wheel, for garnish

Pour all of the ingredients into a Champagne flute. Stir briefly. Add the orange wheel.

Mind Eraser

A sister to the shooter, this cocktail looks like a Pousse-Café but is drunk in one gulp through a straw.

$1/_2$ ounce Kahlúa
$1/_2$ ounce vodka
$1/_2$ ounce club soda

Pour the ingredients, in the order given, over the back of a spoon into a Pousse-Café glass, floating one on top of the other. Place a short straw in the glass and drink from the bottom up in one go.

Minnesota Manhattan

Created by Jaqui Smith, Grange Hall, New York City.

2¹/₂ ounces Stolichnaya Okhotnichya vodka

1 ounce sweet vermouth

2 dashes of Angostura bitters

Maraschino cherry, for garnish

Pour all of the ingredients into a mixing glass two-thirds full
of ice cubes. Stir well. Strain into a chilled Cocktail glass.
Add the cherry.

Mint Julep #1

A drink for the first Saturday in May, when the Kentucky Derby is
run in Louisville, Kentucky, the Mint Julep dates back to at least
the early 1800s. In 1806, Webster's dictionary defined *julep*
as "a kind of liquid medicine," but three years prior to that, an
Englishman described it as "a dram of spirituous liquor that has
mint in it, taken by Virginians of a morning."

It's likely that the Mint Julep was originally made with brandy
and/or peach brandy, but bourbon is now the accepted base liquor.

3 ounces bourbon

1 ounce simple syrup (page 35)

Bouquet of fresh mint

Fill a Julep cup or Highball glass with crushed ice. Add the
liquids, stir, add more ice, and stir again until ice forms on the
outside of the cup. Add the bouquet of mint. Serve with 3 or 4
short straws.

Mint Julep #2

Bouquet of fresh mint

1 ounce simple syrup (page 35)

3 ounces bourbon

Take 5 or 6 leaves from the bouquet of mint and muddle them
with the simple syrup in the bottom of a Julep cup or Highball
glass. Fill the glass with crushed ice, add the bourbon, stir, add
more ice, and stir again until ice forms on the outside of the
vessel. Add the remaining mint as a garnish. Serve with 3 or 4
short straws.

Mint Julep #3
(made ahead of time)
MAKES ABOUT 12 SERVINGS

10 ounces simple syrup (page 35)

8 ounces hot water

Bouquet of fresh mint

1 quart bourbon

Fresh mint, for garnish

Bring the simple syrup and hot water to a boil in a small saucepan. Add the mint and stir briefly. Remove the pan from the heat, cover, and set aside to cool to room temperature, about 1 hour.

Add the mixture to the bourbon. When you build the individual drinks, you will need more fresh mint for garnishes. Build the drinks as described in recipes #1 and #2.

Mirrorball

Adapted from a recipe from Saucebox, Portland, Oregon.

1½ ounces watermelon-infused vodka (see recipe below)

½ ounce Harlequin liqueur

¼ ounce fresh lemon juice

¼ ounce fresh lime juice

¼ ounce simple syrup (page 35)

Splash of cranberry juice

Champagne

Pour the vodka, liqueur, citrus juices, simple syrup, and cranberry juice into a shaker filled two-thirds full of ice cubes. Shake well. Strain into a chilled Cocktail glass. Top with the champagne.

WATERMELON-INFUSED VODKA

Pour a bottle of vodka into a very large jar and fill the jar with chunks of fresh watermelon. Cover and set aside for 1 week. Strain the vodka through a double layer of dampened cheesecloth, pour it back into the original bottle, and refrigerate.

Mischief

Created by me back in 2004.

1 ounce Herradura Silver tequila

1 ounce Charbay key lime vodka

3 ounces fresh orange juice

Orange wheel, for garnish

Pour all of the ingredients into a shaker two-thirds full of ice cubes. Shake well. Strain into a chilled Cocktail glass or a crushed ice–filled Old-Fashioned glass. Add the orange wheel.

Mithering Bastard

1¹/₂ ounces scotch

¹/₂ ounce triple sec

1 ounce orange juice

Build in an ice-filled Rocks glass. Stir well.

Modernista

Adapted from a recipe by Ted Haigh ("Dr. Cocktail"), who in turn adapted it from a formula known as the Modern Cocktail, from The Savoy Cocktail Book.

2 ounces scotch

¹/₂ ounce dark Jamaican rum

¹/₂ ounce fresh lemon juice

Orange bitters, to taste

2 to 3 dashes of absinthe, to taste

Maraschino cherry and a lemon twist, for garnishes

Pour all of the ingredients into a shaker two-thirds full of ice cubes. Shake well. Strain into a chilled Cocktail glass. Add the cherry and the twist.

Mojito

A Cuban drink that probably made its way to the United States during the 1920s, when Americans went to Havana to get a legal drink during Prohibition. The Mojito has been incredibly popular during the past several years, and deservedly so. Hemingway sipped Mojitos at La Bodeguita in Havana, and I've been told that a piece of cardboard hangs behind the bar there, inscribed with the following words, written by him: "My Mojito in La Bodeguita, My Daiquiri in El Floridita."

> **6 to 8 fresh mint leaves**
> **³/₄ ounce simple syrup (page 35)**
> **¹/₂ lime, cut into several wedges**
> **2 ounces light rum**
> **2 ounces club soda**
> **Lime wedge, for garnish**

Place the mint leaves, simple syrup, and lime wedges in the bottom of a Highball glass; muddle well. Fill the glass with crushed ice. Add the rum and club soda; stir briefly. Add the lime wedge.

Monkey Gland Cocktail #1

A popular drink in Europe in the 1920s, this is the American version that calls for Bénédictine. The recipe following is the original formula.

> **2¹/₂ ounces gin**
> **¹/₂ ounce fresh orange juice**
> **¹/₂ ounce Bénédictine**
> **Splash of grenadine**

Pour all of the ingredients into a mixing glass two-thirds full of ice cubes. Stir well. Strain into a chilled Cocktail glass.

Monkey Gland Cocktail #2

> **2¹/₂ ounces gin**
> **¹/₂ ounce fresh orange juice**
> **¹/₂ ounce absinthe**
> **Splash of grenadine**

Pour all of the ingredients into a mixing glass two-thirds full of ice cubes. Stir well. Strain into a chilled Cocktail glass.

Monk's Coffee

Named for the Carthusian monks who first concocted Chartreuse in the 1700s.

> **1¹/₂ ounces green Chartreuse**
> **4 ounces hot coffee**
> **Dollop of whipped cream**

Pour the Chartreuse and coffee into an Irish Coffee glass; stir briefly. Float the whipped cream on top.

Moon Walk

Adapted from a recipe by Joe Gilmore, bartender at the Savoy Hotel, London, to commemorate Neil Armstrong's 1969 walk on the moon.

> **1 ounce fresh grapefruit juice**
> **1 ounce Grand Marnier**
> **Dash of rose water**
> **3¹/₂ ounces chilled champagne**

Build in the order given in a Champagne flute.

The Moonlight Cocktail

Created by Gary Regan, 2007.

> **1¹/₂ ounces gin (Beefeater, Plymouth, or Tanqueray)**
> **1/₂ ounce Cointreau**
> **1/₂ ounce crème de violette**
> **1/₂ ounce fresh lime juice**

Pour all of the ingredients into a shaker two-thirds full of ice cubes. Shake well. Strain into a chilled Cocktail glass.

Moonlight on the Peach

Adapted from a recipe by H. Joseph Ehrmann, owner, Elixir, San Francisco.

> **1/₂ ripe white peach**
> **1/₂ ounce simple syrup (page 35; Ehrmann uses organic sugar syrup)**
> **1¹/₂ ounces Square One organic vodka infused with Numi Organic Ruby Chai tea (see recipe below)**
> **1/₂ ounce Tuaca**
> **Orange twist, for garnish**

Muddle the peach and simple syrup in a shaker until they form a paste. Add the vodka, Tuaca, and lots of ice cubes. Shake well. Strain through a fine sieve into a chilled Cocktail glass. Add the twist.

VODKA INFUSION

In a wide-mouthed bottle or jar, add 1 bag of Numi Organic Ruby Chai tea to each 6 ounces of Square One organic vodka—6 tea bags per 750-ml bottle. Set aside for 2 to 3 hours, shaking the bottle from time to time. Remove the tea bags.

Moonlight over Machu Picchu

Created by Gary Regan, 2008.

>**2^1/$_2$ ounces Acholado pisco brandy**
>**^{1}/$_2$ ounce crème de violette**
>**^{1}/$_2$ ounce Luxardo maraschino liqueur**
>**1 ounce fresh lemon juice**

Pour all of the ingredients into a shaker two-thirds full of ice cubes. Shake well. Strain into a chilled Cocktail glass.

Morning Glory Fizz

>**2 ounces vodka**
>**^{1}/$_2$ ounce white crème de cacao**
>**1 ounce light cream**
>**4 ounces club soda**
>**Freshly grated nutmeg, for garnish**

Pour the vodka, crème de cacao, and cream into a shaker two-thirds full of ice cubes. Shake well. Strain into an ice-filled Collins glass. Add the club soda; stir well. Sprinkle with the nutmeg.

Moscow Mule

Created during the 1940s at the Cock and Bull in Los Angeles, this was the drink that first got Americans drinking vodka on a regular basis. It was originally served in small copper tankards.

> **2 ounces vodka**
> **1 ounce fresh lime juice**
> **4 to 6 ounces ginger beer**
> **Lime wedge, for garnish**

Pour all of the ingredients into an ice-filled Highball glass. Stir briefly. Add the lime wedge.

Mouth Margarita

This is a fun drink to make—I've even heard of a bar in New Jersey where they spin you around in a dentist's chair to properly mix the cocktail.

> **3/4 ounce white tequila**
> **1/2 ounce triple sec**
> **1/4 ounce fresh lime juice**

Pour all of the ingredients into the drinker's mouth. Grasp his or her head and shake vigorously (but not too vigorously). When well blended, the drinker may swallow.

The Moyamensing

Adapted from a recipe by Nicholas R. Jarrett, bartender and manager at the Apothecary Bar and Lounge, Philadelphia.

> **1/2 ounce Ricard, to rinse the glass**
> **2 ounces Brandy de Jerez**
> **1 ounce Dubonnet Rouge**
> **1/2 ounce fresh lemon juice**
> **Dash of Angostura bitters**
> **Dash of Regans' Orange Bitters No. 6**
> **Small pinch of granulated sugar**
> **Small pinch of grated nutmeg**
> **Sparkling water**
> **Lemon twist, for garnish**

Rinse a chilled Cocktail glass with the Ricard. Pour the brandy, Dubonnet, lemon juice, both bitters, sugar, and nutmeg into a shaker two-thirds full of ice cubes. Shake well. Strain into the glass. Add a little sparkling water and the twist.

Muddy Waters

Created by Jimmy Daukas, Maryland.

3 to 4 lime wedges

2 ounces Myers's dark rum

3 ounces fresh grapefruit juice

Squeeze the lime wedges into a Highball glass, and drop them into the glass. Add ice cubes and the rum and juice.

Mudslide

1 ounce Kahlúa

1 ounce vodka

1 ounce Baileys Irish cream liqueur

Pour all of the ingredients into a shaker two-thirds full of ice cubes. Shake well. Strain into a chilled Cocktail glass.

My Favorite Sidecar

Adapted from a recipe by Mark Mendoza, wine director, Sona Restaurant, West Hollywood.

Sugar, for rimming the glass

2 ounces cognac

1 ounce Cointreau or triple sec

$1/4$ ounce Luxardo maraschino liqueur

$1/2$ ounce fresh lemon juice

Dash of Angostura bitters

Lemon twist, for garnish

Prepare a Cocktail glass. Pour all of the ingredients into a shaker two-thirds full of ice cubes. Shake well. Strain into the prepared glass. Add the twist.

Naked Girl Scout

¾ ounce Godiva chocolate liqueur

¾ ounce peppermint schnapps

Pour both ingredients into a mixing glass two-thirds full of ice cubes. Stir well. Strain into a chilled Pony glass.

Naked Martini

"Remember: Conservatism is not desirable where gin and pleasure are concerned." —Isaac Stern

3 ounces gin

Lemon twist or cocktail olive, for garnish

Pour the gin into a mixing glass two-thirds full of ice cubes. Stir well. Strain into a chilled Cocktail glass. Add the garnish.

Navy Grog

Named for eighteenth-century British admiral Edward Vernon, who ordered that rations of rum and water be served to sailors as a restorative. Gordon was known as "Old Grog" because his coat was made from a coarse cloth known as grogram.

½ ounce light rum

½ ounce amber or gold rum

½ ounce dark rum

½ ounce Grand Marnier

1 ounce grapefruit juice

1 ounce orange juice

1 ounce pineapple juice

Pour all of the ingredients into a shaker two-thirds full of ice cubes. Shake well. Strain into an ice-filled Collins glass.

Mark your calendar for Black Tot Day—July 31st. The date marks the anniversary of the end of free daily rum for British soldiers, who had their rations taken away from them in 1970, more than 200 years after the tradition was started by Admiral Edward Vernon, a British naval officer. Because Vernon wore a coat made of grogram, a coarse cloth, his nickname was "Old Grog," and the rations of rum and water he prescribed for the sailors became known as Grog.

Negroni

This variation on the Americano is said to have been the creation of Count Negroni in the late 1800s. Apparently everyone at the Count's local bar was drinking Americanos, and he didn't want to be seen drinking such a common potion. Many people now drink Negronis made with vodka in place of the gin.

> **1 ounce gin**
> **1 ounce sweet vermouth**
> **1 ounce Campari**
> **Orange wheel, for garnish**

Pour all of the ingredients into an ice-filled Rocks glass. Stir briefly. Add the orange wheel.

Nelson's Blood

> **1 ounce ruby port**
> **Chilled champagne or other sparkling wine**

Build in a Champagne flute.

New Amsterdam

Adapted from a recipe from Jim Meehan, owner and bartender, PDT, New York City.

- 2 ounces Bols Oude Genever gin
- 1 ounce Clear Creek Kirschwasser
- 1 barspoon of Demerara sugar syrup (made at a 2:1 sugar to water ratio)
- 2 dashes of Peychaud's bitters
- Lemon twist, for garnish

Pour all of the ingredients into a mixing glass two-thirds full of ice cubes. Stir well. Strain into a chilled Coupe glass. Add the twist.

The New Ideal

Adapted from a recipe by Neyah White, first published in the San Francisco Chronicle, *2008.*

- 1 ounce Bluecoat gin
- $^1/_2$ ounce Punt e Mes
- $^1/_2$ ounce Luxardo maraschino liqueur
- 2 ounces fresh grapefruit juice
- 4 dashes of blackberry root tincture (optional)
- Lemon twist, for garnish

Pour all of the ingredients into a shaker two-thirds full of ice cubes. Shake well. Strain into a chilled Cocktail glass. Add the twist.

New Orleans Cocktail

- 2 ounces bourbon
- $^1/_2$ ounce absinthe
- $^1/_2$ ounce simple syrup (page 35)
- $^1/_2$ ounce fresh lemon juice

Pour all of the ingredients into a shaker two-thirds full of ice cubes. Shake well. Strain into a chilled Cocktail glass.

N

New Orleans Milk Punch

2 ounces bourbon

$1/2$ to 1 ounce dark crème de cacao

3 to 5 ounces milk

Ground nutmeg or cinnamon (optional)

Pour all of the ingredients into a shaker two-thirds full of ice cubes. Shake well. Strain into an ice-filled Rocks or Highball glass. Sprinkle with the nutmeg or cinnamon, if desired.

New Orleans Pink Gin

The Pink Gin is a British drink, but when made with Peychaud's bitters, a product made in New Orleans, and served chilled, it becomes all-American.

3 dashes of Peychaud's bitters

$2^1/2$ ounces Plymouth gin

Pour both ingredients into a mixing glass two-thirds full of ice cubes. Stir well. Strain into a chilled Cocktail glass.

The Nicky Finn

Adapted from a recipe in Cocktail: The Drinks Bible for the 21st Century, *by Paul Harrington and Laura Moorhead.*

1 ounce cognac

1 ounce Cointreau

1 ounce fresh lemon juice

Dash of Pernod

Lemon twist, for garnish

Pour all of the ingredients into a shaker two-thirds full of ice cubes. Shake well. Strain into a chilled Cocktail glass. Add the twist.

Norman's Watermelon Martini

Created by master bartender Norman Bukofzer, New York City.

$2^1/2$ ounces gin

$1/4$ ounce Marie Brizard watermelon liqueur

Juice of a lime wedge

Lemon twist, for garnish

Pour all of the ingredients into a mixing glass two-thirds full of ice cubes. Stir well. Strain into a chilled Cocktail glass. Add the twist.

Nouveau Carre

Adapted from a recipe by Jonny Raglin, bartender, Absinthe Brasserie & Bar, San Francisco. Winner of a 2006 Bastille Day competition for Best Beverage containing B&B.

1¹/₂ ounces Herradura añejo tequila

³/₄ ounce B&B liqueur

¹/₄ ounce Lillet Blanc

4 dashes of Peychaud's bitters

Lemon twist, for garnish

Pour all of the ingredients into a mixing glass two-thirds full of ice cubes. Stir well. Strain into a chilled Cocktail glass. Add the twist.

Nut & Berry Martini

2 ounces Chambord raspberry liqueur

2 ounces Frangelico

Pour both ingredients into a mixing glass two-thirds full of ice cubes. Stir well. Strain into a chilled Cocktail glass.

Nyquil

And this would taste like . . . ? Say goodnight, Gracie.

³/₄ ounce vodka

¹/₄ ounce Jägermeister

2 drops of green food coloring

Pour all of the ingredients into a shaker two-thirds full of ice cubes. Shake well. Strain into a chilled Pony glass.

Oatmeal Cookie

1 ounce Baileys Irish cream liqueur

1 ounce Jägermeister

1 ounce butterscotch schnapps

$^1/_2$ ounce cinnamon schnapps

6 to 8 golden raisins, for garnish

Pour all of the ingredients into a shaker two-thirds full of ice cubes. Shake well. Strain into a chilled Cocktail glass or an ice-filled Highball glass. Thread the raisins onto a cocktail pick and garnish with it.

Oktoberfest Punch

Oktoberfest is usually celebrated by beer drinkers, so this must be for the people who aren't fond of ale or lager. The German festival began in 1810, when Crown Prince Ludwig of Bavaria married Princess Therese of Saxon-Hildburghausen. The festivities lasted for five full days and ended with a horse race held on a green named *Theresienwiese* (Theresa's Green) in honor of the bride. Over the following years the horse race was repeated every October, and Oktoberfest was born.

MAKES ABOUT TWENTY-FOUR 6-OUNCE SERVINGS

1 750-ml bottle dry red wine

2 750-ml bottles dry white wine

3 ounces sweet vermouth

3 ounces dry vermouth

8 ounces applejack

8 ounces citrus vodka

8 ounces peach schnapps

8 ounces cranberry juice

2 ounces simple syrup (page 35)

1 large block of ice

Orange and lemon wheels, for garnish

Pour both wines, both vermouths, the applejack, citrus vodka, peach schnapps, cranberry juice, and simple syrup into a large pan or bowl. Cover and refrigerate for at least 4 hours. Place the block of ice in the center of a large punch bowl. Pour in the punch; add the citrus wheels.

The Old Cuban Cocktail

*Adapted from a recipe by Audrey Saunders, aka "Libation Goddess,"
New York City.*

Audrey makes her own sugared vanilla bean garnishes (see below). But if you don't have one, better to omit the garnish than miss out on this fabulous drink.

> **¹/₂ ounce fresh lime juice**
>
> **³/₄ to 1 ounce simple syrup (page 35)**
>
> **6 fresh mint leaves**
>
> **1¹/₂ ounces Bacardi 8 añejo rum**
>
> **2 dashes of Angostura bitters**
>
> **Moët & Chandon champagne**
>
> **1 sugared vanilla bean, for garnish (see recipe below)**

Muddle the lime juice, simple syrup, and mint leaves in the bottom of an empty shaker. Add the rum and bitters, and ice cubes. Shake and strain into a chilled Cocktail glass. Top with a little champagne. Add the vanilla bean.

SUGARED VANILLA BEANS

Slice the vanilla beans lengthwise; remove the seeds and reserve them for flavoring sugar or other uses. Sprinkle granulated sugar over the beans, and press lightly so the sugar adheres. If you want to make these garnishes in quantity, simply store the sliced beans in a container full of granulated sugar—you'll end up with sugared vanilla bean garnishes, and vanilla-scented sugar to boot.

Old-Fashioned

This classic cocktail has changed greatly over the years: Though many people use blended Canadian whisky, either rye or bourbon is the better choice. Muddling the fruit with the bitters and sugar is essential, although there was no fruit save for a twist of lemon in the original nineteenth-century recipes for this drink.

> **3 dashes of Angostura bitters**
>
> **1 orange slice**
>
> **1 lemon wedge**
>
> **1 maraschino cherry**

1 sugar cube

2¹/₂ ounces straight rye whiskey or bourbon

In a Double Old-Fashioned glass, muddle the bitters, orange slice, lemon wedge, and maraschino cherry into the sugar cube. Fill the glass with ice cubes. Add the whiskey; stir well.

Old San Juan Cocktail

1¹/₂ ounces amber rum

¹/₂ ounce cranberry juice

1 ounce fresh lime juice

Lime wedge, for garnish

Pour all of the ingredients into a mixing glass two-thirds full of ice cubes. Shake well. Strain into a chilled Cocktail glass. Add the lime wedge.

Old-Timer

Adapted from a recipe by Neyah White, Nopa, San Francisco, 2008.

4 fresh thyme sprigs

2 ounces Bols Oude Genever gin

¹/₂ ounce simple syrup (page 35)

¹/₂ ounce fresh lemon juice

2 ounces ginger beer

2 ounces club soda

Slap the thyme sprigs to get the oils going (no need to muddle if they are fresh) and toss into a Collins glass. Add ice cubes, pour in the gin, simple syrup, and lemon juice, and stir. Top with the ginger beer and soda. Stir enough to get the thyme evenly distributed.

Oliver's Twist

Created by Gary Regan for Gourmet magazine's food-pairing challenge, 2004. Named for Garrett Oliver, brewmaster for the Brooklyn Brewery and one of the other competitors.

1 ounce Tanqueray No. Ten gin

1/2 ounce Cointreau

1 ounce pineapple juice

3 dashes of Angostura bitters

Maraschino cherry, for garnish

Pour all of the ingredients into a shaker two-thirds full of ice cubes. Shake well. Strain into a chilled Cocktail glass. Add the cherry.

Olympic Cocktail

1 1/2 ounces brandy

1/2 ounce triple sec

1/2 ounce fresh orange juice

Pour all of the ingredients into a shaker two-thirds full of ice cubes. Shake well. Strain into a chilled Cocktail glass.

Olympic Gold Martini

Created by Michael R. Vezzoni, Four Seasons Hotel, Seattle.

1 ounce Bombay Sapphire gin

1 1/2 ounces Absolut Citron vodka

Splash of Domaine de Canton ginger liqueur

Dash of Martel Cordon Bleu cognac

Lemon twist, for garnish

Pour all of the ingredients into a mixing glass two-thirds full of ice cubes. Stir well. Strain into a chilled Cocktail glass. Add the lemon twist.

1-900-FUK-MEUP

One Internet poll cited this as the most-requested cocktail among its respondents. Hmmmm, I think they just like to say the words.

¹/₂ ounce Absolut Kurant vodka

¹/₄ ounce Grand Marnier

¹/₄ ounce Chambord raspberry liqueur

¹/₄ ounce Midori melon liqueur

¹/₄ ounce Malibu rum

¹/₄ ounce amaretto

¹/₂ ounce cranberry juice

¹/₄ ounce pineapple juice

Pour all of the ingredients into a shaker two-thirds full of ice cubes. Shake well. Strain into a chilled Cocktail glass.

The OP Lemonade Cocktail

Adapted from a recipe by Audrey Saunders, aka "Libation Goddess," New York City.

OP, for all intents and purposes, is a flavored vodka, and a darned good one, too. The sweetening agent here is peach purée, which makes for an interesting dimension. Of OP, Audrey wrote, "It's light, delicate, and has a wonderfully fragrant nose. I created this drink because I wanted to highlight its nuances, instead of masking them with overpowering flavors. The lemon and the peach seem to enhance the flavors nicely in this one."

1¹/₂ ounces OP vodka

¹/₂ ounce (white or regular) peach purée (recipe follows)

¹/₂ ounce fresh lemon juice

¹/₂ ounce simple syrup (page 35)

Lemon wedge, for garnish

Pour all of the ingredients into a shaker two-thirds full of ice cubes. Shake well. Strain into a small ice-filled wine glass. Add the lemon wedge.

PEACH PURÉE

In a blender, purée the flesh, including the skin, of 1 ripe peach, 2 or 3 ice cubes, and ¹/₂ teaspoon of fresh lemon juice.

Opal Cocktail

One 1930s recipe for this drink calls for orange flower water instead of the orange bitters; you might want to give that variation a try.

> 1^1/$_2$ ounces gin
>
> ^{1}/$_2$ ounce triple sec
>
> 1 ounce orange juice
>
> 2 dashes of orange bitters

Pour all of the ingredients into a shaker two-thirds full of ice cubes. Shake well. Strain into a chilled Cocktail glass.

Opening Cocktail

This is a sweet variation on the Manhattan, using Canadian whisky instead of bourbon.

> 2 ounces blended Canadian whisky
>
> ^{1}/$_4$ ounce sweet vermouth
>
> 2 dashes of grenadine
>
> 2 dashes of Angostura bitters

Pour all of the ingredients into a mixing glass two-thirds full of ice cubes. Stir well. Strain into a chilled Cocktail glass.

Opera Cocktail

"Going to the opera, like getting drunk, is a sin that carries its own punishment with it."

—Hannah More (1745–1833), British writer, reformer, philanthropist

> 2 ounces gin
>
> ^{1}/$_2$ ounce Dubonnet Rouge
>
> ^{1}/$_2$ ounce maraschino liqueur

Pour all of the ingredients into a mixing glass two-thirds full of ice cubes. Stir well. Strain into a chilled Cocktail glass.

Oreo Cookie

According to the Oreo Web site, the cookie, which debuted in 1912, could have been named in any of the following ways:

- Some say the name came about because it just seemed like a nice, melodic combination of sounds with just a few catch letters that was easy to pronounce.
- Others attest that the name is based on the French word for gold (*or*), a color used on early package designs.
- There's a tale that the name comes from the Greek word for mountain (*oreo*) and that the name was applied because the first test version was, if you can imagine this, hill shaped.
- Legend also has it that the Oreo was named by taking the "RE" out of *cream* and sandwiching it between the two "O"s from the word *chocolate* . . . just like the cookie.

> **$1/2$ ounce Kahlúa**
> **$1/2$ ounce white crème de cacao**
> **$1/2$ ounce Baileys Irish cream liqueur**
> **Splash of vodka**

Layer all of the ingredients in a Pony glass.

Organized Chaos

Created by Gary Regan, 2004.

> **2 ounces Wild Turkey bourbon (101 proof)**
> **$1^1/2$ ounces Noilly Prat sweet vermouth**
> **$1/2$ ounce Elisir M. P. Roux liqueur**
> **Lemon wedge, for garnish**

Fill a medium-size wine goblet with ice cubes, and add the bourbon, vermouth, and liqueur. Squeeze the lemon wedge into the drink and drop it into the glass. Stir briefly.

Oriental Cocktail

> **$1^1/2$ ounces bourbon**
> **$1/2$ ounce sweet vermouth**
> **$1/2$ ounce triple sec**
> **$1/2$ ounce fresh lime juice**

Pour all of the ingredients into a shaker two-thirds full of ice cubes. Shake well. Strain into a chilled Cocktail glass.

Pacific Rim #1

The gin version, created by Ginger DiLello, Philadelphia Fish and Company, Philadelphia.

2 ounces gin
1 ounce Domaine de Canton ginger liqueur
Strip of crystallized ginger

Pour the gin and liqueur into a mixing glass two-thirds full of ice cubes. Stir well. Strain into a chilled Cocktail glass. Add the crystallized ginger.

Pacific Rim #2

The vodka version, also created by Ginger DiLello, Philadelphia Fish and Company, Philadelphia.

3 ounces vodka
$1/2$ ounce Domaine de Canton ginger liqueur
Strip of crystallized ginger

Pour the vodka and liqueur into a mixing glass two-thirds full of ice cubes. Stir well. Strain into a chilled Cocktail glass. Add the crystallized ginger.

Paddy Cocktail

A variation on the Manhattan, this one stars Irish whiskey.

$1^1/2$ ounces Irish whiskey
1 ounce sweet vermouth
2 dashes of Angostura bitters

Pour all of the ingredients into a mixing glass two-thirds full of ice cubes. Stir well. Strain into a chilled Cocktail glass.

Palmer Cocktail

There was a drink with this name in the 1930s made with whiskey, lemon juice, and bitters. This version is far more interesting.

$2^1/2$ ounces gin
$1/2$ ounce sweet vermouth

$^1/_2$ ounce maraschino liqueur

$^1/_2$ ounce fresh lemon juice

Pour all of the ingredients into a shaker two-thirds full of ice cubes. Shake well. Strain into a chilled Cocktail glass.

PAMA Rose Cocktail

Adapted from a recipe by Victoria Damato-Moran, bartender at Joe DiMaggio's Italian Chophouse, San Francisco.

1 ounce PAMA pomegranate liqueur

1 ounce Skyy Citrus vodka

$^3/_4$ ounce Shaker's Rose vodka

$^1/_4$ ounce crème de cacao

$^1/_4$ ounce Cointreau

$^1/_2$ ounce fresh lemon juice

Rose petal and a lemon twist, for garnishes

Pour all of the ingredients into a shaker two-thirds full of ice cubes. Shake well. Strain into a chilled Cocktail glass. Add the rose petal and the twist.

Pam's Very Sexy Cocktail

Adapted from a recipe by Tony Abou-Ganim, 2004. Does he know my sister?

$1^1/_2$ ounces Belvedere Cytrus vodka

$^3/_4$ ounce Marie Brizard Cassis de Bordeaux

1 ounce fresh lemon juice

$^1/_2$ ounce simple syrup (page 35)

Moët & Chandon White Star champagne

3 fresh raspberries marinated in Grand Marnier, for garnish

Pour the vodka, cassis, lemon juice, and simple syrup into a shaker two-thirds full of ice cubes. Shake well. Strain into a chilled Cocktail glass. Top with the champagne. Add the raspberries.

Pan Galactic Gargle Blaster

What does this name mean?

$^1/_2$ ounce vodka

$^1/_2$ ounce triple sec

$^1/_2$ ounce Yukon Jack liqueur

$^1/_2$ ounce peach schnapps

$^1/_2$ ounce Jack Daniel's Tennessee whiskey

$^1/_2$ ounce fresh lime juice

$^1/_2$ ounce cranberry juice

Lemon-lime soda

Pour all of the ingredients into an ice-filled Collins glass, filling it with the soda. Stir with a long straw.

Panama Cocktail

This was the predecessor to the Brandy Alexander.

1 ounce brandy

1 ounce white crème de cacao

1 ounce light cream

Pour all of the ingredients into a shaker two-thirds full of ice cubes. Shake well. Strain into a chilled Cocktail glass.

Paradise Cocktail

Paradise comes from the Persian word *pardes*, meaning a "pleasure-ground" or "king's garden."

2 ounces gin

1 ounce apricot brandy

1 ounce orange juice

Dash of lemon juice

Pour all of the ingredients into a shaker two-thirds full of ice cubes. Shake well. Strain into a chilled Cocktail glass.

Paraguayan Pineapple Punch

Adapted from a recipe by Colby Spath, "Spiritual Advisor" at LeNell's wine and spirits boutique, Red Hook, Brooklyn.

1¹/₂ ounces Papagayo spiced rum
¹/₂ ounce Maraska maraschino liqueur
¹/₂ ounce PAMA pomegranate liqueur
1¹/₂ ounces Goya pineapple juice
¹/₂ ounce fresh orange juice
1 ounce Coco Rico coconut soda

Pour the rum, liqueurs, and juices into a mixing glass two-thirds full of ice cubes. Stir well. Strain into an ice-filled Collins glass while adding the coconut soda.

Paris Is Burning

Named for Jennie Livingston's universally acclaimed documentary about Harlem's drag queen balls. The film won many awards, including the Grand Jury Prize at the Sundance Film Festival and the 1990 San Francisco International Lesbian & Gay Film Festival Audience Award for Best Documentary.

2 ounces cognac
¹/₂ ounce Chambord raspberry liqueur
Lemon twist, for garnish

Pour the cognac and Chambord into a Brandy snifter. Heat in a microwave for 20 seconds on high power. Garnish with the twist.

Parisian Cocktail

This formula dates back to London in the 1920s.

1 ounce gin
1 ounce dry vermouth
1 ounce crème de cassis

Pour all of the ingredients into a mixing glass two-thirds full of ice cubes. Stir well. Strain into a chilled Cocktail glass.

PB&J

The first patent for peanut butter was submitted in 1895 by the Kellogg brothers, who eventually discarded the product; Joseph Lambert, one of their former employees, started selling the machines they had used to grind the peanuts.

In 1904 at the Universal Exposition, a businessman named C. H. Summer introduced peanut butter to the American nation at large, and four years later, Krema Products started selling peanut butter. Krema is the oldest peanut butter company still in operation.

> $1/2$ ounce vodka
> $1/2$ ounce Chambord raspberry liqueur
> $1/2$ ounce Frangelico

Pour all of the ingredients into a mixing glass two-thirds full of ice cubes. Stir well. Strain into a chilled Pony glass.

Peach and Lemon Champagne Punch

MAKES THIRTY TO FORTY 6-OUNCE SERVINGS

> 16 ounces chilled simple syrup (page 35)
> 1 750-ml bottle chilled citrus vodka or rum
> 1 750-ml bottle chilled dry sherry
> 8 ounces chilled peach schnapps
> 4 ounces maraschino liqueur
> 4 750-ml bottles chilled champagne or sparkling wine
> 1 liter chilled lemon-lime soda
> 1 large block of ice
> 6 peaches, pitted and sliced, for garnish

Stir all of the liquids together in a large punch bowl. Add the block of ice; garnish with the peach slices.

Peach Brandy Julep

It's very probable that peach brandy was the base of America's earliest Juleps.

3 ounces peach brandy

2 dashes of Angostura bitters

3 large mint sprigs, for garnish

Pour both ingredients into a crushed ice–filled Julep Cup. Stir until a film of ice appears on the exterior of the cup. Add the mint sprigs.

Peaches & Cream Martini

1¹/₂ ounces Baileys Irish cream liqueur

1¹/₂ ounces peach schnapps

Pour both ingredients into a shaker two-thirds full of ice cubes. Shake well. Strain into a chilled Cocktail glass.

The Peachy Keen

Adapted from a recipe created by John Sheely, Mockingbird Bistro Wine Bar, Houston, Texas.

1¹/₂ ounces Citadelle or Cîroc vodka

1 ounce Mathilde Pêche liqueur

Wedge of fresh Texas peach, for garnish

Pour both ingredients into a mixing glass two-thirds full of ice cubes. Stir well. Strain into a chilled Cocktail glass. Add the peach wedge.

The Pear Martini

Adapted from a recipe in Cocktails in New York, *by Anthony Giglio. Served at Blue Ribbon restaurant, New York City, circa 2004.*

2 ounces Belle de Brillet liqueur

1 ounce citrus vodka

1 ounce fresh lime juice

Pour all of the ingredients into a shaker two-thirds full of ice cubes. Shake well. Strain into a chilled Cocktail glass.

The Pearl

Adapted from a recipe by Jon Santer, bartender at Bourbon & Branch, San Francisco.

> 1¹/₂ ounces Plymouth gin
> ³/₄ ounces Aperol
> ¹/₂ ounce Lillet Blanc
> 2 ounces Prosecco or any dry sparkling wine
> 5 silver dragées
> 1 drop of lemon oil

Pour the gin, Aperol, and Lillet into a mixing glass two-thirds full of ice cubes. Stir well. Strain into a chilled Champagne flute, and add the Prosecco. Drop the dragées to the bottom and add the lemon oil (eyedroppers are available at the Container Store and some pharmacies).

Pegu Club Cocktail

This drink was created at the Pegu Club in Burma sometime prior to 1930.

> 2 ounces gin
> ¹/₂ ounce Cointreau or other triple sec
> ¹/₂ ounce fresh lime juice
> 2 dashes of Angostura bitters
> 2 dashes of orange bitters

Pour all of the ingredients into a shaker two-thirds full of ice cubes. Shake well. Strain into a chilled Cocktail glass.

Pegu Club (Redux)

Adapted from a recipe by Thad Vogler, bar manager at Jardiniere, San Francisco.

> 1¹/₂ ounces gin
> ³/₄ ounce Qi White liqueur
> ³/₄ ounce fresh lime juice
> 2 dashes of Angostura bitters
> 1 demitasse spoon organic raw sugar

Pour all of the ingredients into a shaker two-thirds full of ice cubes. Shake well. Strain into a chilled Cocktail glass.

Pennie Colada

Adapted from a recipe by Pennie Fuller, The Rack, Boston.

> 1¹/₂ ounces Bacardi O rum
> ³/₄ ounce Fruja mango liqueur
> 3 ounces pineapple juice
> 1¹/₂ ounces coconut cream

Pour all of the ingredients into a blender and add 1 cup ice cubes. Blend until smooth. Pour into a Hurricane glass.

The Percy Special

A variation on the Blood and Sand submitted by a certain Ann Harris: "Fox-hunting in England a few years ago, I had a similar concoction [to the Blood and Sand] called a 'Percy Special.' The alcoholic ingredients were the same, but a splash of 7UP was added instead of orange juice. After making it safely home, it was henceforth referred to as 'liquid courage'!"

> ³/₄ ounce scotch
> ³/₄ ounce sweet vermouth
> ³/₄ ounce cherry brandy
> ³/₄ ounce 7UP

Pour the scotch, vermouth, and brandy into a shaker two-thirds full of ice cubes. Shake well. Strain into a chilled Cocktail glass. Add the 7UP.

The Peruvian Elder-Sour

Created by Gary Regan, 2007.

> 2 ounces Peruvian pisco brandy
> 1 ounce St-Germain Elderflower liqueur
> 1/2 ounce fresh lime juice
> 1/2 lime wheel, for garnish

Pour all of the ingredients into a shaker two-thirds full of ice cubes. Shake well. Strain into a chilled Cocktail glass. Add the lime wheel.

Pesca Di Milano

Adapted from a recipe by Brian MacGregor, bartender at Jardinière, San Francisco, 2008.

> $1/3$ **ripe peach, diced**
> $3/4$ **ounce Bluecoat gin**
> $1^1/2$ **ounces Dimmi liqueur**
> $3/4$ **ounce fresh lemon juice**

Muddle the peaches in an empty shaker to form a paste. Add ice cubes and all of the remaining ingredients. Shake well. Strain into an ice-filled Highball glass.

Pesca Matta

Adapted from a recipe by Joe Alessandroni, bartender at Perbacco, San Francisco, 2008.

> **4 to 5 fresh mint leaves**
> $1/4$ **ripe peach, diced**
> $1/2$ **ounce simple syrup (page 35)**
> $1^1/2$ **ounces Gin No. 209**
> $1/2$ **ounce fresh lemon juice**
> **Club soda**

Lightly muddle the mint leaves in an empty shaker. Add the diced peach and simple syrup and muddle again to form a paste. Add ice cubes, the gin, and the lemon juice. Shake well. Strain into an ice-filled Highball glass. Top with club soda.

Phantasm Fizz

Adapted from a recipe by cocktail historian "Dr. Cocktail" (Ted Haigh), who sees phantasms with great regularity.

> $1^1/2$ **ounces Kirschwasser**
> $1/2$ **ounce parfait amour liqueur**
> **Chilled champagne**
> **Dash of orange bitters**
> **Stemless maraschino cherry, for garnish**

Combine all of the ingredients in a Champagne flute and stir lightly. Garnish with the cherry.

Phoebe Snow Cocktail

This drink was not named for the popular singer from the 1960s; it's been around since the early 1900s, and was probably named for a fictional character used to promote a railroad that boasted that its trains were fueled by anthracite, the highest-grade and cleanest-burning form of coal.

1¹/₂ ounces Dubonnet Rouge
1¹/₂ ounces brandy
Dash of absinthe

Pour all of the ingredients into a mixing glass two-thirds full of ice cubes. Stir well. Strain into a chilled Cocktail glass.

Pierce Brosnan

Oh, to be a Bond girl.

Adapted from a recipe created for Pierce Brosnan by Salvatore Calabrese, The Lanesborough Hotel, London.

1¹/₂ ounces vodka, straight from the freezer
¹/₂ ounce chilled champagne
1 sugar cube
¹/₄ ounce absinthe

Pour the vodka into a well-chilled Martini glass. Add the champagne and stir briefly (don't shake!). Place the sugar cube onto a barspoon or teaspoon, soak it with the absinthe, and ignite it with a match. Drop the flaming sugar cube into the drink.

Pierced Navel

This is simply a Woo Woo without the vodka.

2 ounces peach schnapps
4 ounces cranberry juice

Pour both ingredients into an ice-filled Highball glass; stir briefly.

Pimm's Cup

Pimm's Cup liqueurs were invented by James Pimm, a restaurateur in London who opened his first restaurant in 1823. No. 1, the gin-based drink flavored with fruit liqueurs and herbs, was Pimm's original recipe, but at one time you could also get Pimm's No. 2 Cup, made with scotch, No. 3 with brandy, No. 4 with rum, No. 5 with rye, and No. 6 with vodka. He started bottling his gin-based drink circa 1859.

4 ounces Pimm's No. 1 Cup

8 ounces ginger ale, club soda, ginger beer, or lemon-lime soda

Cucumber spear, for garnish

Pour the Pimm's and the soda into an ice-filled 20-ounce beer tankard; stir briefly. Add the cucumber spear.

Piña Colada

Created in 1954 by bartender Ramón "Monchito" Marrero at the Caribe Hilton Hotel, San Juan, Puerto Rico.

2 ounces light rum

6 ounces pineapple juice

2 ounces coconut cream, such as Coco Lopez

Pineapple spear, for garnish

Pour all of the ingredients into a shaker two-thirds full of ice cubes. Shake well. Strain into an ice-filled wine goblet. Add the pineapple spear.

The Pine Box

Adapted from a recipe by Neyah White, bartender at Nopa, San Francisco.

2 ounces fino sherry

1/2 ounce Zirbenz Stone Pine liqueur

Smallest dash of peach bitters

Pour all of the ingredients into a mixing glass two-thirds full of ice cubes. Stir well. Strain into a chilled Sherry Copita glass.

Pink Gin #1

A this-side-of-the-pond version of the British classic.

2 ounces Plymouth gin
3 dashes of Angostura bitters

Pour both ingredients into a mixing glass two-thirds full of ice cubes. Stir well. Strain into a chilled Cocktail glass.

Pink Gin #2

Reportedly created as a medicinal tonic for nineteenth-century British naval officers.

3 dashes of Angostura bitters
2$^1/_2$ ounces gin

Coat the interior of a small wine goblet with the bitters, and discard the excess. Add the gin.

Pink Lady

The original 1930 recipe for this drink didn't call for heavy cream, so this version is a revised formula.

2 ounces gin
$^1/_2$ ounce heavy cream
2 dashes of grenadine
1 egg white

Pour all of the ingredients into a shaker two-thirds full of ice cubes. Shake very well. Strain into a chilled Cocktail glass.

Pink Lemonade

Created by Bryna O'Shea, San Francisco.

2 ounces Bacardi Limón rum
$^1/_2$ ounce triple sec
$^1/_2$ ounce fresh lemon juice
$^1/_2$ ounce cranberry juice
$^1/_2$ slice lemon, for garnish

Pour all of the ingredients into a shaker two-thirds full of ice cubes. Shake well. Strain into a chilled Cocktail glass. Add the lemon slice.

The Pink Sink

Adapted from a recipe by Michelle McLaughlin, The Hi-Life restaurant, Seattle, circa 2005.

> 2 ounces Absolut Kurant vodka
> 3/4 ounce peach schnapps
> 1/2 ounce fresh lemon juice
> 1/2 ounce cranberry juice

Pour all of the ingredients into a shaker two-thirds full of ice cubes. Shake well. Strain into a chilled Cocktail glass.

Pink Squirrel

If you can't find crème de noyaux, use amaretto instead.

> 2 ounces crème de noyaux
> 1 ounce white crème de cacao
> 1 ounce light cream

Pour all of the ingredients into a shaker two-thirds full of ice cubes. Shake well. Strain into a chilled Cocktail glass.

Pisco Sour

This classic cocktail was reputedly created in 1915 by Victor Morris, an American bartender from Berkeley who owned the Morris Bar in Lima, Peru.

> 2 ounces pisco brandy
> 3/4 ounce fresh lime juice
> 1/2 ounce simple syrup (page 35)
> 1 egg white
> 2 to 3 dashes of Angostura bitters, for garnish

Pour the brandy, juice, syrup, and egg white into an empty shaker. Dry-shake for about 10 seconds. Add ice cubes and shake very well. Strain into a chilled Cocktail glass. Dash the bitters on top as an aromatic garnish.

Piscorita Aromatica

Created by Gary Regan, 2006.

> 2¹/₂ ounces BarSol Quebranta pisco brandy
>
> 1¹/₂ ounces Cointreau
>
> ³/₄ ounce fresh lime juice
>
> 2 dashes of Angostura bitters
>
> Orange twist, for garnish (optional)

Pour all of the ingredients into a shaker two-thirds full of ice cubes. Shake well. Strain into a chilled Cocktail glass. Carefully flame the twist over the drink, if desired.

Piscorita Milanese

Created by Gary Regan, 2008.

> 2 ounces BarSol Quebranta pisco brandy
>
> ¹/₂ ounce Cointreau
>
> ¹/₂ ounce Grand Marnier
>
> ¹/₂ ounce Campari
>
> ¹/₂ ounce fresh lime juice
>
> Orange twist, for garnish (optional)

Pour all of the ingredients into a shaker two-thirds full of ice cubes. Shake well. Strain into a chilled Cocktail glass. Carefully flame the twist over the drink, if desired.

The Planter's Cocktail

Created for Captain Morgan by Gary Regan, circa 1998.

> 2 ounces Captain Morgan's Private Stock rum
>
> ¹/₂ ounce Godiva chocolate liqueur
>
> Maraschino cherry, for garnish

Pour both ingredients into a mixing glass two-thirds full of ice cubes. Stir well. Strain into a chilled Cocktail glass. Add the cherry.

Planter's Punch

2 ounces dark rum

2 ounces fresh grapefruit juice

1 ounce pineapple juice

1 ounce fresh lime juice

$1/2$ ounce simple syrup (page 35)

1 ounce club soda

Pineapple spear, for garnish

Pour the rum, fruit juices, and simple syrup into a shaker two-thirds full of ice cubes. Shake well. Pour into an ice-filled Collins glass. Pour in the club soda; stir briefly. Add the pineapple spear.

Pomegranate Julep

Adapted from a recipe by Jonathan Pogash and Herman Allenson, Prime Grill, Manhattan.

5 to 6 mint leaves

1 teaspoon Sugar in the Raw

1 ounce simple syrup (page 35)

$1^1/2$ ounces Basil Hayden bourbon

1 ounce pomegranate juice

Mint sprigs, for garnish

Muddle the mint leaves, sugar, and simple syrup in an empty mixing glass. Add ice cubes, the bourbon, and pomegranate juice. Stir very well. Pour directly into a Rocks glass. Garnish with the mint sprigs.

Pompier Cocktail

Based on the Pompier Highball, the gin is an additional ingredient.

$2^1/2$ ounces dry vermouth

$1/2$ ounce gin

$1/2$ ounce crème de cassis

Lemon twist, for garnish

Pour all of the ingredients into a mixing glass two-thirds full of ice cubes. Stir well. Strain into a chilled Cocktail glass. Add the twist.

Pompier Highball

In French, *pompier* means "fireman." This is sure to put your fire out.

> **1½ ounces dry vermouth**
> **½ ounce crème de cassis**
> **Club soda**
> **Lemon twist, for garnish**

Pour the vermouth and cassis into a mixing glass two-thirds full of ice cubes. Stir well. Strain into an ice-filled Highball glass. Top with the club soda. Add the twist.

Pom-Pom

Adapted from a recipe by Sean Bigley, bartender at the Fontana Bar, Bellagio, Las Vegas.

> **3 fresh raspberries**
> **½ ounce Marie Brizard Cassis de Bordeaux**
> **1½ ounces Belvedere Pomarancza vodka**
> **1½ ounces fresh orange juice**
> **⅔ ounce fresh lemon juice**
> **⅓ ounce simple syrup (page 35)**

Muddle the raspberries and cassis in an empty shaker. Add ice cubes, and all of the remaining ingredients. Shake well. Strain into a chilled Cocktail glass.

Pony's Neck

> **Lemon peel spiral (page 41)**
> **6 to 8 ounces ginger ale**
> **Dash of Angostura bitters**

Place the lemon peel spiral into a Collins glass; fill the glass with ice cubes. Pour the ginger ale and bitters into the glass; stir briefly.

Port & Brandy

This potion used to be my favorite remedy for an upset tummy, but I'd be the last one to tell you to drink alcohol medicinally.

1¹/₂ ounces ruby port

1¹/₂ ounces brandy

Pour both ingredients into a small wine goblet; stir briefly.

Port & Brandy Cobbler

1¹/₂ ounces ruby port

1¹/₂ ounces brandy

¹/₂ ounce simple syrup (page 35)

Fresh fruit in season (your choice), for garnish

Pour all of the ingredients into a wine goblet filled with crushed ice. Stir briefly. Add the fruit.

Port Cooler

Adapted from a recipe by Rick Pitcher, Bolo, Manhattan.

2 lime wedges

6 fresh mint leaves

2 ounces Lillet Blanc

¹/₂ ounce Fonseca white port

Tonic water

Muddle the lime wedges and mint leaves in an empty shaker. Add ice cubes, the Lillet, and port. Shake well. Strain into an ice-filled Double Old-Fashioned glass. Top with the tonic water.

Port Wine Sangaree

2 ounces ruby port

¹/₂ ounce simple syrup (page 35)

Freshly grated nutmeg, for garnish

Pour both ingredients into a mixing glass two-thirds full of ice cubes; stir well. Strain into a chilled wine goblet. Sprinkle with the nutmeg.

Porteño

Adapted from a recipe by Murray Stenson, Zig Zag Café, Seattle, circa 2006.

$3/4$ ounce bourbon

$1/2$ ounce Fernet-Branca

$1/2$ ounce cherry brandy

$1/2$ ounce fresh lime juice

$1/2$ ounce Falernum liqueur or simple syrup (page 35)

Pour all of the ingredients into a shaker two-thirds full of ice cubes. Shake well. Strain into a chilled Cocktail glass.

Porto Champagne Cocktail

1 sugar cube

2 to 3 dashes Angostura bitters

1 ounce ruby port

5 ounces champagne

Lemon twist, for garnish

Drop the sugar cube into the bottom of a Champagne flute; sprinkle with the bitters. Add the port; carefully pour in the champagne. Add the twist.

Portuguese General

Adapted from a recipe by Patrick McCormick, bartender at The Oceanaire, Baltimore, Maryland.

1 orange wedge

$1/4$ ounce simple syrup (page 35)

$2^{1}/2$ ounces Citadelle gin

$3/4$ ounce ruby port

Muddle the orange wedge, simple syrup, and some ice in an empty shaker until all the juices have been extracted from the orange. Add ice cubes, the gin, and port. Shake well. Strain into a chilled Cocktail glass.

Pousse-Café

The Pousse-Café is actually a category of drinks, not a specific one. This one's good for starters. *Pousse-café* translates to "push the coffee."

1/2 ounce grenadine
1/2 ounce green crème de menthe
1/2 ounce light rum

Pour the ingredients, in the order given, over the back of a spoon into a Pousse-Café glass, floating one on top of the other.

Praguetive

Adapted from a recipe by Joe McCanta, barman and sommelier at Saf Organic Restaurant & Martini Bar, Istanbul.

Turkish raki, to rinse the glass
2 1/2 ounces straight rye whiskey
1 ounce Becherovka liqueur
Orange twist, for garnish

Coat the interior of a chilled Cocktail glass with the raki; discard any excess. Pour the rye and liqueur into a mixing glass two-thirds full of ice cubes. Stir well. Strain into the prepared glass. Carefully flame the twist over the drink.

Prairie Dog

Created by Gary Regan, 2008, as a cocktail to serve next to a chocolate dessert.

1 1/2 ounces Hendrick's gin
1/2 ounce Domaine de Canton ginger liqueur
1/4 ounce fresh lemon juice
Lemon twist, for garnish

Pour all of the ingredients into a shaker two-thirds full of ice cubes. Shake well. Strain into a chilled Cocktail glass. Add the twist.

Prairie Oyster

Some say this cures hangovers. I say that only vegetable soup cures hangovers. Oyster lovers should give this one a try anyway.

> 1 egg
> 1/4 ounce fresh lemon juice
> Dash of hot sauce
> Salt and pepper

Break the egg into a large Rocks glass; add the lemon juice, hot sauce, and salt and pepper to taste. Drink in one go.

Preakness Cocktail

In 1873, the year after a horse named Preakness won the very first race to be held at the Pimlico track, Governor Oden Bowie of Maryland, a horseman and racing entrepreneur, named the then-new race for three-year-olds after the horse. The word *preakness* comes from the language of the Minisi, a northern New Jersey tribe of Native Americans, who called their area *Pra-qua-les*, meaning "quail woods." The name just evolved into "Preakness."

> 2 ounces blended Canadian whisky
> 1 ounce sweet vermouth
> 2 dashes of Bénédictine
> Dash of Angostura bitters
> Lemon twist, for garnish

Pour all of the ingredients into a mixing glass two-thirds full of ice cubes. Stir well. Strain into a chilled Cocktail glass. Add the twist.

Presbyterian

For my money, it's tasty no matter what your religion.

> 2 1/2 ounces blended Canadian whisky
> 2 ounces ginger ale
> 2 ounces club soda
> Lemon twist, for garnish

Pour all of the ingredients into an ice-filled Highball glass; stir briefly. Add the twist.

Pretty in Pink

Created by Gary Regan for Brook Wilkinson on March 30, 2002.

> **2 ounces Van Gogh Wild Appel vodka**
> **³/₄ ounce crème de noyaux**
> **³/₄ ounce fresh lemon juice**
> **Club soda**

Pour the vodka, crème de noyaux, and juice into a shaker two-thirds full of ice cubes. Shake well. Strain into an ice-filled Collins glass. Top with club soda.

Prince of Wales Champagne Cocktail

Bonnie Prince Charlie? David? Charles? William?

> **1 sugar cube**
> **2 to 3 dashes of Angostura bitters**
> **¹/₂ ounce Drambuie**
> **5 ounces champagne or other sparkling wine**
> **Lemon twist, for garnish**

Drop the sugar cube into the bottom of a Champagne flute; sprinkle with the bitters. Add the Drambuie; carefully pour in the champagne. Add the twist.

The Prince of Wales's Cocktail

Adapted from a recipe in Imbibe From Absinthe Cocktail to Whiskey Smash, A Salute in Stories and Drinks to "Professor" Jerry Thomas, *by David Wondrich.*

> **1 teaspoon superfine sugar**
> **Dash of Angostura bitters**
> **¹/₂ teaspoon water**
> **1¹/₂ ounces straight rye whiskey**
> **¹/₄ teaspoon maraschino liqueur**
> **1 pineapple chunk (rinse well if using canned)**
> **1 ounce chilled brut champagne**
> **Lemon twist, for garnish**

This methodology is verbatim from *Imbibe:*

"Put the sugar in the mixing glass with the bitters and ¹/₂ teaspoon of water. Stir briefly until it has dissolved. Add the rye, the maraschino, and the pineapple chunk, fill two-thirds full of cracked ice and shake brutally to crush the pineapple. Strain into a chilled cocktail glass, add the cold champagne, and deploy the twist. Then smile."

Princeton Cocktail

Named for the university, which was founded in 1746, an early version of a drink with this name calls for sweetened gin with orange bitters and club soda, and yet another calls for gin, port, and orange bitters. This recipe is the twenty-first-century version.

> 1½ ounces gin
> ½ ounce dry vermouth
> ½ ounce fresh lime juice
> ½ ounce simple syrup (page 35)

Pour all of the ingredients into a shaker two-thirds full of ice cubes. Shake well. Strain into a chilled Cocktail glass.

Priority Cocktail

Created by Gary Regan, circa 2005.

> 2 ounces Cîroc vodka
> ¾ ounce Busnel calvados
> ¼ ounce Kahlúa
> Lemon twist, for garnish

Pour all of the ingredients into a mixing glass two-thirds full of ice cubes. Stir well. Strain into a chilled Cocktail glass. Add the twist.

The Pumpkin Martini

Adapted from a recipe created by David Pennachetti, beverage director at Maggiano's Little Italy, New York City.

> Granulated sugar and ground cinnamon for rimming the glass
> 3 ounces Bols Pumpkin Smash liqueur
> 1 ounce Captain Morgan spiced rum
> Dash of half-and-half
> Ground cinnamon, for garnish

Prepare a Cocktail glass. Pour all of the ingredients into a shaker two-thirds full of ice cubes. Shake well. Strain into the prepared glass. Sprinkle a little cinnamon on top.

The Punch and Judy

Adapted from a recipe by Charlotte Voisey, winner of the 2008 Official Cocktail of Tales of the Cocktail.

> **1 ounce Martell VSOP**
> **1/4 ounce Old New Orleans Crystal rum**
> **1/2 ounce Hendrick's gin**
> **1/2 ounce Bols orange curaçao**
> **2 ounces pineapple juice**
> **1/2 ounce fresh lime juice**
> **1/2 ounce orange juice**
> **1/2 ounce Partida agave nectar**
> **2 dashes of Angostura bitters**
> **4 mint leaves**
> **Lime wheel and freshly grated nutmeg, for garnishes**

Pour all of the liquid ingredients and the mint leaves into a shaker two-thirds full of ice cubes. Shake well. Strain into an ice-filled Highball glass. Float the lime wheel on top; sprinkle with the nutmeg.

Punt e Mes Fizz

Adapted from a recipe by Audrey Saunders, "Libation Goddess," New York City.

> **3/4 ounce Punt e Mes**
> **1 1/2 ounces sweet vermouth**
> **1 1/2 to 2 ounces Prosecco**
> **Lemon twist, for garnish**

Pour the Punt e Mes and vermouth into a mixing glass two-thirds full of ice cubes. Stir well. Strain into a chilled Cocktail glass. Top with the Prosecco. Add the twist.

Purgatory

Adapted from a recipe by Ted Kilgore, bartender and bar manager at Monarch Restaurant, Maplewood, Missouri.

> **2 1/2 ounces Rittenhouse straight rye whiskey (100 proof)**
> **3/4 ounce Bénédictine**
> **3/4 ounce green Chartreuse**
> **Lemon twist, for garnish**

Pour all of the ingredients into a mixing glass two-thirds full of ice cubes. Stir well. Strain into a chilled Cocktail glass. Add the twist.

Purple Haze

2 ounces vodka

2 ounces blackberry schnapps

2 ounces fresh orange juice

Pour all of the ingredients into a shaker two-thirds full of ice cubes. Shake well. Strain into a chilled Cocktail glass.

Purple Penis

This drink is popular with bartenders far and wide. Many of them suggest that when it is ordered, the barkeep should pretend not to hear. The object? To make the drinker shout out its name even louder.

2 ounces vodka

1¹/₂ ounces blue curaçao

1¹/₂ ounces Chambord raspberry liqueur

2 ounces cranberry juice

1 ounce fresh lemon juice

1 ounce simple syrup (page 35)

Pour all of the ingredients into a shaker two-thirds full of ice cubes. Shake well. Strain into a chilled Collins glass.

Pussyfoot

A nonalcoholic drink named for a Prohibition activist known as "Pussyfoot" Johnson.

6 ounces orange juice

1 ounce fresh lime juice

1 ounce fresh lemon juice

1 egg yolk

Pour all of the ingredients into a shaker two-thirds full of ice cubes. Shake very well. Strain into an ice-filled wine goblet.

A Quick Little Pick-Me-Up

Adapted from a recipe by Audrey Saunders, "Libation Goddess,"
New York City—this one's a shooter.

> ³/₄ ounce Maker's Mark bourbon
> ¹/₄ ounce Fernet-Branca Menta liqueur
> ¹/₂ ounce fresh lemon juice
> ³/₄ ounce simple syrup (page 35)
> Maraschino cherry, for garnish

Pour all of the ingredients into a shaker two-thirds full of ice
cubes. Shake well. Strain into a chilled Cocktail glass. Add
the cherry.

Ramos Gin Fizz

The Ramos Gin Fizz originated in the Big Easy, but making one
isn't so easy at all. Your upper body must be in good shape
because this drink requires shaking for a full three minutes—no
cheating allowed.

> 2 ounces gin
> ¹/₄ ounce fresh lime juice
> ¹/₄ ounce fresh lemon juice
> ¹/₂ ounce simple syrup (page 35)
> 4 drops of orange flower water
> 1 egg white
> 1 ounce light cream
> 2 ounces club soda

Pour the gin, citrus juices, simple syrup, orange flower water,
egg white, and cream into a shaker two-thirds full of ice cubes.
Shake very well for at least 3 minutes. Strain into a chilled wine
goblet. Add the club soda; stir briefly.

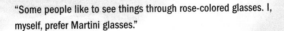

"Some people like to see things through rose-colored glasses. I,
myself, prefer Martini glasses."

—Michel Roux, late chairman and C.E.O., Crillon Importers Ltd.

Rauch

Adapted from a recipe by Laila Darwich and Helmut Adam, bartenders at Salz, Berlin, Germany, circa 2005.

   1/3 ounce Laphroaig 10-year-old single-malt scotch
   1 1/2 ounces Black Mozart chocolate liqueur
   2 1/2 ounces tamarind juice
   Slice of star anise, for garnish

Pour all of the ingredients into a shaker two-thirds full of ice cubes. Shake well. Strain into a crushed ice–filled Double Old-Fashioned glass. Add the star anise.

The RBS Special Cocktail

Adapted from a recipe created by David Wondrich in 2001 for New York's RBS Gazette, a "paper put out by the Rubber Band Society, a New York–based coalition of writers and artists, many of whom are Russian."

   2 ounces Wild Turkey straight rye whiskey
   1/4 ounce Gilka Kümmel
   1/2 ounce fresh lemon juice
   1/4 ounce grenadine

Pour all of the ingredients into a shaker two-thirds full of ice cubes. Shake well. Strain into a chilled Cocktail glass.

The Red Delicious

Adapted from a recipe by Eric Schreiber, bar manager at Chaya Brasserie, San Francisco, circa 2003.

   1 1/2 ounces Van Gogh Wild Appel vodka
   3/4 ounce de Kuyper Sour Apple Pucker or Van Gogh Applefest
   1/2 ounce fresh lime juice
   1/2 ounce cranberry juice

Pour all of the ingredients into a shaker two-thirds full of ice cubes. Shake well. Strain into a chilled Cocktail glass.

Red Snapper

In 1934, when Vincent Astor hired Fernand "Pete" Petiot as a bartender at New York City's St. Regis Hotel, Astor wasn't keen on the name of Petiot's signature drink, the Bloody Mary, and changed it to the Red Snapper. The original name remained its popular moniker, though.

2 ounces tomato juice

2 ounces vodka

Dash of Worcestershire sauce

Pinch of salt

Pinch of cayenne pepper

Dash of fresh lemon juice

Pour all of the ingredients into a shaker two-thirds full of ice cubes. Shake well. Strain into an ice-filled Highball glass.

Red Wine Cooler

4 ounces dry red wine

4 ounces lemon-lime soda

Lemon twist, for garnish

Pour both ingredients into an ice-filled Collins glass. Stir briefly; add the twist.

Redheaded Whore

1¹/₂ ounces brandy

1¹/₂ ounces sloe gin

¹/₂ ounce peach schnapps

Pour all of the ingredients into a mixing glass two-thirds full of ice cubes. Stir well. Strain into a chilled Cocktail glass or an ice-filled Rocks glass.

The Rembrandt

Adapted from a recipe by Ryan Magarian, Kathy Casey Food Studios/ Liquid Kitchen, Seattle, circa 2005.

2 ounces genever gin

1 ounce dry vermouth

¹/₄ ounce Drambuie

3 Drambuie-marinated raisins on a cocktail pick, for garnish

Pour all of the ingredients into a mixing glass two-thirds full of ice cubes. Stir well. Strain into a chilled Cocktail glass. Add the garnish.

Remember the *Maine*

Adapted from a recipe in The Gentleman's Companion: An Exotic Drinking Book, *by Charles H. Baker, Jr.*

2 ounces bourbon
$^3/_4$ ounce sweet vermouth
$^1/_4$ ounce cherry brandy
1 to 2 dashes absinthe, to taste
Angostura bitters, to taste

Pour all of the ingredients into a mixing glass two-thirds full of ice cubes. Stir well. Strain into a chilled Cocktail glass.

Remsen Cooler

An early cooler, this drink was originally made with Old Tom gin, but the base was changed circa 1900, when a cocktail book of the time called for scotch as the base.

$2^1/_2$ ounces Old Tom or London Dry gin
6 to 7 ounces club soda
Lemon twist, for garnish

Pour both ingredients into an ice-filled Collins glass. Stir briefly. Add the twist.

Renaissance Negroni

Adapted from a recipe by Duggan McDonnell, bar manager at Frisson, San Francisco, circa 2005.

$1^1/_2$ ounces Plymouth gin
1 ounce Germain-Robin Liqueur de Poète
$^3/_4$ ounce Campari
Orange twist, for garnish

Pour all of the ingredients into a mixing glass two-thirds full of ice cubes. Stir well. Strain into a chilled Cocktail glass. Add the twist.

Rick Moonen's Lemon-Ginger Grog

Adapted from a recipe from Rick Moonen, rm restaurant, New York City.

1/2 ounce shaved fresh ginger

1 tablespoon dark brown sugar

4 whole black peppercorns

1 thin lemon slice

4 ounces boiling water

2 ounces dark rum (use spiced rum for added depth of flavor)

Muddle the ginger and the sugar in a glass cup or mug. Add the peppercorns, lemon slice, and boiling water; let steep for 1 minute. Add the rum; stir briefly.

Ritz of New York

Created by Dale DeGroff, New York City.

1 ounce cognac

1/2 ounce triple sec

2 splashes of maraschino liqueur

1/2 ounce fresh lemon juice

2 1/2 to 3 ounces chilled dry champagne or other
  sparkling wine

Orange twist, for garnish

Pour the cognac, triple sec, maraschino liqueur, and lemon juice into a mixing glass two-thirds full of ice cubes. Stir well. Strain into a chilled Champagne flute. Add the champagne. Carefully flame the orange peel over the drink and discard.

Riveredge Cocktail

Adapted from a recipe by James Beard.

MAKES 4 SERVINGS

Grated zest of 1 orange

2 ounces orange juice

6 ounces gin

2 ounces dry vermouth

Pour all of the ingredients into a blender filled with 4 to 6 ice cubes. Blend until the ice is broken up and the ingredients are well combined. (This is not meant to be a frozen drink.) Divide among 4 chilled Cocktail glasses.

Rob Roy

This drink was created at the Waldorf-Astoria hotel, New York City, and named for the 1913 Broadway musical of the same name.

2¹/₂ ounces scotch
¹/₂ ounce sweet vermouth
Maraschino cherry, for garnish

Pour both ingredients into a mixing glass two-thirds full of ice cubes. Stir well. Strain into a chilled Cocktail glass. Add the cherry.

Rob Roy, Dry

2¹/₂ ounces scotch
¹/₂ ounce dry vermouth
Lemon twist, for garnish

Pour both ingredients into a mixing glass two-thirds full of ice cubes. Stir well. Strain into a chilled Cocktail glass. Add the twist.

Rob Roy, Perfect

2¹/₂ ounces scotch
¹/₄ ounce sweet vermouth
¹/₄ ounce dry vermouth
Lemon twist, for garnish

Pour all of the ingredients into a mixing glass two-thirds full of ice cubes. Stir well. Strain into a chilled Cocktail glass. Add the twist.

Rolls Royce Cocktail

A drink from the U.K., circa 1930.

2¹/₂ ounces gin
¹/₄ ounce sweet vermouth
¹/₄ ounce dry vermouth
Dash of Bénédictine

Pour all of the ingredients into a mixing glass two-thirds full of ice cubes. Stir well. Strain into a chilled Cocktail glass.

The Rose

Based on an early-twentieth-century Parisian cocktail, this is Dave Wondrich's formula for this spectacular drink.

> 2 ounces Noilly Prat dry vermouth
>
> 1 ounce Trimbach Kirschwasser
>
> 1 teaspoon raspberry syrup

Pour all of the ingredients into a mixing glass two-thirds full of ice cubes. Stir well. Strain into a chilled Cocktail glass.

Rosé the Riveter

Adapted from a recipe by LeNell Smothers, 2006.

> 1¹/₂ ounces Hendrick's gin
>
> ¹/₂ ounce PAMA pomegranate liqueur
>
> ¹/₄ ounce honey syrup (see recipe below)
>
> 3 ounces dry rosé wine
>
> Lime wheel, for garnish

Pour all of the ingredients into a shaker two-thirds full of ice cubes. Shake well. Strain into a chilled Collins glass. Add the lime wheel.

HONEY SYRUP

Mix equal parts of honey and water for a simple syrup. Do not heat; let dissolve naturally.

Rosebud

"'Rosebud.' The most famous word in the history of cinema. It explains everything, and nothing. Who, for that matter, actually heard Charles Foster Kane say it before he died?" —Roger Ebert

> 2 ounces red or pink grapefruit juice
>
> 2 ounces citrus vodka
>
> ¹/₂ ounce triple sec
>
> 1 ounce lime juice cordial, such as Rose's

Pour the grapefruit juice into an ice-filled Collins glass. Pour the vodka, triple sec, and lime juice cordial into a shaker two-thirds full of ice. Shake well. Strain into the Collins glass so the mixture floats on the grapefruit juice.

Rosita

1¹/₂ ounces white tequila

1 ounce Campari

¹/₂ ounce sweet vermouth

¹/₂ ounce dry vermouth

Dash of Angostura bitters

Lemon twist, for garnish

Pour all of the ingredients into a Double Old-Fashioned glass filled with crushed ice. Stir briefly. Add the twist.

Royale

Created by Peter Brown, Craigellachie Hotel, Scotland.

2 ounces scotch

1 ounce apple schnapps

4 ounces ginger ale

Build in a large crushed–ice–filled wine goblet.

The Ruby Delicious

Created by Gary Regan, circa 2004.

2 ounces cognac

2 ounces ruby port

1¹/₂ ounces Monin apple syrup

Apple slice, for garnish

Pour all of the ingredients into a shaker two-thirds full of ice cubes. Shake well. Strain into a chilled Cocktail glass. Add the apple slice.

Ruby Fizz

Adapted from a recipe by Symington Family Estates in Portugal.

6 ounces champagne

¹/₂ ounce Dow's ruby port

¹/₂ ounce cognac

Pour the champagne into a chilled Champagne flute. Add the port and cognac, and do not stir; let it mingle.

Ruby Sunday

Created by Gary Regan, 2008.

2 ounces Bombay Sapphire gin
1 ounce Domaine de Canton ginger liqueur
1 ounce rhubarb simple syrup (see recipe below)
$^1/_2$ ounce fresh lemon juice
6 fresh mint leaves

Pour all of the ingredients into a shaker two-thirds full of ice cubes. Shake well. Strain into a chilled Cocktail glass.

RHUBARB SIMPLE SYRUP

Combine 4 cups roughly chopped rhubarb with water to cover (about 2 cups) in a nonreactive saucepan set over moderately high heat. Add $^1/_2$ cup sugar and bring to a boil. Reduce the heat and simmer for a few minutes, until the rhubarb is tender. Strain the rhubarb syrup through a double layer of dampened cheesecloth; discard the solids.

Rum Runner

2 ounces Bacardi 151-proof rum
$1^1/_2$ ounces blackberry brandy
1 ounce crème de banane
$^1/_2$ ounce fresh lime juice
Splash of grenadine
Lime wedge, for garnish

Pour all of the ingredients into a blender. Add 4 to 6 ice cubes; blend until frozen. Pour into a wine goblet. Add the lime wedge.

Rum Swizzle

2 ounces dark rum
$^1/_2$ ounce fresh lemon juice
$^1/_2$ ounce triple sec
5 to 6 ounces ginger ale
Lemon wheel, for garnish

Pour the rum, lemon juice, and triple sec into a shaker two-thirds full of ice cubes; shake well. Strain into an ice-filled Collins glass. Add the ginger ale; stir briefly. Add the lemon wheel and a swizzle stick.

The Bartender's Best Friend

Russian Quaalude

This drink caught on in the late 1980s.

1 ounce vodka
1 ounce Baileys Irish cream liqueur
1 ounce Frangelico

Pour all of the ingredients into a shaker two-thirds full of ice cubes. Shake well. Strain into a Pony glass. It's also good sipped from an ice-filled Rocks glass.

Russian Walnut Martini

Adapted from 2087 An American Bistro, Thousand Oaks, California.

2 ounces Stolichnaya vodka
1 ounce Nocello walnut liqueur
1/2 ounce dark crème de cacao

Pour all of the ingredients into a mixing glass two-thirds full of ice cubes. Stir well. Strain into a chilled Cocktail glass.

Rusty Gate

Adapted from a recipe by Wes Bouchia, bar manager at Yoshi's, San Francisco, 2008.

2 ounces Wild Turkey 101-proof bourbon
1/4 ounce Wild Turkey American Honey liqueur
1/4 ounce Cinzano sweet vermouth
Dash of Stirrings Blood Orange Bitters
Blood orange twist, for garnish

Pour all of the ingredients into a mixing glass two-thirds full of ice cubes. Stir well. Strain into a chilled Cocktail glass. Add the twist.

Rusty Nail

"The latest [cocktail made with a liqueur], the Rusty Nail, is also one of the most mellow—a simple libation of Scotch on the rocks with a float of Drambuie."—Thomas Mario, *Playboy*, April 1968

2 ounces scotch
1/2 ounce Drambuie
Lemon twist, for garnish

Pour both ingredients into an ice-filled Rocks glass. Stir briefly. Add the twist.

Rye & Ginger

Though this drink is usually built with blended Canadian whisky, it really should contain straight rye whiskey.

2¹/₂ ounces straight rye whiskey

4 ounces ginger ale

Build in an ice-filled Highball glass. Stir briefly.

The Sage Margarita

Adapted from a recipe by Ryan Magarian, Restaurant Zoe, Seattle.

2 ounces Sauza Hornitos tequila

1/2 ounce Cointreau

3/4 ounce fresh lime juice

1/4 ounce simple syrup (page 35)

3 large fresh sage sprigs (preferably pineapple sage)

Sage leaf, for garnish

Pour all of the ingredients, including the sage sprigs, into a shaker two-thirds full of ice cubes. Shake well. Strain into a chilled Cocktail glass. Add the sage leaf.

Saketini

2¹/₂ ounces gin or vodka

1/4 ounce saké

Anchovy-stuffed olive, for garnish

Pour both ingredients into a mixing glass two-thirds full of ice cubes. Stir well. Strain into a chilled Cocktail glass. Garnish with the olive.

Salty Chihuahua

Inspired by the Salty Dog, this one is especially for small-dog lovers.

Salt and a lime wedge, for rimming the glass

2¹/₂ ounces tequila

4 ounces grapefruit juice

Prepare a Highball glass and fill it with ice. Pour both ingredients into the prepared glass. Stir briefly.

Salty Dog

If you don't salt the rim of the glass, it's a Greyhound.

Salt and a lime wedge, for rimming the glass

2¹/₂ ounces vodka

4 ounces grapefruit juice

Prepare a Highball glass and fill it with ice. Pour both ingredients into the prepared glass. Stir briefly.

Sangria

Usually made with red wine, the name of this punch probably comes from the Spanish *sangre*, meaning "blood."

MAKES ABOUT FOURTEEN 6-OUNCE SERVINGS

1¹/₂ 750-ml bottles dry red wine

1/₂ 750-ml bottle white wine

6 ounces brandy

6 ounces triple sec

6 ounces simple syrup (page 35)

6 ounces fresh orange juice

6 ounces cranberry juice

Diced apples and pears, plus orange and lemon wheels, for garnishes

Pour all of the ingredients into a large bowl; stir well. Cover and refrigerate until chilled, at least 4 hours. Pour the sangria into a large pitcher. Add all of the garnishes and stir to mix.

Santa Barbara

Created by Yvan D. Lemoine, New York City, 2008.

4 to 5 mint leaves

1 ounce St-Germain Elderflower liqueur

1¹/₂ ounces Chopin vodka

2¹/₂ ounces fresh Fiji apple juice

1 lemon wedge

Splash of club soda

Muddle the mint in an empty Collins glass. Add ice cubes, the liqueur, vodka, and apple juice. Stir well. Squeeze the lemon on top and top with the club soda. Stir briefly.

Sappho

Adapted from a recipe by Rafael Ballesteros, Spain, circa 2007.

> **Green Chartreuse, to rinse the glass**
> **2 1/2 ounces gin**
> **1/2 ounce Campari**
> **1/4 ounce Cointreau**
> **Orange twist, for garnish**

Coat the interior of a chilled Cocktail glass with the Chartreuse; discard any excess. Pour all of the remaining ingredients into a mixing glass two-thirds full of ice cubes. Stir well. Strain into the glass. Add the twist.

Sargasso

Created by Don Lee, PDT, New York City, who won second place in the 2008 Rhum Clément Cocktail Challenge.

> **2 ounces Clément V.S.O.P. rum**
> **3/4 ounce Lustau East India sherry**
> **1/2 ounce Aperol**
> **2 dashes of Angostura bitters**

Pour all of the ingredients into a mixing glass two-thirds full of ice cubes. Stir well. Strain into a chilled Cocktail glass.

The Sassentini

Adapted from a recipe by Brian Sassen, New York, 2002.

> **2 ounces Hennessy cognac**
> **3/4 ounce Martini & Rossi dry vermouth**
> **1/2 ounce peach schnapps**
> **1/4 ounce fresh lemon juice**
> **Lemon twist, for garnish**

Pour all of the ingredients into a shaker two-thirds full of ice cubes. Shake well. Strain into a chilled Cocktail glass. Add the twist.

The Bartender's Best Friend

Satan's Whiskers

¹/₂ ounce gin

¹/₂ ounce dry vermouth

¹/₂ ounce sweet vermouth

¹/₂ ounce Grand Marnier

¹/₂ ounce fresh orange juice

Dash of orange bitters

Pour all of the ingredients into a shaker two-thirds full of ice cubes. Shake well. Strain into a chilled Cocktail glass or an ice-filled Rocks glass.

Sazerac

The Sazerac was created in New Orleans in the mid-1800s and originally contained brandy as a base liquor. Bourbon or rye whiskey usually replace it now.

¹/₂ ounce absinthe

2 ounces bourbon or straight rye whiskey

¹/₂ ounce simple syrup (page 35)

2 dashes of Peychaud's bitters

Lemon twist, for garnish

Coat the interior of a Rocks glass with the absinthe. Fill the glass with crushed ice. Pour all of the remaining ingredients into a mixing glass two-thirds full of ice cubes. Stir well. Discard the crushed ice and absinthe from the Rocks glass; strain the drink into the glass. Add the twist.

Schnapp, Crackle, & Pop

1 ounce Van Gogh Wild Appel vodka

¹/₂ ounce cinnamon schnapps

4 to 5 ounces champagne or other sparkling wine

Pour all of the ingredients into a chilled Champagne flute.

Scofflaw Cocktail

A French creation from the 1920s, when *scofflaw* was a brand-new word.

2 ounces dry vermouth
1 ounce fresh lemon juice
$^1/_2$ ounce grenadine
Dash of orange bitters or triple sec

Pour all of the ingredients into a shaker two-thirds full of ice cubes. Shake well. Strain into a chilled Cocktail glass or an ice-filled Rocks glass.

Scorched Earth

Adapted from a recipe by Nicholas Gray Hearin, bartender, Restaurant Eugene, Atlanta, Georgia.

$1^1/_2$ ounces cognac
$^1/_2$ ounce sweet vermouth
$^1/_2$ ounce Cynar liqueur
Lemon twist, for garnish

Pour all of the ingredients into a mixing glass two-thirds full of ice cubes. Stir well. Strain into a chilled Cocktail glass. Carefully flame the twist over the glass.

Scorpion

Can you say "tiki bar"?

2 ounces dark rum
$^1/_2$ ounce brandy
$^1/_2$ ounce dry vermouth
$^1/_4$ ounce gin
1 ounce orange juice
1 ounce fresh lemon juice
Dash of orgeat syrup
Mint sprig, for garnish

Pour all of the ingredients into a shaker two-thirds full of ice cubes. Shake well. Strain into a large, ice-filled wine goblet. Add the mint sprig.

S

The Bartender's Best Friend

Scotch Mist

This drink is in the style of a Frappé, although most drinks in that category contain just one ingredient.

2 ounces scotch
1/2 ounce Drambuie

Fill a Sour glass with crushed ice; add the scotch and Drambuie.

Screamin' Carl

Adapted from a recipe by Neyah White, Nopa, San Francisco.

3/4 ounce ruby port (such as Carl Sutton's Solera)
1/2 ounce Cointreau
3 dashes of Angostura bitters
4 ounces chilled sparkling wine
Fresh strawberry, for garnish

Build in a chilled Champagne flute. Add the (critical, according to Neyah) strawberry.

Screwdriver

Garnish with a screwdriver.

2 1/2 ounces vodka
4 ounces orange juice

Build in an ice-filled Highball glass; stir briefly.

Seabreeze

2 ounces vodka
2 ounces grapefruit juice
1 1/2 ounces cranberry juice
Lime wedge, for garnish

Pour all of the ingredients into an ice-filled Highball glass. Stir briefly. Add the lime wedge.

Seelbach Cocktail

Created at Louisville's Seelbach Hotel in Kentucky, around 1917, when a bartender reportedly spilled champagne into a Manhattan cocktail.

> 1 ounce bourbon
> $1/2$ ounce triple sec
> 7 dashes of Angostura bitters
> 7 dashes of Peychaud's bitters
> Chilled champagne
> Orange twist, for garnish

Build in a Champagne flute. Add the twist.

7 & 7

> $2^1/2$ ounces Seagram's 7 whiskey
> 4 ounces 7UP
> Lemon twist, for garnish

Pour both ingredients into an ice-filled Highball glass. Stir briefly. Add the twist.

7 Leguas Margarita

Adapted from a recipe by Thad Vogler, bar manager at Jardiniere, San Francisco.

> Salt, for rimming the glass
> $1^1/2$ ounces 7 Leguas silver tequila
> $3/4$ ounce Qi White liqueur
> $3/4$ ounce fresh lime juice
> 1 demitasse spoon raw organic sugar

Prepare a Cocktail glass. Pour all of the remaining ingredients into a shaker two-thirds full of ice cubes. Shake well. Strain into the prepared glass.

Sex on a Peach

Created by Gary Regan, 2007.

> $1/2$ ounce Bénédictine, to rinse the glass
> $2^1/2$ ounces Bombay Sapphire gin

1/2 ounce Cointreau

1/2 ounce peach schnapps

1/2 ounce fresh lemon juice

Rinse a chilled Cocktail glass with the Bénédictine; discard the excess. Pour all of the remaining ingredients into a shaker two-thirds full of ice cubes. Shake well. Strain into the prepared glass.

Sex on the Beach

Peach schnapps, OJ, CJ, vodka, and Sex on the Beach—yum.

2 ounces vodka

1 ounce peach schnapps

2 ounces orange juice

1 1/2 ounces cranberry juice

Build in an ice-filled Highball glass; stir briefly.

Sex with the Bartender Martini

Enough said.

3/4 ounce Bacardi Limón rum

3/4 ounce triple sec

3/4 ounce fresh lime juice

1/2 ounce grenadine

Pour all of the ingredients into a shaker two-thirds full of ice cubes. Shake well. Strain into a chilled Cocktail glass.

Shagadelic Shooter

Adapted from 2087 An American Bistro, Thousand Oaks, California.

2 ounces white tequila

1/2 ounce blue curaçao

1/2 ounce fresh lemon juice

Maraschino cherry, for garnish

Pour all of the ingredients into a shaker two-thirds full of ice cubes. Shake well. Strain into a Pony glass. Garnish with the cherry.

S

DRINKS A TO Z

Shandy Gaff

A drink that dates back to at least the 1880s.

8 ounces lemon-lime soda

8 ounces amber ale

Carefully pour the soda and ale into a 16-ounce beer glass.

Shanghai Tea

Adapted from a recipe created by Evelyn Hsu for Peacock Alley,
Waldorf-Astoria, New York City, 2006.

2 ounces Hennessey XO cognac

1 ounce infused sweet vermouth (see recipe below)

1 ounce brewed green tea

1 ounce PAMA pomegranate liqueur

Splash of fresh lime juice

Lime wedge, for garnish

Pour all of the ingredients into a shaker two-thirds full of ice
cubes. Shake well. Strain into an ice-filled Highball glass. Add
the lime wedge.

INFUSED SWEET VERMOUTH

Pour 1 750-ml bottle of sweet vermouth, 6 cardamom pods,
6 whole cloves, and 1 cinnamon stick. into a nonreactive
saucepan set over moderately high heat. Bring to a boil. Set
aside to cool to room temperature. Strain through a double layer
of dampened cheesecloth; discard the solids. Refrigerate.

Shark Bite

Shades of *Jaws*.

³/₄ ounce spiced rum, such as Captain Morgan's

³/₄ ounce light rum

¹/₂ ounce blue curaçao

1 ounce fresh lime juice

¹/₂ ounce simple syrup (page 35)

3 drops of grenadine, for garnish

Pour the rums, curaçao, lime juice, and simple syrup into a
shaker two-thirds full of ice cubes. Shake well. Strain into a
chilled Cocktail glass. Garnish with the drops of grenadine.

Sherman's Revenge

Adapted from a recipe by Eric Simpkins, bartender at Pegu Club, New York City.

> 3 orange twists
> 2¹/₂ ounces Old Overholt rye whiskey
> 1 ounce Pedro Ximénez Sweet Cream sherry
> Dash of Regans' Orange Bitters No. 6

One at a time, flame 2 of the orange twists over a chilled Cocktail glass; discard both twists. Pour all of the remaining ingredients into a mixing glass two-thirds full of ice cubes. Stir well. Strain into the glass. Carefully flame the remaining twist on top, and drop it into the drink.

Sherry Sangaree

> 2 ounces dry sherry
> ¹/₂ ounce simple syrup (page 35)
> Freshly grated nutmeg, for garnish

Pour both ingredients into a mixing glass two-thirds full of ice cubes; stir well. Strain into a chilled wine goblet. Sprinkle with the nutmeg.

Shirley Temple

Shirley Temple made almost 50 movies between 1932 and 1943. In the late 1960s, she ran for Congress, and although she lost the election, as Shirley Temple Black she went on to have a successful career with the United Nations and the State Department.

> 1 ounce orange juice
> ¹/₂ ounce fresh lemon juice
> Splash of fresh lime juice
> 6 ounces lemon-lime soda
> Dash of grenadine
> Maraschino cherry, for garnish

Pour the citrus juices into a shaker two-thirds full of ice cubes. Shake well. Strain into an ice-filled Collins glass. Add the soda and the grenadine; stir briefly. Add the cherry.

Shirley Temptress

Adapted from a recipe by Tarcísio Costa, wine and spirits director at Alfama, New York City.

1 orange twist
2¹/₂ ounces Rainha Santa tawny port
1 ounce Ponte de Amarante brandy
¹/₂ ounce grenadine
¹/₂ ounce fresh lime juice
Small dash of Pernod

Carefully flame the twist over a chilled Cocktail glass; drop the twist into the glass. Pour all of the remaining ingredients into a shaker two-thirds full of ice cubes. Shake well. Strain into the prepared glass.

Sidecar

Reportedly created in Paris during World War I, this classic cocktail was named for a customer at the bar where it was invented, who was driven to and from the bar in the sidecar of a motorcycle.

Superfine sugar and a lemon wedge, for rimming the glass
2 ounces cognac or brandy
¹/₂ ounce Cointreau
¹/₂ ounce fresh lemon juice

Prepare a Cocktail glass. Pour all of the remaining ingredients into a shaker two-thirds full of ice cubes. Shake well. Strain into the prepared glass.

Silver Bullet

There are many different versions of the Silver Bullet, although gin seems to be the base for all of them. This scotch-laced formula dates back to the early 1960s.

2¹/₂ ounces gin
2 dashes of scotch
Lemon twist, for garnish

Pour the gin and scotch into a mixing glass two-thirds full of ice cubes. Stir well. Strain into a chilled Cocktail glass. Add the twist.

The Singapore Sling

Note that there are two versions of this drink: This first recipe originally went under the banner of the Straights Sling. The formula was found by Ted "Dr. Cocktail" Haigh. It calls for kirsch, a dry cherry brandy. The second recipe is the kind of drink you'll get at the Raffles Hotel in Singapore, where the drink is said to have been created by bartender Ngiam Tong Boon in 1915.

RECIPE #1

2 ounces gin
$1/2$ ounce Bénédictine
$1/2$ ounce kirsch
$3/4$ ounce fresh lemon juice
Orange bitters, to taste
Angostura bitters, to taste
Club soda

Pour the gin, Bénédictine, kirsch, lemon juice, and both bitters into a shaker two-thirds full of ice cubes. Shake well. Strain into an ice-filled Collins glass. Top with the club soda.

RECIPE #2

This drink doesn't contain club soda when served at the Raffles Hotel.

2 ounces Beefeater gin
$1/2$ ounce Cherry Heering
$1/4$ ounce Bénédictine
$1/2$ ounce Cointreau
2 ounces pineapple juice
$3/4$ ounce fresh lime juice
Angostura bitters, to taste
Club soda

Pour the gin, Cherry Heering, Bénédictine, Cointreau, both juices, and the bitters into a shaker two-thirds full of ice cubes. Shake well. Strain into an ice-filled Collins glass. Top with the club soda.

Single-Malt Scotch Martini

Created by master bartender Norman Bukofzer, New York City.

> **3 ounces single-malt scotch**
> **1/2 ounce fino sherry**
> **Lemon twist, for garnish**

Pour both ingredients into a mixing glass two-thirds full of ice cubes. Stir well. Strain into a chilled Cocktail glass. Add the twist.

The Sleeve

Adapted from a recipe by Neyah White, Nopa, San Francisco, 2008.

> **1 ounce Plymouth or Beefeater gin**
> **1 ounce Pineau de Charente wine**
> **2 dashes of orange bitters**
> **Orange slice, for garnish**

Pour all of the ingredients into a mixing glass two-thirds full of ice cubes. Stir gently. Strain into a chilled Sherry glass. Add the orange slice.

Sloe Comfortable Screw

The simple version.

> **3/4 ounce sloe gin**
> **3/4 ounce Southern Comfort**
> **3/4 ounce vodka**
> **3 to 5 ounces orange juice**

Pour all of the ingredients into a shaker two-thirds full of ice cubes. Shake well. Strain into an ice-filled Highball glass.

Sloe Comfortable Screw Against the Wall with Satin Pillows

The party version.

> **1/2 ounce sloe gin**
> **1/2 ounce Southern Comfort**
> **1/2 ounce vodka**

1/2 ounce Galliano

1/2 ounce Frangelico

3 to 5 ounces orange juice

Pour all of the ingredients into a shaker two-thirds full of ice cubes. Shake well. Strain into an ice-filled Highball glass.

Sloe Gin Fizz

What everybody used to order the minute they reached legal drinking age.

2 ounces sloe gin

1 ounce fresh lemon juice

1/2 ounce simple syrup (page 35)

5 to 6 ounces club soda

Fresh fruit in season (your choice), for garnish

Pour the sloe gin, lemon juice, and simple syrup into a shaker two-thirds full of ice cubes. Shake well. Strain into a chilled wine goblet. Add the club soda; stir briefly. Add the fruit.

Smurf Piss

Don't ask.

1/2 ounce light rum

1/2 ounce blueberry schnapps

1/2 ounce blue curaçao

1/2 ounce fresh lemon juice

Lemon-lime soda

Pour the rum, schnapps, curaçao, and lemon juice into a shaker two-thirds full of ice cubes. Shake well. Strain into an ice-filled Highball glass. Top with the soda. Stir with a sip-stick.

Snake Bite #1

This drink is very popular in the U.K., and it really packs a punch.

8 ounces hard cider

8 ounces amber ale

Carefully pour the cider and ale into a 16-ounce beer glass.

Snake Bite #2

8 ounces hard cider

8 ounces brown ale

Carefully pour the cider and ale into a 16-ounce beer glass.

Snake Bite #3

This version of the Snake Bite is American and made its debut in the early 1970s.

2 ounces blended Canadian whisky

1/2 ounce white crème de menthe

Pour both ingredients into a mixing glass two-thirds full of ice cubes. Stir well. Strain into a chilled Pony glass.

S.O.C.

Adapted from a recipe by Jonathan Abogado, bartender on the cruise ship Paul Gauguin, sailing out of Tahiti.

2 1/2 ounces cognac

3/4 ounce Chambord raspberry liqueur

3/4 ounce Frangelico

2 dashes of Angostura bitters (optional)

Lemon twist, for garnish

Pour all of the ingredients into a mixing glass two-thirds full of ice cubes. Stir well. Strain into a chilled Cocktail glass. Add the twist.

The Social

Created by "King Cocktail," Dale DeGroff, New York City, 1998.

2 ounces Jack Daniel's Tennessee whiskey

3/4 ounce fresh lemon juice

1/2 ounce Cherry Heering

1/2 ounce simple syrup (page 35)

Maraschino cherry and a lemon twist, for garnishes

Pour all of the ingredients into a shaker two-thirds full of ice cubes. Shake well. Strain into a chilled Cocktail glass. Add the cherry and the twist.

The Bartender's Best Friend

The Soiree

Adapted from a recipe by Duggan McDonnell, Jeff Hollinger, and H. Joseph Ehrmann for San Francisco Cocktail Week, 2008.

1 1/2 ounces Partida Blanco tequila

1/2 ounce St-Germain Elderflower liqueur

1/2 ounce green Chartreuse

1/2 ounce fresh lemon juice

2 dashes of cinnamon-chile tincture (see recipe below)

Jalapeño pepper slice, for garnish

Pour all of the ingredients into a shaker two-thirds full of ice cubes. Shake well. Strain into a chilled Cocktail glass. Add the jalapeño.

CINNAMON-CHILE TINCTURE

5 cinnamon sticks, broken up

1 cup cacao nibs

1 red bell pepper, cored, seeded, and finely diced

2 Fresno chiles, cored, seeded, and finely diced

1 1/2 dried Thai dragon chiles, finely diced

1 750-ml bottle Partida Blanco tequila

Place all of the ingredients into a large jar with a tight-fitting lid. Shake the jar twice daily for 4 days. Strain the mixture through a double layer of dampened cheesecloth; discard the solids. Bottled, the tincture should last at room temperature for at least 1 year.

Sol y Sombre

The Sol y Sombre is a Spanish creation—play with the ratios to vary the level of sweetness.

1 1/2 ounces brandy

1 1/2 ounces anisette

Pour both ingredients into a mixing glass two-thirds full of ice cubes. Stir well. Strain into a snifter.

Sombrero

2 ounces Kahlúa

1¹/₂ ounces light cream

Pour both ingredients into a shaker two-thirds full of ice cubes. Shake well. Strain into an ice-filled Rocks glass.

Sophistication

Adapted from a recipe by Ray Srp, bartender at the Allegro Bar, Bellagio, Las Vegas.

1 ounce Dubonnet Rouge

1 ounce Bacardi Limón rum

¹/₂ ounce fresh lime juice

1 teaspoon granulated sugar

Champagne

Pour the Dubonnet, rum, lime juice, and sugar into a shaker two-thirds full of ice cubes. Shake well. Strain into a chilled Champagne flute. Top with the champagne.

Sortie's Green Tea Martini

Adapted from a recipe created by Juan Coronado, Sortie Restaurant, New York City.

2 ounces Charbay Green Tea vodka

1¹/₂ ounces Zen Green Tea liqueur

Whole shiso leaf, for garnish

Pour both ingredients into a shaker two-thirds full of ice cubes. Shake well. Strain into a chilled Cocktail glass. Add the shiso leaf.

Soul Kiss Cocktail

The Soul Kiss Cocktail was served at London's Savoy Hotel in the 1920s, where they also had a variation on the drink that contained no whisky.

2 ounces blended Canadian whisky

¹/₄ ounce dry vermouth

¹/₂ ounce Dubonnet Rouge

¹/₂ ounce orange juice

The Bartender's Best Friend

Pour all of the ingredients into a shaker two-thirds full of ice cubes. Shake well. Strain into a chilled Cocktail glass.

South Beach Martini

Deco, palm trees, hot sand, yes.

> 1¹/₂ ounces orange vodka
> 1¹/₂ ounces citrus vodka
> ¹/₂ ounce Cointreau
> ¹/₂ ounce fresh lime juice
> Orange twist, for garnish

Pour all of the ingredients into a shaker two-thirds full of ice cubes. Shake well. Strain into a chilled Cocktail glass. Add the twist.

Southern Comfort Manhattan

This drink is a fairly sweet variation on the Manhattan—it was very popular in the late 1970s.

> 2¹/₂ ounces Southern Comfort
> ¹/₂ ounce sweet vermouth
> 2 dashes of Angostura bitters
> Maraschino cherry, for garnish

Pour all of the ingredients into a mixing glass two-thirds full of ice cubes. Stir well. Strain into a chilled Cocktail glass. Add the cherry.

Southside Cocktail

The Southside has been around for decades, but it has made quite a comeback in recent years.

> 2 ounces gin
> 1 ounce fresh lemon juice
> ¹/₂ ounce simple syrup (page 35)
> 2 mint sprigs, for garnish

Pour all of the ingredients into a shaker two-thirds full of ice cubes. Shake well. Strain into a chilled Cocktail glass. Add the mint sprigs.

Spanish Main

Adapted from a recipe by David Wondrich, author of Killer Cocktails.

1¹/₂ ounces Mount Gay Eclipse rum

1 ounce fino sherry

Scant ¹/₂ ounce Velvet Falernum liqueur

Pinch of cayenne pepper and an orange twist, for garnishes

Pour all of the ingredients into a mixing glass two-thirds full of ice cubes. Stir well. Strain into a chilled Cocktail glass. Dust with the cayenne pepper and then carefully flame the twist over the drink.

The Spanish Rose

Adapted from a recipe by David Nepove, bar manager, Enrico's, San Francisco.

1 rosemary sprig

³/₄ ounce fresh lemon juice

1¹/₂ ounces Plymouth gin

³/₄ ounce Quarenta y Tres Licor 43

¹/₂ ounce cranberry juice

Strip the leaves from the bottom half of the rosemary sprig and place them in an empty shaker. Add the lemon juice and muddle well. Add ice cubes, the gin, and the Licor 43. Shake well. Strain into an ice-filled wine goblet, and place the rosemary stem with its remaining leaves in the glass. Top with the cranberry juice.

Speyside

Created by Gary Regan, 2001.

2 ounces The Macallan 12-year-old single-malt scotch

1 ounce apple schnapps

Pour both ingredients into a mixing glass two-thirds full of ice cubes. Stir well. Strain into a chilled Cocktail glass.

Spice Market

*Created by my darling Naren Young for the B&B 70th Anniversary
Master Mixologist Showcase, March 25, 2008.*

1¹/₂ ounces Wild Turkey rye whiskey

³/₄ ounce B&B liqueur

¹/₂ ounce clove and vanilla syrup (see recipe below)

³/₄ ounce fresh lemon juice

1 egg white

Freshly grated nutmeg, for garnish

Pour all of the ingredients into an empty shaker. Dry-shake to
emulsify. Add ice cubes and shake well. Strain into a small wine
glass. Add the nutmeg.

CLOVE AND VANILLA SYRUP

Combine 2 cups hot water, 2 cups sugar, 2 vanilla beans, and
6 whole cloves in a nonreactive saucepan over moderate heat.
Bring to a simmer, stirring frequently until the sugar dissolves.
Set aside to cool. Strain through a double layer of dampened
cheesecloth. Bottle and refrigerate.

Spiced Cider

Spike individual servings at will.

MAKES ABOUT EIGHT 6-OUNCE SERVINGS

1 quart unsweetened apple cider

4 whole cloves

1 cinnamon stick (about 3 inches long), broken

¹/₂ teaspoon freshly grated nutmeg

12 ounces pear nectar

1 large block of ice

Apple and pear slices, for garnishes

Pour the apple cider into a large saucepan set over high heat. Add
the cloves, cinnamon, and nutmeg and bring the mixture to a boil.
Reduce the heat to low, cover, and simmer for 20 minutes.

Strain the mixture through a sieve lined with a double layer of
dampened cheesecloth; discard the solids. Set aside to cool to
room temperature. Pour in the pear nectar. Cover and refrigerate
until chilled.

Place the block of ice into a punch bowl. Add the chilled punch.
Add the apple and pear slices.

The Stanford Cocktail

Adapted from a recipe by Colin Field, head barman at the Hemingway Bar, Ritz Hotel, Paris.

1¹/₂ ounces amontillado sherry
1 ounce cognac
Angostura bitters, to taste

Pour all of the ingredients into a mixing glass two-thirds full of ice cubes. Stir well. Strain into a chilled Cocktail glass.

The Star Gazer

Adapted from a recipe by H. Joseph Ehrmann, owner, Elixir, San Francisco.

2 ounces Night Harvest Chardonnay
1 ounce dark rum
¹/₂ ounce vanilla bean syrup
¹/₂ ounce pineapple juice
Lime wedge, for garnish

Pour all of the ingredients into a shaker two-thirds full of ice cubes. Shake well. Strain into an ice-filled Highball glass. Squeeze the lime over the top of the drink, and drop it in to finish the drink.

The Starfish Cooler

Adapted from a recipe by Stacy Smith, bartender at G. W. Fins, New Orleans.

1 orange slice
1 mint leaf
1 ounce limoncello
1 ounce PAMA pomegranate liqueur
1 ounce unsweetened iced tea
¹/₂ ounce simple syrup (page 35)
1 ounce Moët & Chandon White Star champagne
Mint sprig, for garnish

Muddle the orange slice and mint leaf in an empty Collins glass. Add ice cubes and all of the remaining ingredients. Stir briefly. Add the mint sprig.

Starlight

Created by Tony Abou-Ganim, Bellagio, Las Vegas.

> $1^{1}/_{4}$ ounces Campari
> $^{1}/_{2}$ ounce Cointreau
> $^{1}/_{2}$ ounce fresh lemon juice
> $^{1}/_{2}$ ounce orange juice
> $^{1}/_{4}$ ounce simple syrup (page 35)
> Club soda
> $^{1}/_{2}$ ounce brandy
> Lemon wheel and a lime wheel, for garnishes

Pour the Campari, Cointreau, lemon juice, orange juice, and simple syrup into a shaker two-thirds full of ice cubes. Shake well. Strain into a Collins glass half-filled with ice. Add club soda to almost fill the glass; float the brandy on top. Garnish with the citrus wheels.

The Starlight 200

Adapted from a recipe by Jacques Bezuidenhout, bartender at Tres Agaves, San Francisco.

> $1^{1}/_{2}$ ounces Plymouth gin
> $^{3}/_{4}$ ounce Leacock's Madeira
> $^{1}/_{2}$ ounce Otima 10-year-old tawny port
> Dash of Angostura bitters
> Orange twist, for garnish

Pour all of the ingredients into a mixing glass two-thirds full of ice cubes. Stir well. Strain into a chilled Cocktail glass. Add the twist.

The Starry Night Cocktail

Created by Gary Regan for Van Gogh gin.

> $2^{1}/_{2}$ ounces Van Gogh gin
> 1 ounce Goldschlager

Pour both ingredients into a mixing glass two-thirds full of ice cubes. Stir well. Strain into a chilled Cocktail glass.

Stiletto

The flavors in this cocktail come together beautifully. This drink can also be served over ice in a Rocks glass.

> 2¹/₂ ounces bourbon
> ¹/₄ ounce amaretto
> ¹/₄ ounce fresh lime juice

Pour all of the ingredients into a shaker two-thirds full of ice cubes. Shake well. Strain into a chilled Cocktail glass.

Stinger

This is the one drink that's traditionally shaken, even though it contains no dairy products or fruit juices.

> 2¹/₂ ounces brandy
> ¹/₂ ounce white crème de menthe

Pour both ingredients into a shaker two-thirds full of ice cubes. Shake well. Strain into a crushed ice–filled wine goblet.

Stout Sangaree

The classic Sangaree.

> 10 ounces stout
> 2 ounces ruby port
> Freshly grated nutmeg, for garnish

Pour both ingredients into a large wine goblet; sprinkle with the nutmeg.

Suffering Bastard

Created by Joe Scialom, Shepheard's Hotel, Cairo, Egypt, circa 1945. This formula is adapted from a recipe in Esquire Drinks: An Opinionated and Irreverent Guide to Drinking, *by David Wondrich, 2002.*

> 1 ounce bourbon
> 1 ounce gin
> 1 teaspoon fresh lime juice
> Dash of Angostura bitters

Ginger ale

2 fresh mint sprigs, for garnish

Pour the bourbon, gin, lime juice, and bitters into a shaker two-thirds full of ice cubes. Shake well. Strain into an ice-filled Collins glass. Top with the ginger ale. Add the mint sprigs.

The Sultana

Adapted from a recipe created by Matthew Colling, Ponzu, San Francisco, 2005.

$1/2$ ounce yuzu juice

$1/2$ ounce fresh lime juice

1 ounce simple syrup (page 35)

10 to 15 fresh mint leaves

3 ounces Stolichnaya Vanil vodka

Muddle the yuzu juice, lime juice, simple syrup, and all of the mint leaves except for 1 in an empty shaker. Add ice cubes and the vodka. Shake well. Strain into a chilled Cocktail glass. Garnish with the reserved mint leaf.

Summer Berries

Adapted from a recipe by Xavier Herit, Francesco at Mix, Manhattan, this nonalcoholic drink is so tasty and refreshing. If you want to fancy it up, substitute champagne for the lemon-lime soda.

2 fresh raspberries, coarsely chopped

1 fresh strawberry, coarsely chopped

1 tablespoon brown sugar

1 tablespoon simple syrup (page 35)

1 tablespoon fresh lime juice

4 ounces lemon-lime soda

Fresh raspberry and a fresh mint sprig, for garnishes

Muddle the berries, sugar, simple syrup, and lime juice in an empty shaker. Add ice cubes, shake, and strain into an ice-filled Highball glass. Top with the lemon-lime soda, and stir briefly. Add the raspberry and mint sprig.

Summertime

Adapted from a recipe by Mathew Hewitt, head bartender, The Bowery, Brisbane, Australia, circa 2005.

> 1¹/₂ ounces bourbon
> ¹/₂ ounce Massenez crème de mûre
> ¹/₄ ounce sweet vermouth
> Dash of Grand Marnier

Pour all of the ingredients into a mixing glass two-thirds full of ice cubes. Stir well. Strain into a chilled Cocktail glass.

The Sun Salutation

Adapted from a recipe by David Nepove, Enrico's Bar & Restaurant, San Francisco.

> 10 mint leaves
> 1¹/₂ ounces Soho lychee liqueur
> ³/₄ ounce fresh lemon juice
> Club soda
> Fresh berries in season (your choice) and a mint sprig,
>   for garnishes

Muddle the mint leaves in an empty shaker until broken into flecks. Fill the shaker two-thirds full of ice; add the liqueur and lemon juice. Shake well. Strain into an ice-filled Collins glass. Top with the club soda. Add the berries and mint sprig.

Sunset on Dunnigan

Adapted from a recipe by H. Joseph Ehrmann, owner, Elixir, San Francisco.

> 2 ounces Night Harvest Sauvignon Blanc
> 1 ounce citrus-forward, light juniper gin, such as Bluecoat or
>   Tanqueray No. Ten
> ¹/₂ ounce St-Germain Elderflower liqueur
> Grapefruit twist, for garnish

Pour all of the ingredients into a mixing glass two-thirds full of ice. Stir well. Strain into a chilled Cocktail glass. Twist the twist to spray the oils over the surface of the cocktail. Drop the twist into the drink.

The Bartender's Best Friend

Sunsplash

Created by Tony Abou-Ganim, Bellagio, Las Vegas.

2^1/$_2$ ounces Stolichnaya Ohranj vodka
^{1}/$_2$ ounce Cointreau
1 ounce fresh lemon juice
1 ounce orange juice
^{1}/$_2$ ounce cranberry juice
^{1}/$_2$ ounce simple syrup (page 35)
Orange slice and lemon twist, for garnish

Pour all of the ingredients into a shaker two-thirds full of ice cubes. Shake well. Strain into a chilled Cocktail glass. Garnish with the orange slice and the twist.

Swamp Gas

Adapted from a recipe by Dawn Clemens, general manager of Cobalt, New Orleans.

1 ounce light rum
^{1}/$_2$ ounce Hpnotiq
^{1}/$_2$ ounce Cointreau
^{1}/$_3$ ounce fresh lime juice
Lime wedge, for garnish

Pour all of the ingredients into a shaker two-thirds full of ice cubes. Shake well. Strain into a chilled Cocktail glass. Add the lime wedge.

Sweet Dream

Created to celebrate 2003's Fashion Group International's Night of Stars.

2 ounces Maker's Mark bourbon
^{3}/$_4$ ounce Drambuie
^{1}/$_2$ ounce white crème de cacao
^{1}/$_2$ ounce fresh lemon juice
Lemon twist, for garnish

Pour all of the ingredients into a shaker two-thirds full of ice cubes. Shake well. Strain into a chilled Cocktail glass. Add the twist.

The Sweetie Pie

Created by Lydia Reissmueller, Elettaria, New York City, third-place winner in the Rhum Clément Cocktail Challenge.

2 ounces Clément V.S.O.P. rum
1/4 ounce St. Elizabeth Allspice Dram
1 1/2 ounces fresh-pressed apple juice
2 dashes of Angostura bitters
Pinch of sea salt

Build over ice, stir, and strain into a chilled Champagne Saucer glass.

Tabby Cat

2 ounces Dubonnet Rouge
1 ounce Belvedere Pomarancza vodka
2 dashes of Regans' Orange Bitters No. 6
Lemon twist, for garnish

Pour all of the ingredients into a mixing glass two-thirds full of ice cubes. Stir well. Strain into a chilled Cocktail glass. Add the twist.

TAMI

Created by Gary Regan, 2007. The Palais Bénédictine in Fécamp, France, represents tradition, modernity, art, and industry. TAMI was named for these four features after the initials were rearranged a little. TAMI was born on October 18, 2007, at Maxim's, Paris.

1/2 ounce Bénédictine or B&B, to rinse the glass
2 1/2 ounces cognac
1 ounce Noilly Prat sweet vermouth
Dash of Angostura bitters

Rinse a chilled Cocktail glass with the liqueur; discard any excess. Pour all of the remaining ingredients into a mixing glass two-thirds full of ice cubes. Stir well. Strain into the glass.

Tangerine Martini

From the Morton's of Chicago Martini Club.

3 ounces Tanqueray Sterling vodka
1/2 ounce Mandarine Napoléon
Orange slice, for garnish

Pour both ingredients into a mixing glass two-thirds full of ice cubes. Stir well. Strain into a chilled Cocktail glass. Add the orange slice.

The Tangier Tartini

Adapted from a recipe by Farnoush Deylamian, Aziza, San Francisco, circa 2003.

2 ounces Charbay Ruby Red Grapefruit vodka
1 ounce guava nectar
1/4 ounce simple syrup (page 35)
1/2 ounce tonic water
Mango slice with peel, for garnish

Pour the vodka, nectar, and syrup into a shaker two-thirds full of ice cubes. Shake well. Strain into a chilled Cocktail glass. Top with the tonic water; add the mango slice.

The Tao of Love

Adapted from a recipe by George Delgado, New York City, circa 2003.

3 red raspberries
1/2 ounce simple syrup (page 35)
1/2 ounce fresh lime juice
1 ounce Raynal Tao liqueur
Chilled champagne

Muddle the raspberries and simple syrup in an empty shaker. Pour in the lime juice and liqueur; add ice. Shake vigorously. Strain into a chilled Champagne flute. Top with the champagne.

Tart Gin Cooler

The Tart Gin Cooler, created by Gary Regan and me in the 1990s, is a wonderfully refreshing drink.

>2 ounces gin
>
>2 ounces fresh pink grapefruit juice
>
>3 ounces tonic water
>
>2 dashes of Peychaud's bitters

Build in an ice-filled Collins glass. Stir with a straw.

Tea Tini

Adapted from a recipe from the Peninsula Grill, Charleston, South Carolina.

>Superfine sugar and a lemon wedge, for rimming the glass
>
>1³/₄ ounces Stolichnaya Ohranj vodka
>
>1 ounce sweetened iced tea
>
>1/4 ounce fresh lemon juice
>
>Lemon wedge, for garnish

Prepare a Cocktail glass. Pour all of the remaining ingredients into a shaker two-thirds full of ice cubes. Shake well. Strain into the prepared glass. Add the lemon wedge.

> "The little rum we had was a great service but our nights were particularly distressing. I generally served a teaspoon or two to each person and it was joyful tidings when they heard my intentions."
>
> —Captain William Bligh, 1789, after being set adrift with 18 sailors from *HMS Bounty* and not sighting land for more than six weeks

Tea Whiskey Highball

Adapted from a recipe by James Meehan, bartender at Gramercy Tavern, New York City.

>2¹/₂ ounces chilled Lapsang Souchong tea
>
>1¹/₄ ounces The Glenlivet single-malt scotch
>
>1 ounce mint syrup (recipe follows)

¹/₂ ounce Fernet-Branca Menta liqueur
Lemon twist, for garnish

Pour all of the ingredients into a mixing glass two-thirds full of ice cubes. Stir well. Strain into an ice-filled Collins glass. Add the twist.

MINT SYRUP

1 cup granulated sugar
1 cup water
40 mint leaves

Combine the sugar and water in a saucepan over moderate heat, Cook, stirring frequently, until the sugar dissolves completely. Remove from the heat and add the mint leaves. Set aside to cool. Transfer the mixture to a container; cover, and refrigerate overnight. Strain the mint leaves from the syrup the following day and store in a resealable container for up to 3 weeks.

Tea with the Brokers

Created by Gary Regan, 2008.

2 ounces Broker's gin (47% abv)
2 ounces chilled peach tea
1 ounce Domaine de Canton ginger liqueur
¹/₂ ounce fresh lemon juice
2 dashes of orange bitters
Lemon twist, for garnish

Pour all of the ingredients into a shaker two-thirds full of ice cubes. Shake well. Strain into a chilled Cocktail glass. Add the twist.

Tequila Conquistador

2 ounces white tequila
2 ounces fresh grapefruit juice
4 ounces tonic water

Build in an ice-filled Collins glass. Stir with a sip-stick or straw.

Tequila Mockingbird

2^1/$_2$ ounces white tequila

^{1}/$_2$ teaspoon white crème de menthe

^{1}/$_2$ ounce fresh lime juice

Pour all of the ingredients into a shaker two-thirds full of ice cubes. Shake well. Strain into a chilled Cocktail glass.

Tequila Neat

As easy as 1, 2, 3.

1 lime wedge

Pinch of salt

2 ounces tequila

Rub the lime wedge onto the back of your hand where the thumb meets the forefinger.

Sprinkle the salt onto the damp area of your hand.

Lick the salt from your hand, knock the tequila straight back, and then bite down on the lime wedge.

Tequila Punch #1

2 ounces white tequila

2 ounces fresh orange juice

2 ounces pineapple juice

^{1}/$_2$ ounce fresh lime juice

2 to 3 ounces club soda

Pour the tequila and all of the fruit juices into a shaker two-thirds full of ice cubes. Shake well. Strain into an ice-filled Collins glass. Add the club soda.

Tequila Punch #2

2 ounces white tequila

3 ounces pineapple juice

^{1}/$_2$ ounce fresh lemon juice

^{1}/$_4$ ounce grenadine

Pour all of the ingredients into a shaker two-thirds full of ice cubes. Shake well. Strain into an ice-filled Rocks glass.

Tequila Sunrise

2¹/₂ ounces white tequila

4 ounces fresh orange juice

¹/₄ ounce grenadine

Pour the tequila and orange juice into an ice-filled Highball glass; stir briefly. Pour the grenadine directly into the center of the drink.

Teresa

Adapted from a recipe by Rafael Ballesteros, Spain.

2 ounces Campari

³/₄ ounce crème de cassis

1 ounce fresh lime juice

Pour all of the ingredients into a shaker two-thirds full of ice cubes. Shake well. Strain into a chilled Cocktail glass.

Thai Boxer

Adapted from a recipe by Scott Beattie, bar manager at Cyrus restaurant, Healdsburg, California, circa 2005.

10 fresh cilantro leaves

10 fresh mint leaves

12 fresh Thai basil leaves

1 ounce fresh lime juice

¹/₂ ounce Thai coconut milk

¹/₂ ounce simple syrup (page 35)

1¹/₂ ounces Charbay Tahitian Vanilla Bean rum

2 to 3 ounces Cock 'n Bull ginger beer

Tear the cilantro, mint, and 10 of the basil leaves into small pieces. Add them to an empty mixing glass along with the lime juice, coconut milk, and simple syrup. Muddle well. Add ice cubes, the rum, and the ginger beer. Stir together. Strain into an ice-filled Collins glass. Garnish with the 2 reserved basil leaves.

Thai Lady

Adapted from a recipe by Jamie Terrell, Lab Bar, London.

> 1¹/₂ ounces Plymouth gin
> ¹/₂ ounce Cointreau
> 1 ounce fresh lemon juice
> ¹/₂ ounce lemongrass syrup (see recipe below)

Pour all of the ingredients into a shaker two-thirds full of ice cubes. Shake well. Strain into a chilled Cocktail glass.

LEMONGRASS SYRUP

Dissolve 1 cup of granulated sugar into 1 cup of water in a saucepan set over moderate heat. Let cool to room temperature. Pour the syrup into a blender and add 4 lemongrass stalks. Blend until smooth. Strain through a double layer of dampened cheesecloth. Store in the refrigerator.

Third Rail Cocktail

There used to be two versions of this drink, but this formula is the one that withstood the test of time.

> 1 ounce dark rum
> 1 ounce applejack
> 1 ounce brandy
> 2 dashes of absinthe

Pour all of the ingredients into a mixing glass two-thirds full of ice cubes. Stir well. Strain into a chilled Cocktail glass.

The Thoroughbred Martini

Adapted from a recipe by Nick Burns, Arterra restaurant at the San Diego Marriott, circa 2004.

> 2 ounces Hangar 1 Mandarin Blossom vodka
> 1 ounce Cointreau
> Splash of blue curaçao
> Splash of fresh grapefruit juice
> Orange twist, for garnish

Pour all of the ingredients into a shaker two-thirds full of ice cubes. Shake well. Strain into a chilled Cocktail glass. Add the twist.

3 Tenors

Adapted from a recipe by Jeff Grdinich, bartender at Stonehurst Manor, North Conway, New Hampshire.

3 ounces Tuaca

1/2 ounce amontillado sherry

2 ounces fresh blood orange juice

1 teaspoon orange flower water

2 dashes of Regans' Orange Bitters No. 6

Pinch of grated nutmeg and a blood orange slice, for garnishes

Pour all of the ingredients into a shaker two-thirds full of ice cubes. Shake well. Strain into a chilled Cocktail glass. Add the nutmeg and orange slice.

Tidal Wave

The original Tidal Wave was created at Pedro's, an Upper East Side Manhattan bar, in the early 1970s.

1 ounce dark rum

1 ounce brandy

1/2 ounce vodka

1/2 ounce tequila

2 ounces pineapple juice

1 ounce fresh lime juice

1/4 ounce grenadine

Pour all of the ingredients into a shaker two-thirds full of ice cubes. Shake well. Strain into a large, ice-filled wine goblet.

Tipperary Cocktail

1 1/2 ounces Irish whiskey

1/2 ounce sweet vermouth

1/2 ounce green Chartreuse

Pour all of the ingredients into a mixing glass two-thirds full of ice cubes. Stir well. Strain into a chilled Cocktail glass. Sing while you drink it.

T

DRINKS A TO Z

The Tiramisu Martini

Adapted from a recipe by Alan Kearney and Salvatore Como, Pen-Top Bar, New York City.

1 ounce Godiva White Chocolate liqueur

1 ounce Stolichnaya Vanil vodka

1 ounce Kahlúa

$1/2$ ounce DiSaronno amaretto

$1/2$ ounce heavy cream

Chocolate shavings, for garnish

Pour all of the ingredients into a shaker two-thirds full of ice cubes. Shake well. Strain into a chilled Cocktail glass. Add the chocolate shavings.

Toasted Almond

1 ounce amaretto

1 ounce Kahlúa

$1^1/2$ ounces light cream

Pour all of the ingredients into a shaker two-thirds full of ice cubes. Shake well. Strain into an ice-filled Rocks glass.

Tom & Jerry

This drink was supposedly created by a nineteenth-century bartender, Jerry Thomas, and it's said that he refused to make it until after the first snowfall of the year.

MAKES ABOUT TWENTY-FOUR 6-OUNCE SERVINGS

12 eggs, separated

$1^1/2$ cups granulated sugar

1 teaspoon baking soda

16 ounces dark rum

16 ounces brandy

$1/2$ gallon plus 1 cup milk, scalded

Freshly grated nutmeg, for garnish

In a mixing bowl, combine the egg yolks, $1^1/4$ cups of the sugar, and the baking soda. Whisk until creamy and thick.

In another mixing bowl, beat the egg whites until frothy. Sprinkle on the remaining $1/4$ cup sugar and continue beating until soft peaks form. Fold the egg whites into the egg yolk mixture to lighten it. Gradually whisk in the rum and brandy.

TO SERVE: Divide the drink among 24 Tom & Jerry cups or punch cups. Add some of the hot milk to each cup. Dust each serving with nutmeg.

Tom Collins

Early recipes for this drink called for Old Tom, a sweetened gin that's finally back on the market.

"This is a long drink, to be consumed slowly with reverence and meditation." —*The Fine Art of Mixing Drinks*, by David Embury, 1958.

2 ounces gin
$1/2$ ounce fresh lemon juice
$1/2$ ounce simple syrup (page 35)
5 to 6 ounces club soda
Fresh fruit in season (your choice), for garnish

Pour the gin, lemon juice, and simple syrup into a shaker two-thirds full of ice cubes. Shake well. Strain into an ice-filled Collins glass. Pour in the club soda; stir briefly. Add the fruit.

Torino

Adapted from a recipe by Umberto Gibin, owner, Perbacco, San Francisco.

$1^1/2$ ounces Carpano Antica Formula vermouth
$1^1/2$ ounces Cinzano dry vermouth
Dash of Aperol
Orange slice, for garnish

Pour the two vermouths into a cracked ice–filled Double Old-Fashioned glass. Stir well. Add the Aperol and the orange slice.

The Touchable

Created by John Myers for the B&B 70th Anniversary Master Mixologist Showcase, March 25, 2008. This was the winning recipe.

1 ounce B&B

1 ounce Bacardi 8 rum

1 ounce Noilly Pratt dry vermouth

$1/2$ ounce pure maple syrup

$1/2$ ounce fresh lime juice

Cinnamon stick, for garnish

Pour all of the ingredients into a shaker two-thirds full of ice cubes. Shake well. Strain into a chilled Cocktail glass. Add the cinnamon stick.

Trembling Martini

Adapted from a recipe created by Steven Izzo, beverage manager at One Market, San Francisco, 2006.

$1/2$ ounce Vya extra-dry vermouth

3 ounces No. 209 gin

Olive, for garnish

Coat the interior of a chilled Cocktail glass with the vermouth; discard any excess. Pour the gin into a cocktail shaker two-thirds full of ice cubes. Shake well. Strain into the prepared cocktail glass, and add the olive.

Trilby Cocktail

This drink was named after the heroine in George du Maurier's novel *Trilby*, which was later seen on the big screen as *Svengali*, but the drink wasn't the only object to adopt the name—along with the Trilby hat, there used to be ice cream, shoes, sausages, cigars, and cigarettes named for Trilby.

2 ounces gin

1 ounce sweet vermouth

2 dashes of orange bitters

Pour all of the ingredients into a mixing glass two-thirds full of ice cubes. Stir well. Strain into a chilled Cocktail glass.

Trinity Cocktail

1 ounce gin

1 ounce sweet vermouth

1 ounce dry vermouth

Pour all of the ingredients into a mixing glass two-thirds full of ice cubes. Stir well. Strain into a chilled Cocktail glass.

Tropical Cocktail

A drink with this name that dates back to the 1930s called for entirely different ingredients than these—this is a more up-to-date formula.

2 ounces dark rum

1 ounce pineapple juice

$1/2$ ounce fresh lime juice

Dash of grenadine

Pour all of the ingredients into a shaker two-thirds full of ice cubes. Shake well. Strain into a chilled Cocktail glass.

Tru Blu Martini

Adapted from a recipe by Adam Seger at Tru Blu restaurant, Chicago.

$2^{1}/2$ ounces Bombay Sapphire gin

$1/2$ ounce blue curaçao

3 drops of grenadine

Splash of tonic water

Juice from 1 lime wedge

Champagne

3 skewered blueberries, for garnish

Pour the gin, curaçao, grenadine, tonic, and lime juice into a shaker two-thirds full of ice cubes. Shake well. Strain into a chilled Cocktail glass. Top with the champagne. Add the garnish.

The Tsar's Champagne Cocktail

A recipe from spirits writer Herb Silverman, who says that in 1945 a Russian friend claimed this was a favored drink of the tsars.

2 ounces chilled vodka

3 1/2 ounces chilled champagne

Build in the order given in a Champagne flute.

Tulio Oro

Adapted from a recipe from Turo restaurant, Seattle, Washington.

1 lemon twist

3/4 ounce limoncello

1/2 ounce Punt e Mes

6 ounces Prosecco

In a shaker half-filled with ice cubes, combine the lemon twist, limoncello, and Punt e Mes. Shake well. Strain into a Champagne flute. Add the Prosecco.

Tuscan Sidecar

Adapted from a recipe by Jon Connors, head bartender at Country Restaurant, New York City.

Superfine sugar, for rimming the glass

2 dashes of orange bitters

1 orange slice

2 ounces V.S. cognac

1 ounce Faretti Biscotti Famosi liqueur

1 ounce fresh lemon juice

Prepare a Cocktail glass. Muddle the orange bitters and orange slice in an empty shaker until all of the juices have been extracted from the orange. Add ice cubes and all of the remaining ingredients. Shake well. Strain into the prepared glass.

The Tuxedo

Created by Gary Regan, 2008.

1 ounce bourbon
1 ounce Kahlúa
3 ounces chilled espresso
Whipped cream

Pour the bourbon, Kahlúa, and coffee into a shaker two-thirds full of ice cubes. Shake well. Strain into a chilled Champagne flute. Float the whipped cream on top.

The Twentieth-Century Cocktail

Detailed in *Café Royal Cocktail Book*, 1937, this drink was created by a certain C. A. Tuck.

1¹/₂ ounces gin
¹/₂ ounce Lillet Blanc
¹/₂ ounce white crème de cacao
¹/₂ ounce fresh lemon juice

Pour all of the ingredients into a shaker two-thirds full of ice cubes. Shake well. Strain into a chilled Cocktail glass.

21st Martini

Adapted from a recipe by Matt Navarro, co-owner and general manager at Cuatro, Chicago, where it is served in a glass rimmed with guava sugar.

2¹/₂ ounces 10-Cane rum
2 ounces fresh guava juice
2 ounces fresh-pressed sugarcane juice
Laurent-Perrier Brut L-P champagne

Pour the rum, guava juice, and sugarcane juice into a shaker two-thirds full of ice cubes. Shake well. Strain into a chilled Cocktail glass. Top with the champagne.

21 Hayes

Created by Rob Schwartz, bar manager at Absinthe Brasserie & Bar, San Francisco, circa 2004.

3 cucumber slices (each about 1/4 inch thick)
1/4 ounce Pimm's Cup #1
1 1/2 ounces gin
1/4 ounce fresh lemon juice
Splash of simple syrup (page 35)

Muddle 4 or 5 small ice cubes in a shaker with 2 of the cucumber slices and the Pimm's. Keep at it until the cucumber is almost liquid—some of the skin will be left. Add ice cubes, the gin, lemon juice, and simple syrup. Shake well. Strain into a chilled Cocktail glass. Garnish with the remaining cucumber slice.

Under the Mexican Sun

Adapted from a recipe by David Touye, bartender at Restaurant Gary Danko, San Francisco, where the glass is rimmed with lavender-scented sugar and the drink is garnished with candied orange peel. Oh, so tasty.

2 ounces Herradura Silver tequila
1 ounce Sonoma Lavender Syrup
1/2 ounce fresh lime juice
1/4 ounce Cointreau
Orange twist, for garnish

Pour all of the ingredients into a shaker two-thirds full of ice cubes. Shake well. Strain into a chilled Cocktail glass. Add the twist.

The Universal Cocktail

Created by Gary Regan and me in 2004.

1 1/2 ounces Herradura Reposado tequila
1/2 ounce Navan liqueur
3/4 ounce orange juice
1/4 ounce fresh lemon juice
2 dashes of Angostura bitters
Orange twist, for garnish

Pour all of the ingredients into a shaker two-thirds full of ice cubes. Shake well. Strain into a chilled Cocktail glass. Carefully flame the twist over the drink.

The Uptown Manhattan

Adapted from a recipe by Marcovaldo Dionysos, Harry Denton's Starlight Room, San Francisco.

2 ounces Maker's Mark bourbon

1/2 ounce Amaro Nonino

2 dashes of orange bitters

1 barspoon cherry brandy from brandied cherries

Large orange twist and a brandied cherry, for garnishes

Pour all of the ingredients into a shaker two-thirds full of ice cubes. Shake well. Strain into a chilled Cocktail glass. Carefully flame the twist over the drink. Add the cherry.

Uva Maria

Adapted from a recipe created by mixologist Jacques Bezuidenhout for Urbana Restaurant and Wine Bar, Washington, D.C.

1/4 ounce fresh lime juice

6 seedless white grapes

1 1/2 ounces Milagro Blanco tequila

1 1/2 ounces muscat wine

1/4 ounce simple syrup (page 35)

3 seedless white grapes skewered on a cocktail pick, for garnish

Muddle the lime juice and grapes in an empty shaker until all of the juices are extracted from the grapes. Add ice cubes and all of the remaining ingredients. Shake well. Strain into a chilled Cocktail glass. Add the garnish.

V Sting

Adapted from a recipe by Albert Trummer, bar chef at Trummer Home, Greenpoint, New York, circa 2004.

2 ounces Navan liqueur

2 ounces Hennessy Paradis Extra or Hennessy VSOP Privilège cognac

2 dashes of Angostura bitters (optional)

Orange slice and a vanilla bean, for garnishes

Fill a Double Old-Fashioned glass with ice and add the Navan, cognac, and bitters. Stir briefly. Add the orange slice and vanilla bean.

DRINKS A TO Z

Valentino

This is a variation on the Negroni. *See also* Vodka Valentino.

2¹/₂ ounces gin
¹/₂ ounce Campari
¹/₂ ounce sweet vermouth
Orange twist, for garnish

Pour all of the ingredients into a mixing glass two-thirds full of ice cubes. Stir well. Strain into a chilled Cocktail glass. Add the twist.

Velvet Hammer

2 ounces vodka
³/₄ ounce white crème de cacao
³/₄ ounce heavy cream

Pour all of the ingredients into a shaker two-thirds full of ice cubes. Shake well. Strain into a chilled Cocktail glass.

Velvet Peach

Adapted from a recipe by cocktail historian "Dr. Cocktail" (Ted Haigh), who is himself a peach.

2 ounces light rum
1 ounce Tuaca
1 ounce fresh lime juice
2 dashes of peach bitters

Pour all of the ingredients into a shaker two-thirds full of ice cubes. Shake well. Strain into a chilled Cocktail glass.

Vento Vortex

Adapted from a recipe by Eben Klemm, director of cocktail development at New York City's B. R. Guest, Inc. Served at Vento Trattoria.

1¹/₂ ounces vodka or Plymouth gin
¹/₄ ounce maraschino liqueur
¹/₄ ounce crème de griotte (cherry-flavored liqueur)
¹/₂ ounce fresh lime juice
¹/₂ ounce fresh grapefruit juice

Pour all of the ingredients into a shaker two-thirds full of ice cubes. Shake well. Strain into a chilled Cocktail glass.

Vermouth Cassis

This drink is also known as the Pompier Highball.

2¹/₂ ounces dry vermouth
¹/₂ ounce crème de cassis
4 to 6 ounces club soda
Lemon twist, for garnish

Pour the vermouth and cassis into an ice-filled Collins glass. Add club soda to fill the glass; stir briefly. Add the twist.

Vermouth Cocktail

1¹/₂ ounces sweet vermouth
1¹/₂ ounces dry vermouth
2 dashes of Angostura bitters
Maraschino cherry, for garnish

Pour all of the ingredients into a mixing glass two-thirds full of ice cubes. Stir well. Strain into a chilled Cocktail glass. Add the cherry.

Vesper Martini

One of the few clear drinks that should be shaken, this Martini variation uses both gin and vodka and was ordered in *Casino Royale*, the only film in which David Niven, the late British actor, played James Bond. Ursula Andress played Vesper Lynd in that version, and the drink is named for her character.

2 ounces gin
1¹/₄ ounces vodka
¹/₂ ounce Lillet Blanc
Lemon twist, for garnish

Pour all of the ingredients into a shaker two-thirds full of ice cubes. Shake well. Strain into a chilled Cocktail glass. Add the twist.

Vieux Carré

¾ ounce straight rye whiskey

¾ ounce brandy

¾ ounce sweet vermouth

⅛ ounce Bénédictine

Dash of Peychaud's bitters

Dash of Angostura bitters

Build over ice in an Old-Fashioned glass; stir briefly.

Virgin Caesar

6 ounces Clamato juice

½ ounce fresh lemon juice

Pinch of ground black pepper

Pinch of celery salt

Dash of hot sauce

Dash of Worcestershire sauce

Lemon wedge, for garnish

Pour the Clamato juice and lemon juice into a shaker two-thirds full of ice cubes; add the pepper, celery salt, hot sauce, and Worcestershire. Shake well. Strain into an ice-filled Highball glass. Add the lemon wedge.

Virgin Mary

6 ounces tomato juice

½ ounce fresh lemon juice

¼ teaspoon freshly milled black pepper

Pinch of salt

¼ teaspoon celery seeds

¼ teaspoon ground cumin

2 dashes of Worcestershire sauce

2 dashes of hot sauce

Lemon wedge, for garnish

Pour the tomato juice and lemon juice into a shaker two-thirds full of ice cubes; add the pepper, salt, celery seeds, cumin, Worcestershire, and hot sauce. Shake well. Strain into an ice-filled Highball glass. Add the lemon wedge.

The Bartender's Best Friend

Virgin Peach Daiquiri

2 ounces fresh lime juice

1 ounce simple syrup (page 35)

1 ripe peach, pitted, cut into 6 pieces

Place all of the ingredients into a blender containing 1 cup of ice cubes. Blend well. Pour into a chilled wine goblet.

Virgin Piña Colada

7 ounces pineapple juice

2 ounces orange juice

2¹/₂ ounces coconut cream, such as Coco Lopez

1 cup pineapple chunks

Pineapple spear, for garnish

Place all of the ingredients into a blender containing 1 cup of ice cubes. Blend well. Pour into a chilled wine goblet. Add the pineapple spear.

Vodka Gibson

The vodka version of the gin-based classic.

3 ounces vodka

¹/₂ ounce dry vermouth

3 pearl onions, for garnish

Pour the vodka and vermouth into a mixing glass two-thirds full of ice cubes. Stir well. Strain into a chilled Cocktail glass. Add the onions.

Vodka Gimlet

2¹/₂ ounces vodka

¹/₂ ounce lime juice cordial, such as Rose's

Lime wedge, for garnish

Pour both ingredients into an ice-filled Rocks glass; stir briefly. Add the lime wedge.

Vodka Martini, Dry

Make your Vodka Martini the way you like it by experimenting with gin-to-vermouth ratios, and when making Martinis for others, ask how they like theirs to be made. The recipe below works if a simple "Dry Martini" is called for. Use less vermouth for an Extra-Dry Martini, and more for a Medium Martini.

> **3 ounces vodka**
> **$1/2$ ounce dry vermouth**
> **Lemon twist or cocktail olive, for garnish**

Pour both ingredients into a mixing glass two-thirds full of ice cubes. Stir well. Strain into a chilled Cocktail glass. Add the garnish.

Vodka Valentino

The vodka version of the gin-based Valentino.

> **2 ounces vodka**
> **$1/2$ ounce Campari**
> **$1/2$ ounce sweet vermouth**
> **Orange twist, for garnish**

Pour all of the ingredients into a mixing glass two-thirds full of ice cubes. Stir well. Strain into a chilled Cocktail glass. Add the twist.

The Voodoo Priestess

Adapted from a recipe by Thayer Lund, Forbidden Island, Alameda, California, 2006. At Forbidden Island this drink is served in a glass rimmed with red sanding sugar, that is, red-colored superfine sugar. If you have it, try it.

> **$1^1/_2$ ounces Cruzan dark rum**
> **$1^1/_2$ ounces VooDoo spiced rum**
> **$1/2$ ounce brandy**
> **2 ounces fresh orange juice**
> **1 ounce fresh lime juice**
> **1 ounce fresh lemon juice**
> **2 ounces VooDoo Priestess Spice syrup (see recipe below)**
> **Dash of orange bitters**

The Bartender's Best Friend

Pour all of the ingredients into a shaker two-thirds full of ice cubes. Shake well. Strain into a large, ice-filled goblet.

VOODOO PRIESTESS SPICE SYRUP

1 tablespoon pumpkin pie spice

2 cups pure cane sugar

1 cup boiling water

In a heatproof bowl, stir together the pumpkin pie spice and the sugar. Add the boiling water and stir until the sugar dissolves. Set aside to cool to room temperature.

Waldorf Sunset

Adapted from a recipe by bartender Cenko "Sonny" Koltovski, the Waldorf-Astoria, New York City.

$1^1/_2$ ounces Tanqueray No. Ten gin

3 ounces fresh orange juice

$^1/_2$ ounce white crème de cacao

3 to 4 drops of grenadine

Maraschino cherry, for garnish

Pour all of the ingredients into a shaker two-thirds full of ice cubes. Shake well. Strain into a chilled Cocktail glass. Add the cherry.

Ward Eight

The Ward Eight was created at Boston's Locke-Ober restaurant, "the place where Caruso cooked his own sweetbreads; where John F. Kennedy habitually ordered the lobster stew, drank the broth and gave the meat to the waiter; where a dying man came for his last lunch; and where, when regular customers pass away, their plates are turned over and their chairs are cocked against the table." —www.lockeober.com

2 ounces bourbon

1 ounce orange juice

1 ounce fresh lemon juice

Dash of grenadine

Pour all of the ingredients into a shaker two-thirds full of ice cubes. Shake well. Strain into a chilled Cocktail glass.

DRINKS A TO Z

Wentworth

Adapted from a recipe by Sharon Cooper, The Harvest restaurant, Connecticut.

> 1 ounce Very Special Old Fitzgerald bourbon
>
> 1¹/₂ ounces Dubonnet Rouge
>
> 1 ounce cranberry juice
>
> Orange slice and 3 dried cranberries, for garnishes

Pour all of the ingredients into a shaker two-thirds full of ice cubes. Shake well. Strain into a chilled Cocktail glass. Add the orange slice and cranberries.

The Wet Spot

Adapted from a recipe by Will Shine and Aisha Sharpe, mixologists at B.E.D., New York City, 2006.

> 1¹/₂ ounces Plymouth gin
>
> ¹/₂ ounce apricot brandy
>
> 1 ounce apple juice
>
> ³/₄ ounce fresh lemon juice
>
> ¹/₂ ounce elderflower syrup
>
> Lemon twist, for garnish

Pour all of the ingredients into a shaker two-thirds full of ice cubes. Shake well. Strain into a chilled Cocktail glass. Add the twist.

Whisky Mac

A Scottish antidote for a cold winter night.

> 2 ounces scotch
>
> 1 ounce green ginger wine

Build in an ice-filled Rocks glass.

Whisky Sour

Some of us like to substitute bourbon for the Canadian whisky.

> 2 ounces blended Canadian whisky
>
> ³/₄ ounce fresh lemon juice
>
> ¹/₂ ounce simple syrup (page 35)
>
> Orange wheel and a maraschino cherry, for garnishes

Pour all of the ingredients into a shaker two-thirds full of ice cubes. Shake well. Strain into a chilled Sour glass. Add the orange wheel and cherry.

White Diamonds

Adapted from a recipe by Paul Morganelli, bartender at envy, the Steakhouse at the Renaissance in Las Vegas. At envy, the drink is garnished with a demitasse sugar stick.

1¹/₂ ounces Cîroc vodka

2 ounces icewine

Lemon twist, for garnish

Pour both ingredients into a shaker two-thirds full of ice cubes. Shake well. Strain into a chilled Cocktail glass. Add the twist.

White Iced Tea

¹/₂ ounce vodka

¹/₂ ounce gin

¹/₂ ounce light rum

¹/₂ ounce tequila

¹/₂ ounce triple sec

¹/₂ ounce lemon juice

Lemon-lime soda

Lemon wedge, for garnish

Pour the vodka, gin, rum, tequila, triple sec, and lemon juice into a shaker two-thirds full of ice cubes. Shake well. Strain into an ice-filled Collins glass. Top with the soda. Add the lemon wedge.

White Lady Cocktail

2¹/₂ ounces gin

1 ounce light cream

1 egg white

¹/₂ ounce simple syrup (page 35)

Pour all of the ingredients into a shaker two-thirds full of ice cubes. Shake very well. Strain into a chilled Cocktail glass.

White Russian

"Listen, Maude, I'm sorry if your stepmother is a nympho, but I don't see what it has to do with—do you have any Kahlúa?"

—From *The Big Lebowski*, the movie in which Jeff Bridges, as "The Dude," drinks more White Russians than you might think possible

2 ounces vodka

1 ounce Kahlúa

1 ounce light cream

Pour all of the ingredients into a shaker two-thirds full of ice cubes. Shake well. Strain into an ice-filled Rocks glass.

White Spider

Though it's actually a Vodka Stinger, this drink is better known by this creepier name. Shake this; don't stir it.

2 ounces vodka

$1/2$ ounce white crème de menthe

Pour both ingredients into a shaker two-thirds full of ice cubes. Shake well. Strain into an ice-filled Rocks glass or a crushed ice–filled wine goblet.

White Wine Spritzer

6 ounces white wine

1 to 2 ounces club soda

Lemon twist, for garnish

Pour the wine and club soda into an ice-filled Collins glass. Stir briefly; add the twist.

Widow's Kiss #1

The Widow's Kiss is a Prohibition-era drink created in Europe while Americans were enduring the Great Drought.

1 ounce calvados

$1/2$ ounce yellow Chartreuse

$1/2$ ounce Bénédictine

Dash of Angostura bitters

Pour all of the ingredients into a mixing glass two-thirds full of ice cubes. Stir well. Strain into a chilled Cocktail glass.

Widow's Kiss #2

1 1/2 ounces brandy

1/2 ounce yellow Chartreuse

1/2 ounce Bénédictine

2 dashes of Angostura bitters

Pour all of the ingredients into a mixing glass two-thirds full of ice cubes. Stir well. Strain into a chilled Cocktail glass.

Windex

Because it looks like what?

2 ounces vodka

1/2 ounce blue curaçao

1/2 ounce triple sec

Pour all of the ingredients into a mixing glass two-thirds full of ice cubes. Stir well. Strain into a chilled Cocktail glass or chilled spray bottle.

Winter Tale

Adapted from a recipe by Ektoras Binikos, head bartender at Aureole New York, New York City.

1 cardamom pod

2 to 3 dashes of Regans' Orange Bitters No. 6

1 ounce Churchill's white port

1/2 ounce aquavit

1/2 ounce Belle de Brillet liqueur

Muddle the cardamom and bitters in an empty shaker, grinding until the pod releases the seeds. Add ice cubes and all of the remaining ingredients. Shake well. Strain into a chilled Reisling glass.

Witch's Tit

2 ounces Kahlúa

Dollop of whipped cream

1/2 maraschino cherry, for garnish

Pour the liqueur into a Pousse-Café glass. Top with the cream; add the cherry.

Woo Woo

2 ounces vodka

1/2 ounce peach schnapps

4 ounces cranberry juice

Build in an ice-filled Highball glass; stir briefly.

The World Peace Cocktail

Adapted from a recipe by Jonathan Pogash, director of cocktail development at the World Bar, New York City. At the World Bar this drink is garnished with a "dove of peace" made from white chocolate. We substituted a lemon twist.

1 1/2 ounces Bombay Sapphire gin

2 drops of blue curaçao

2 drops of orgeat syrup

1/2 ounce fresh lemon juice

Splash of elderflower syrup

Lemon twist, for garnish

Pour all of the ingredients into a shaker two-thirds full of ice cubes. Shake well. Strain into a chilled Cocktail glass. Add the twist.

XYZ Cocktail

2 ounces light rum

1 ounce triple sec

1 ounce fresh lemon juice

Pour all of the ingredients into a shaker two-thirds full of ice cubes. Shake well. Strain into a chilled Cocktail glass.

Yale Cocktail

This cocktail has changed because its original recipe included crème Yvette, a violet-flavored liqueur, but it's no longer available.

2 1/2 ounces gin

1/4 ounce dry vermouth

1/4 ounce blue curaçao

Dash of Angostura bitters

Pour all of the ingredients into a mixing glass two-thirds full of ice cubes. Stir well. Strain into a chilled Cocktail glass.

Yellowbird

A Caribbean drink that will take you to sandy shores.

> **2 ounces light rum**
> **$1/2$ ounce Galliano**
> **$1/2$ ounce triple sec**
> **$1/2$ ounce fresh lime juice**

Pour all of the ingredients into a shaker two-thirds full of ice cubes. Shake well. Strain into a chilled Cocktail glass.

Zaza Cocktail

The Zaza Cocktail was named for a nineteenth-century Broadway play, not for the character in *La Cage aux Folles*.

> **$1^1/2$ ounces gin**
> **$1^1/2$ ounces Dubonnet Rouge**
> **Orange twist, for garnish**

Pour both ingredients into a mixing glass two-thirds full of ice cubes. Stir well. Strain into a chilled Cocktail glass. Add the twist.

Zenzero Rossi

Adapted from a recipe by Jerri Banks, Taj restaurant, New York City.

> **3 fresh ginger slices**
> **2 lemon wedges**
> **2 teaspoons granulated sugar**
> **3 ounces Martini & Rossi sweet vermouth**
> **Club soda**
> **Lemon twist, for garnish**

Muddle the ginger, lemon wedges, and sugar in an empty shaker. Add ice cubes and the vermouth. Shake well. Strain into an ice-filled Collins glass. Top with the club soda. Add the twist.

Zig Zag Cocktail

Adapted from a recipe by Kacy Fitch, owner and bartender, Zig Zag Café, Seattle.

- 1¹/₂ ounces Cazadores reposado tequila
- ¹/₄ ounce Bénédictine
- ¹/₄ ounce apricot brandy
- ¹/₄ ounce fresh lime juice

Pour all of the ingredients into a shaker two-thirds full of ice cubes. Shake well. Strain into a chilled Cocktail glass.

Zipperhead

The term *zipperhead* originated at IBM, where it was used to describe people with closed minds.

- 1 ounce vodka
- 1 ounce Chambord raspberry liqueur
- 1 ounce lemon-lime soda

Layer in an ice-filled Rocks glass. Sip through a straw.

Zombie

The king of all tiki bar drinks, the Zombie was created by Donn the Beachcomber, originator of the tiki bar–themed restaurant in the United States. It made its debut at the Hurricane Bar at the 1939 World's Fair.

- 2 ounces añejo rum
- 1 ounce dark rum
- 1 ounce light rum
- ¹/₂ ounce applejack
- 1 ounce fresh lime juice
- ¹/₂ ounce pineapple juice
- ¹/₂ ounce papaya nectar
- ¹/₂ ounce simple syrup (page 35)
- ¹/₂ ounce 151-proof Demerara rum
- Pineapple spear, maraschino cherry, and a mint sprig, for garnishes

Pour the añejo, dark, and light rums, the applejack, lime juice, pineapple juice, papaya nectar, and simple syrup into a shaker two-thirds full of ice cubes. Shake well. Strain into an ice-filled Zombie or Hurricane glass. Float the 151-proof rum on top. Add the pineapple spear, cherry, and mint sprig.

THE PROFESSIONAL BARTENDER: HOW TO BE THE BEST

AAAH, THE LIFE OF A BARTENDER: Holding court behind two feet of shining mahogany every night; shaking and stirring while customers watch in wonder at the delectable nectars that cascade from the shaker into sleek cocktail glasses; being the fountain of knowledge, the baroness of bar lore, the princess of trivia, and the sage whose knowledge knows no bounds; constantly attending swank parties where multimillionaires proudly introduce you as their bartender; unclogging the toilet in the ladies' room. So who said it would always be glamorous?

I married a bartender. I've been a bartender, but never for very long and never at a place that forced me to do my homework or make an effort to develop a style for myself. I've rarely met a bartender I didn't like. I've met bad bartenders, and I've been privileged to sit across from the best, and I've noted that all of them—the good, the bad, and the middling—exhibit that gene that makes them yearn for a good Boston shaker and an audience to play to—and I give good audience, no doubt about it.

The role of a professional bartender is much more complex than most people think. And though it sometimes remains a job one seeks out while looking for that Broadway break or finishing that MBA, bartending is a craft that can—and should—garner praise and recognition equal to that of a well-respected and talented chef. But before you get that good, you need to acquire knowledge, style, and most of all, experience.

The Bar Chef and the Bartender

There's nothing wrong with calling yourself a bar chef if you think that you are pretty much expert in knowing your ingredients, being very creative, understanding the intricacies of methodology, and mixing and matching flavors to astound your guests at the drop of a hat. Being a bar chef, or a cocktailian or a master mixologist, or whatever you want to call yourself, doesn't necessarily make you a bartender. Bartenders need to know how to do far more than mix drinks in order to qualify for the title. Bartenders have to know how to manage people, they must be able to wear at least a dozen hats during the course of a single shift, and they must truly care about the well-being of their guests. Many bar chefs are also bartenders, of course, but bartenders who aren't too accomplished in the craft of mixology, in my opinion, stand head and shoulders above mixologists who don't care about their customers.

The Qualities of a Good Professional Bartender

Not just any Regular Joe off the street can become a good professional bartender—at least not without a good deal of work. However, there are some general qualities and recommendations that apply to the job, whether it's at a high-end restaurant or at a beach bar where sandals and bikinis are standard attire.

Be punctual: In fact, be more than punctual: Get to work early. If you are the opening bartender, you will be setting up for the entire day's business—restocking everything from liquor to bottled beers to wines, ingredients, paper goods, and cleaning supplies; counting banks or floats (the money that you start with at the beginning of your shift); cutting fruit garnishes; polishing bottles and glasses; and doing whatever else is necessary at that particular place of business.

Be organized: Without getting overly picky about the order in which things are done, doesn't it make sense to restock items that need to chill and to get any messy tasks out of the way first? You bet. If you have chores to do in the basement or stockroom—lugging huge buckets of ice to chill ingredients and use for serving, for example—do those things before you start cutting fruit garnishes and fanning out a tall stack of cocktail napkins. (Indeed, many opening bartenders arrive at work wearing grungy clothes because they know that the early part of their work is messy. They change into work clothes once those chores are out of the way.) As a rule, do anything and everything that requires your being away from the bar first. After that, get behind your bar and set it up to work for you.

Be physically strong: Unless barbacks do all of the heavy lifting—keg changing, ice hauling, and restocking—a certain amount of strength is necessary to do the job well.

Be generous and kind to barbacks: Typically, barbacks are lower-paid workers who do the scut work behind the bar. If one keeps his or her eyes open and shows real interest, this is an excellent way to break into the bartending business. Pray you get the chance to work with someone worth emulating. Established bartenders need to take notice of ambitious barbacks: Tip them well and train them to help you offer the best service possible. Encourage them.

Be honest: A bartender's pay is usually the combination of a low hourly wage and all the tips that he or she can make. Stories of bartender thievery are legion, but if you are good at your job, you shouldn't need to supplement your income by cheating the management and owners.

Be hard-working: Although it's not necessary to be a perpetual-motion machine, there's always something that can be done behind the bar—polishing or washing glasses, straightening bottles, getting rid of all that superfluous matter that continually gathers.

Be tactful and diplomatic: Though it depends on the bar itself, bartenders generally keep the party rolling by trading quips, introducing one customer to the next, and having a good time while they work. But since the business involves serving alcoholic beverages, sooner or later a customer will get out of control. A good bartender will cut customers off before they become belligerent and will make sure that they know they can come back another time. Alternatively, a bartender has the power to "eighty-six"—permanently ban—a customer from the premises. When this becomes necessary, be sure that all of the staff and management are aware of the circumstances and the identity of the eighty-sixed former patron.

Be personable: Ideally, a bartender must get along well with the floor staff, the kitchen staff, the managers, and every single customer who walks through the door. He or she knows when to talk to people, when to keep his mouth shut, which customers have had enough drinks, who is becoming a nuisance to other customers, and who is merely trying to be friendly and break into the local scene.

Be well-groomed: Since the bartender is often the first person a customer sees upon entering a restaurant or bar, he or she should be presentable at all times. Many places have a uniform requirement or a dress code that must be followed. Just be sure that your hands and nails are clean and tidy at all times. Wash your hands after handling sticky ingredients or dusty bottles.

Be a gymnast: It is absolutely vital that a bartender be able to vault over the bar—one-handed—in order to handle any situation on the opposite side. Nah, just kidding.

Be able to prioritize: Don't think this won't happen to you: It's the middle of a busy shift. What are you going to do first? Deliver food to your bar customers, serve the waitpeople, prepare a couple of drinks for the customers who just walked in, or answer the telephone? You need to be able to handle it all, without losing your cool or your temper. Most people don't understand just how complicated and stressful it can be to work behind a bar.

Be sober at work: Let's face it, some people want to be bartenders because they love to drink and hang out in bars. However, there is no such thing as a good professional bartender who is tipsy or, worse, drunk while on the job. Wait until your shift is over to imbibe.

Be a good manager: At many restaurants, the man or woman behind the mahogany needs be able to take control of the entire restaurant at the drop of a hat. It's often the case that at the exact moment that the manager pops out to the bank, the deep fryer will catch fire, a table of three will try to walk out on their check, and a busperson will spill coffee on a haughty customer's white linen suit. Someone must take charge of the situation, and the fact is, when a problem arises, the entire staff and the majority of customers will often run straight to the bartender—even if the manager is standing right there. Bartenders are authority figures. "The bar is the pilot house of the restaurant," says Dale DeGroff, former head bartender and beverage manager at New York City's Rainbow Room, "and the bartender is captain of the ship. Some people say that if there isn't a priest around, a bartender can marry people—that's authority for you."

Thus, given all of the above, the ideal bartender is punctual, presentable, fairly strong, trustworthy, and able to read minds, judge characters, set the atmosphere, take control, make decisions, deal with troublemakers, command respect, and remain sober for eight hours at a stretch. Strangely enough, the majority of restaurateurs believe that knowing how to mix drinks is way down on the list of priorities when it comes to hiring a bartender. I don't agree.

Behind the Professional Bar

You need to be able to make drinks—confidently, properly, and, ideally, quickly. That's where the layout of the bar is key to your success. Unfortunately, however, every bar layout is different. Naturally, some aspects are constant.

Most bars will have a number of stainless-steel sinks;

usually at least two are used for glass washing, some are used as tubs to contain ice for serving, and some are used as tubs for chilling wine, bottled beers, and other ingredients that need to be kept cold.

Most bars will have a soda gun, a push-button nozzle that dispenses cola, lemon-lime soda, tonic water, club soda, and usually water, ginger ale, or another ingredient.

Virtually every bar will have at least one cash register; many will have a service area at one end where the bartender serves the waitstaff's drink orders.

Most bars will have beer engines that dispense one or more draft beers; many will also have commercial espresso machines that are plumbed into the water system.

A number of refrigerated cabinets are the norm behind most bars; often there are display shelves for backup bottles of high-volume, popular liquor brands; drawers usually provide a haven for supplies of cocktail napkins, sip-sticks, straws, and other necessities.

At sink level it's important to have plenty of storage and work space; blenders might await use there, and certainly whole fruit like bananas or pineapples will be kept there for use when needed.

Most bars will have what's called a speed rack, a long metal trough affixed at sink level that holds the most-often-used ingredients—so-called well liquors—that are poured when customers don't specify a brand name. Speed racks can be arranged in whatever order is most useful to that individual bar; for an all-around bar, the lineup from left to right is usually vodka, gin, tequila, rum, triple sec, blended whisky, scotch, bourbon, brandy, and then sweet and dry vermouths. Each of these bottles, as well as all of the most-often-requested brands, should be fitted with speed pourers, each facing with the open end of the spout to the left when looking at the bottle's front label. Any bottles that are visible to the public should be placed with front labels facing out; labels and bottles facing every which way are the sign of a sloppy bartender.

Plastic bottles with different colored pour spouts are excellent containers for juices and simple syrup; color-code them so you know what's inside at a glance. These might also be kept in the speed rack.

WINE BOTTLE VOLUMES

$1/2$ standard wine bottle: 375 ml

Standard wine/liquor bottle: 750 ml

Magnum: 1.5 liters

Double Magnum: 3 liters

Rehoboam: approximately 4.5 liters

Jeroboam: 4.5 liters

Imperial: approximately 6 liters

Methuselah: approximately 6 liters

Salmanazar: approximately 9 liters

Balthazar: approximately 12 liters

Nebuchadnezzar: approximately 14 liters

HOW MANY DRINKS ARE IN THE BOTTLE?

One 750-ml bottle of wine = a little over five 5-ounce glasses of wine.

One 750-ml bottle of liquor = seventeen $1^1/2$-ounce shots.

One 1-liter bottle of liquor = twenty-two-and-a-half $1^1/2$-ounce shots.

One liter of soda or juice = seven 12-ounce Highball glasses, each filled with ice and one shot of liquor.

Most bars span the area from the customer's side to four or five inches from the bartender's side and then step down an inch or so. In that space sits a rubber bar mat with a stubby rubber surface that looks like an invention of Dr. Scholl. This bar mat is where a bartender lines up the glassware for the specific order being prepared. The mat provides a flat area directly in front of the customer, and the bar mat sops up any liquids that are splashed outside the glasses.

However the brand-name liquors are displayed—usually in multileveled shelves on the back bar—their arrangement should be sensible; that is, all vodkas together, all gins together, and so forth. Bottles that are not frequently poured will not be fitted with speed pourers. When using them, the bartender can do one of several things: insert a speed pourer spout, free pour, or use a jigger for measuring. After use, every item behind the bar should be returned to its normal location so that other bartenders will find it where it's supposed to be.

And now we come to making the drinks. For specific techniques, refer to Bartending Techniques (page 41) and Drink-Making Techniques (page 44). There you'll learn everything you need to know to handle the experience effectively. *Efficiency* is the key word in drink making. If you are ambidextrous, you are extremely lucky. For those of us who are not capable of functioning equally well with our right and left hands, learning to use both hands is a most worthwhile expenditure of time. Practice is key. Making a Highball by pouring the liquor with one hand and simultaneously operating the soda gun with the other is a must. When one hand frees up, it can next grab a sip-stick or garnish or place a cocktail napkin in front of a customer. Go out and watch a few good bartenders; you'll be surprised at the efficiency of their movements.

When you have a busy bar with a number of customers clamoring for your attention, the best, most practical way to cope is to first acknowledge everyone so that they know you are aware of them, then keep your head down and work as quickly as possible on the order at hand. Glance up only to serve and accept payment. Then make eye contact with the next customer and keep going. Getting flustered doesn't help; keeping a cool head does.

Should You Attend Bartending School?

Gee, I don't know. Certainly some of them are excellent for conveying the basics of cocktail making in a functioning bar or restaurant. I've spoken to graduates who glowed about the course they took, but like everything else, bartending schools are sure to run the gamut from really good to poor. I know one person who paid good money to attend a bartending school, and he showed me his "textbook" after completing the classes. I am not exaggerating when I say that more than 65 percent of the information in the "manual" was downright incorrect—even some of the classic drink recipes. If I were seriously considering a bartending school, I would ask for the names of former students and phone them to ask about the course and their opinion of its worth. If the school is not willing to furnish the names of satisfied graduates, I'd look for another.

In the twenty-first century, though, there are many more decent schools than were in existence a couple of decades ago, and by doing just a little research on the Internet, visiting bartender forums such as chanticleersociety.org, and asking the right questions of seasoned professionals, you'll probably find yourself guided in the right direction.

Or, it's sometimes best to just jump in there and get your basic training in whatever way is possible. Go out and beg for a job—as a barback, as a trainee, or in any position that affords the opportunity to watch the accomplished and learn the moves and processes. In this case, experience is the best teacher. Practicing with a bottle of water and a few simple tools can make a huge difference to the budding bartender. In addition, start reading cocktail books—especially old ones to see how it was done and compare it to how it's done now. All of the recipes included here need not be memorized, but anyone serious about learning the craft of bartending should acquaint himself or herself with the classic recipes and classic ingredients while keeping up with what's going on right now. For those who are seriously interested in learning about cocktail recipes, I highly recommend Gary Regan's book, *The Joy of Mixology.*

Experimentation and practice, in this case at least, make perfect.

Would You Hire This Guy?

My friend Julien, a recent college graduate, wants to be a bartender in New York City. Asked to write why, here's his e-mail response:

I've been looking for work these past few months, with little to no luck even getting a warm welcome to most bars. The moment I say I want to drop off a résumé, I get a little bit of a cold shoulder and a dismissive "I'll leave it for the manager," who has no idea what I'm talking about when I call back.

This wouldn't bother me so much if I could see that the people who already have the job actually cared about what they were doing. By and large the men (and women) I've seen behind the bar are there because they look good from the waist up and they can splash some whiskey into a glass of coke. The other flavor of bartender I've encountered is the snobby elitist who knows how to build a decent cocktail but does it without smiling and shoots mean looks at anyone who takes too long with an order.

Only very infrequently have I seen a bartender who can laugh and joke while pouring and mixing, who can make a drink as easily as he or she can make a customer smile. That's the kind of bartender I've always wanted, and the kind I'd like to be. I'd love to be taught how to make complicated and obscure drinks and how to look good while doing it, and I'm enthusiastic about learning the trade in general. . . . But really I just want to be someone who can tell a joke, recommend a drink, be patient, be a listener, be funny when it's called for, and be silent when that's more appropriate. I would like to be able to read my customers, and to do my damnedest to help them with whatever it is they need that night.

I'd hire him in a minute.

A BARTENDER'S GLOSSARY

Absinthe: A high-proof spirit with a predominant anise flavor. Absinthe was made illegal in the United States in 1912 because the chemical thujone in the spirit was thought to have a similar effect on the body as the THC in cannabis. This, however, has been proven to be untrue, and absinthe with low thujone content is now legal again. Most experts agree that the absinthes available prior to 1912 also had low thujone content, so we can now experience bottlings that are very similar, at least, to nineteenth-century absinthes.

Ale: A group of beers that are made using a strain of yeast that ferments at the top of a vat. A number of styles of ale exist, amber ales, barley wines, bitter ales, cream ales, India pale ales, lambics, porters, Scotch ales, stouts, Trappist ales, and wheat beers among them.

Apéritif: A single beverage or combination of ingredients that usually includes an alcoholic component and that is drunk before dinner as an appetite stimulant.

Armagnac: A French grape-based aged brandy made in Gascony.

Aromatized wines: Wines that are flavored by any of several methods with herbs, spices, and other botanical ingredients. Vermouth is a prime example, as are several apéritifs, Dubonnet and Lillet among them.

Barspoon: A long-handled spoon with a twisted shaft that is used to stir cocktail ingredients during their preparation.

Beer: Generally, this term refers to alcoholic beverages made by fermenting cooked grains, hops, and yeast. Lagers and ales are styles of beer.

Bitters: Alcoholic-based infusions of a base spirit and, usually, a number of herbs, spices, other botanicals, and other flavorings that are produced as proprietary brands by a few producers. Cocktail bitters, such as Angostura, orange bitters, and Peychaud's, are used in very small quantities to add complexity to a drink mixture. Many new bottlings of bitters in many guises are now available.

Blended whisk(e)y: A spirit made by combining one or more flavorful whisk(e)ys with flavorless neutral whisk(e)y to produce a particular flavor profile.

Boston shaker: A cocktail-shaking tool comprised of two parts: a metal cone and a 16-ounce mixing glass. The two parts fit snugly together to allow shaking, while the glass portion is used alone for stirring ingredients together.

Botanicals: A collective term describing the fresh and dried herbs, fruits, spices, and other components used to flavor some usually aromatic liquors, beers, and wines.

Bourbon: Any whiskey made in the United States, distilled from a fermented mash of grains that contains at least 51 percent corn and aged in new oak barrels for a minimum of two years.

Brandy: A spirit distilled from fermented grape or other fruit juice.

Buck: A Highball made of a base spirit, the juice of a squeezed lemon wedge, and ginger ale.

Calvados: An aged brandy made in a specific geographical area of Normandy, France, from a fermented mash of apples, although a small percentage of pears is usually included.

Champagne: A sparkling wine made according to the *méthode champenoise* in a specific geographical area of the Champagne district of northeastern France.

Chaser: A beverage that immediately follows the drinking of another, as in a Boilermaker.

Churchkey: A tool that has a rounded bottle opener at one end and a V-shaped piercing can opener at the end. Generally, the V-shaped end is used to open cans of liquid, such as tomato juice or beef bouillon.

Cobbler: A cocktail made of a base spirit or wine and simple syrup that's shaken with a slice or two of orange in the shaker, and then strained into a wine goblet full of crushed ice and garnished with fresh fruit.

Cocktail: Originally cocktails were made with spirits, water, sugar, and bitters, but now the name can be applied to any combination of ingredients that have been shaken or stirred with ice and strained into a chilled V-shaped glass.

Collins: A mixed drink made from a base spirit, lemon juice, simple syrup, and club soda, which is served in an ice-filled Collins glass with a fresh fruit garnish (optional).

Cooler: A drink made of a base spirit, wine, and/or liqueur topped with a carbonated beverage, and sometimes a fruit juice, which is served in an ice-filled glass and often is garnished with fruit or a lemon twist.

Cordial: Also known as a liqueur, a bottled beverage made from liquor, one or more sweetening agents, and other flavorings.

Crusta: A mixed drink made from a base spirit, lemon juice, and curaçao, which is shaken over ice and then strained into a sugar-rimmed glass that is lined with a lemon peel spiral.

Daisy: A mixed drink made from a base spirit, lemon juice, and either an orange liqueur, such as curaçao, or grenadine. Daisies are shaken and strained into a cocktail glass. Liqueurs other than curaçao —maraschino, for instance—can be used also. A fresh fruit and/or fresh mint garnish is optional.

Dash: An inexact, small measure shaken from the bottle that should equal about $1/16$ teaspoon.

Digestif: A single beverage or combination of ingredients that usually has an alcoholic component and is drunk after dinner to stimulate digestion.

Eaux-de-vie: The French name for un-aged, colorless brandies distilled from fermented fruit juices.

Fermentation: When yeast is introduced to sugar or simple starches in a mash, or "soup," of fruits, grains, sugars, or vegetables, it feeds on the sugar and produces heat, carbon dioxide, and beverage alcohol, and this process is known as fermentation.

Fix: A mixed drink made from a base spirit, lemon juice, and simple syrup, curaçao, or pineapple syrup that is built over crushed ice in a Highball glass or a wine goblet, with fresh fruit for garnish.

Fizz: A mixed drink made from a base spirit, lime or lemon juice, simple syrup, and club soda that is served straight up in a Sour glass with fresh fruit for garnish (optional).

Flip: A mixed drink made from a base wine, spirit, or beer, a whole raw egg, and simple syrup that is served straight up in a wine goblet or beer glass with grated nutmeg as a garnish.

Fortified wine: A wine that has had brandy added to it, such as Madeira, port, or sherry.

Frappé: A drink composed solely of a base liqueur or spirit that is served over crushed ice in a Champagne Saucer glass or a Sour glass.

Garnish: An ingredient, usually fruit or vegetable, that is added to a mixed drink or cocktail just before serving.

Gin: A spirit usually made from a fermented mash of grains that is flavored at some step in its manufacture with juniper and other botanical ingredients.

Hawthorne strainer: A bar tool with a spring coil that is used to strain liquids from the metal half of a Boston shaker.

Highball: The simplest form of a mixed drink, which comprises just two ingredients, such as scotch and soda or vodka and tonic, that are poured directly into a Highball glass for serving. Garnishes are optional, depending on the ingredients in the Highball; so, for instance, a Gin and Tonic Highball automatically gets a lime wedge garnish, but in the case of a Scotch and Soda, a lemon twist would be optional.

Irish whiskey: A spirit made in Ireland that is distilled from a fermented mash of grains.

Jigger: 1) A liquid measurement equal to $1^1/_2$ fluid ounces; 2) a metal or plastic tool used by a bartender to measure ingredients. Most jiggers measure 1 fluid ounce on one side and $1^1/_2$ fluid ounces on the other side, but jiggers with various other measurements are also available.

Julep strainer: A perforated bar tool that is used to strain ingredients that have been stirred together and chilled in a mixing glass.

Lager: A style of beer made with a bottom-fermenting yeast.

Liqueur: Also sometimes known as a cordial, a bottled beverage made from liquor, one or more sweetening agents, and other flavorings.

Madeira: A wine fortified with brandy, produced on the island of Madeira.

Martini: Originally a drink made with gin, vermouth, and bitters, the word is now commonly applied to any drink that is stirred or shaken over ice and strained into a V-shaped cocktail glass.

Mash: The word used to describe the fruits, fruit juices, or cooked grains that are fermented with yeast to produce wine or beer or the mixture that will be distilled into spirits.

Mixed drink: A combination of two or more liquid ingredients, at least one of them containing alcohol. A Highball is one type of mixed drink.

Mixing glass: A 16-ounce glass designed for stirring together the ingredients for cocktails; also the glass half of a Boston shaker.

Muddling: The process in which a bartender uses a usually wooden pestle to crush together ingredients, such as wedges of fruit, sugar cubes, and bitters, to express their flavorful components.

Neat: Spirits served straight from the bottle without being chilled or mixed with other ingredients.

Perfect: A term that usually describes a cocktail that contains equal parts of both sweet and dry vermouths.

Pony: 1) A 1-fluid-ounce measure of liquid; 2) a serving glass usually used for serving spirits neat or for shooters.

Port: A Portuguese wine that is fortified with brandy and is produced in the Douro region of Portugal.

Proof: In the United States, the alcohol content of a beverage expressed by degree and based on 200 degrees equaling 100 percent. Therefore, 80-proof vodka is 40 percent alcohol by volume. Other countries use different scales, and because of the confusion this presents, bottlings of current products express the alcohol content as the percentage by volume (abv).

Rickey: A cocktail made from a base spirit, fresh lime juice, and club soda that is served over ice in a wine goblet, a Double Old-Fashioned glass, or a Highball glass, with an optional wedge of lime for garnish.

Rum: A spirit distilled from a fermented mash of molasses or sugarcane juice.

Rye whiskey: An aged spirit distilled from a fermented grain mash containing a minimum of 51 percent rye.

Sangaree: A drink made from a base of fortified wine, ale, or porter and a sweetening agent; it is garnished with grated nutmeg. Wine Sangarees are shaken over ice and strained into a small glass; beer Sangarees are served at room temperature in beer glasses.

Scotch: An aged spirit that is distilled in Scotland from a fermented mash of grains.

Shaker: A bar tool that creates a sure seal and is fitted with a built-in strainer that is used to shake together the ingredients for cocktails.

Sherry: A wine fortified with brandy, made in a specific geographical area of Spain that surrounds the city of Jerez.

Shooter: A cocktail meant to be downed in a single gulp.

Shot: Usually a $1^1/_2$-ounce measure of a spirit.

Simple syrup: A solution of sugar dissolved in water that is used to sweeten cocktails. See the recipe on page 35.

Single-malt scotch: A type of whisky produced by a single distillery in Scotland from a fermented mash of malted barley and aged for at least three years in oak barrels.

Sling: A mixed drink made from a base spirit, citrus juice, simple syrup or a liqueur, and club soda (optional) that is served over ice in a Collins glass and usually garnished with fresh fruits.

Smash: A mixed drink made from a base spirit, simple syrup, and mint leaves that are all shaken over ice and strained into a glass filled with crushed ice and garnished with a mint sprig.

Sour: A mixed drink composed of a base spirit, lemon juice, simple syrup, and an optional egg white that is served straight up in a Sour glass or over ice in a Rocks glass or wine goblet.

Sparkling wine: Wine, such as champagne or Prosecco,

that is carbonated by a secondary fermentation that takes place within the bottle.

Spirit: An alcoholic beverage, such as brandy, gin, rum, or vodka, that is made by distilling a fermented mash of grains or fruits to a potency of at least 40 percent alcohol by volume.

Splash: An inexact, small measure that should equal about $1/8$ teaspoon.

Straight up: A drink that is stirred or shaken over ice, then strained from the ice into a chilled glass.

Straight whiskey: A spirit that is distilled from a fermented mash of grains and aged in oak barrels to mature and develop flavor.

Swizzle: A cocktail made with a base spirit, citrus juice, simple syrup or a liqueur, and a carbonated beverage; it is served in a Collins glass with a swizzle stick for stirring.

Tennessee whiskey: A spirit made in Tennessee that is distilled from a fermented mash of grains and filtered through sugar-maple charcoal before aging.

Tequila: A liquor made in specific geographical areas of Mexico from a fermented mash of the *Tequilana Weber* variety of blue agave.

Toddy: A drink made from a base spirit, hot water, sugar or another sweetening agent such as honey, and various spices—cinnamon, allspice, and nutmeg are all popular. Toddies are usually served in Irish Coffee glasses.

Vermouth: A wine slightly fortified with spirits and flavored by various aromatic botanicals.

Vodka: A spirit distilled from a fermented mash of grains, vegetables, fruits, and/or sugar.

Whisk(e)y: A liquor, such as scotch, bourbon, or rye, distilled from a fermented mash of grains that is aged in oak barrels. As a generalization, when the word is spelled without the "e," it refers to products of Scotland and Canada, while those spelled with the "e" are made in Ireland or the United States.

Zest: The colorful outer layer of citrus fruit peels, where the essential oils are located.

BIBLIOGRAPHY

Angostura Bitters Complete Mixing Guide. New York: J. W. Wupperman, 1913.

An Anthology of Cocktails together with Selected Observations by a Distinguished Gathering and Diverse Thoughts for Great Occasions. London: Booth's Distilleries, Ltd., no date.

Arthur, Stanley Clisby. *Famous New Orleans Drinks & how to mix 'em.* Gretna, LA: Pelican Publishing Company, 1989.

Baker, Charles H., Jr. *The Gentleman's Companion.* New York: Crown Publishers, 1946.

————.*The South American Gentleman's Companion.* New York: Crown Publishers, 1951.

Beebe, Lucius. *The Stork Club Bar Book.* New York and Toronto: Rinehart & Company, 1946.

Bergeron, Victor. *Trader Vic's Book of Food & Drink.* Garden City, NY: Doubleday & Company, 1946.

Berry, Jeff, and Annene Kaye. *Beachbum Berry's Grog Log.* San Jose, CA: SLG Publishing, 1998.

Broom, Dave. *Spirits & Cocktails.* London: Carlton, 1998.

Brown, Charles. *The Gun Club Drink Book.* New York: Charles Scribner's Sons, 1939.

Brown, Gordon. *Classic Spirits of the World.* New York: Abbeville Press, 1996.

Brown, John Hull. *Early American Beverages.* New York: Bonanza Books, 1966.

Cotton, Leo, ed. *Old Mr. Boston De Luxe Official Bartender's Guide.* Boston: Berke Brothers Distilleries, Inc., 1949.

————.*Old Mr. Boston De Luxe Official Bartender's Guide.* Boston: Mr. Boston Distiller Inc., 1966.

Craddock, Harry. *The Savoy Cocktail Book.* New York: Richard R. Smith, Inc., 1930.

Crockett, Albert Stevens. *The Old Waldorf-Astoria Bar Book*. New York: A. S. Crockett, 1935.

DeVoto, Bernard. *The Hour*. Cambridge, MA: Riverside Press, 1948.

Dickens, Cedric. *Drinking with Dickens*. Goring-on-Thames, England: Elvendon Press, 1980.

Duffy, Patrick Gavin. *The Official Mixer's Manual*. New York: Alta Publications, Inc., 1934.

Earle, Alice Morse. *Customs and Fashions in Old New England*. New York: Charles Scribner's Sons, 1913.

Edmunds, Lowell. *Martini, Straight Up: The Classic American Cocktail*. Baltimore and London: Johns Hopkins University Press, 1998.

Embury, David A. *The Fine Art of Mixing Drinks*. New revised ed. New York: Doubleday & Company, 1958.

Emmons, Bob. *The Book of Tequila: A Complete Guide*. Chicago and La Salle: Open Court Publishing Company, 1997.

Gaige, Crosby. *Crosby Gaige's Cocktail Guide and Ladies' Companion*. New York: M. Barrows & Company, Inc., 1945.

Grimes, William. *Straight Up or On the Rocks: The Story of the American Cocktail*. New York: North Point Press, 2001.

Grossman, Harold J., revised by Harriet Lembeck. *Grossman's Guide to Wines, Beers, and Spirits*. Sixth revised ed. New York: Charles Scribner's Sons, 1977.

Haigh, Ted, aka Dr. Cocktail. *Vintage Spirits & Forgotten Cocktails: From the Alamagoozlum Cocktail to the Zombie*. Gloucester, MA: Quarry Books, 2004.

Haimo, Oscar. *The Barmen's Bible*. New York: The International Cocktail, Wine, and Spirits Digest, Inc., 1964.

Harwell, Richard Barksdale. *The Mint Julep*. Charlottesville: University Press of Virginia, 1985.

Hastings, Derek. *Spirits & Liqueurs of the World*. Constance Gordon Wiener, consulting ed. London: Footnote Productions, Ltd., 1984.

Jones, Stan. *Jones' Complete Barguide*. Los Angeles: BARGUIDE Enterprises, 1977.

Kappeler, George J. *Modern American Drinks: How to Mix and Serve All Kinds of Cups and Drinks*. New York: The Merriam Company, 1895.

Mario, Thomas. *Playboy's Host & Bar Book*. Chicago: Playboy Press, 1971.

Miller, Anistatia, ed. *Mixologist: The Journal of the American Cocktail, Vol. I*. New York: Mixellany, 2005.

———, ed. *Mixologist: The Journal of the American Cocktail, Vol. II*. New York: Mixellany, 2006.

Mortlock, Geoffrey, and Stephen Williams. *The Flowing Bowl: A Book of Blithe Spirits and Blue Devils*. London: Hutchison & Co., 1948.

Murray, Jim. *The Complete Guide to Whiskey*. Chicago: Triumph Books, 1997.

Pacult, F. Paul. *Kindred Spirits 2*. Walkill, NY: Spirit Journal Inc., 2008.

Ray, Cyril. *Cognac*. London: Peter Davis, Ltd., 1973.

Regan, Gary. *The Joy of Mixology*. New York: Clarkson Potter, 2003.

Sardi, Vincent, with George Shea. *Sardi's Bar Guide*. New York: Ballantine Books, 1988.

Saucier, Ted. *Ted Saucier's Bottoms Up*. New York: The Greystone Press, 1951.

Terrington, William. *Cooling Cups and Dainty Drinks*. London: Routledge and Sons, 1869.

Thomas, Jerry. *How to Mix Drinks or The Bon Vivant's Companion*. New York: Dick & Fitzgerald, 1862.

———. *The Bar-Tender's Guide or How to Mix all Kinds of Plain and Fancy Drinks*. New York: Fitzgerald Publishing Corporation, 1887.

United Kingdom Bartender's Guild, comp. *The U.K.B.G. Guide to Drinks*. London: United Kingdom Bartender's Guild, 1955.

Vermeire, Robert. *Cocktails: How to Mix Them*. London: Herbert Jenkins Limited, no date.

Wondrich, David. *Esquire Drinks: An Opinionated & Irreverent Guide to Drinking*. New York: Hearst Books, 2002.

———. *Imbibe! From Absinthe Cocktail to Whiskey Smash; A Salute in Stories and Drinks to "Professor" Jerry Thomas, Pioneer of the American Bar*. New York: Penguin, 2007.

———. *Killer Cocktails: An Intoxicating Guide to Sophisticated Drinking*. New York: HarperCollins, 2005.

INDEX

Index

Index

377